THE COMPLETE BOOK OF FISHING

THE COMPLETE BOOK OF
FISHING

COARSE • GAME • SEA

INTRODUCTION BY JOHN WILSON

St Michael
FROM
MARKS & SPENCER

First published in 1996

Based on the Art of Fishing
© Eaglemoss Publications Ltd 1992

1 3 5 7 9 8 6 4 2

A CIP catalogue record for this book is
available from the British Library

ISBN 0 583 32529 7

This edition published specially for Marks & Spencer, 1996,
by HarperCollins*Publishers*
London

Printed and bound in Singapore

Contents

Introduction

Do you know how you can use soluble PVA string to get boilies out to distant carp? Or when you might choose a sink-tip fly line as opposed to a sinker? And what the best times are to shore-fish for cod?

You will if you read *The Complete Book of Fishing*. Written by a team of top anglers, it is crammed with everything you'll want to know about the world of fishing – coarse, game and sea. In fact, one of the main things that keeps fishing alive, transforming youngsters into life-long fishermen and fishermen into guardians of the sport, is a continuing knowledge of natural history. No one is denying, of course, that what anglers love above all is to catch fish. But at the same time most of us come to enjoy – and put to practical use – what we learn about the fish, the water and the flora and fauna that share it.

The experts who have contributed to this book – and each is indeed a leading name in his branch of the sport – share the belief that developing this knowledge is the best way not only to get more out of your fishing but also to understand the pressing need to care for the environment on which our fishing depends.

Within its 240 information-packed pages, *The Complete Book of Fishing* contains in one volume all you will want to know about coarse, game and sea fishing techniques. Embracing both modern and traditional approaches, these range from mounting a pop-up boilie, through selecting and casting a trout fly, to wreck fishing for conger. In every case the essentials are explained clearly and with the help of detailed illustrations and superb colour photographs.

As I suggested earlier, the practical skills described in this book have come about through the contributors' willingness to study and learn about the fish they want to catch. Similarly, the sections on the species themselves reflect their enduring enthusiasm for the fish. These pages explain the habitat and physical characteristics of all the species most commonly fished for, and their feeding habits.

Baits are perhaps the most complex subject in angling. That is why *The Complete Book of Fishing* pays special attention to them, offering plentiful advice on both natural and manufactured baits, with hints on collecting, preparing, colouring and preserving them for use in fresh and salt water. Naturally the game enthusiast is not left out, for in addition to an exhaustive run-down of wet and dry flies of all types and for all seasons, there is ample coverage of artificial lures that really catch.

Whether you are a complete beginner or a more experienced fisherman, someone dedicated to just one branch of the sport or perhaps thinking about 'crossing over' to make the fishing year longer and more varied, the important thing to understand is that there is always more to learn. And in my view there is no better place to start than this excellent book.

John Wilson

COARSE FISHING

TACKLE AND TECHNIQUES

Float rods

Casting, controlling the tackle, striking and playing fish are the basic functions which a float rod must do well. Top Midlands matchman, Dave Harrell, helps you to choose the right rod.

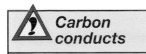

Carbon conducts

Carbon is an excellent conductor of electricity. Don't use a carbon rod anywhere near electricity power lines. The current can arc from the power line to your rod without the rod even touching it and the results could be fatal.

Since carbon fibre replaced glass-fibre as the main rod-building material, the choice of float rods has grown dramatically. Each season, manufacturers are adding new models to the vast range – each with their own advantages and disadvantages.

Rod materials

The action, lightness and feel of a rod depend on the materials it's made of. Split-cane, greenheart, Spanish reed and glass-fibre have all been used to build rods but materials like carbon fibre and kevlar have made them obsolete.

Carbon fibre versus glass-fibre To appreciate the advantages of carbon fibre, go to a tackle shop and compare a carbon float rod with a glass-fibre float rod of the same length and action.

Before picking up the rods, notice that the carbon rod is slimmer – maybe only 10mm (⅜in) at the butt – perhaps half the diameter of a glass rod. This is a great advantage (particularly in windy weather) because it enables the rod to slice through the air, offering less resistance when casting and striking.

Notice too, how much lighter the carbon rod is. A typical weight for a 12ft (3.6m) glass rod is 8-10oz (227-283g) whereas a 12ft (3.6m) carbon rod might weigh 4½-6oz (128-170g). Apart from making the rod suitable for one-handed casting, it means you can hold it for hours without tiring.

If you take the glass rod in one hand and the carbon rod in the other and give each a gentle 'waggle', the carbon rod returns to a state of rest sooner than the glass rod – carbon fibre is a more resilient material. In

Choose the rod to suit the kind of fishing you think you'll be doing. If you expect to floatfish for powerful species like tench or small carp, go for a more powerful rod.

This angler had an enjoyable day bagging-up with roach on light float gear.

Tip Waxing joints

Prevent the joints on your rod from sticking by rubbing a little candle wax or pencil graphite on to the male section. You can pack out loose joints slightly by lightly coating the male section with carbon spray which also prevents sticking.

When fishing, check the joints don`t work loose.

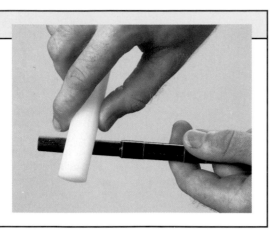

Tip The four hand method

If your rod gets stuck together, don't try to pull it apart by yourself. Get assistance from another angler. Each person then grips the rod on one side of the joint with one hand, and on the other side of the joint with the other hand. A steady pull should bring the rod apart without too much difficulty.

fishing terms this means that it is more responsive – making accurate casting easier and giving a crisper strike, which is useful when bites are fast.

Finally, compare the prices. Carbon fibre is a more expensive material so you must be prepared to pay more for the rod. Some manufacturers expect you to pay more for their name alone but you should buy a rod strictly on its merits.

Carbon composites Some carbon fibre float rods include kevlar in their construction. Kevlar – a combination of polymers and nylon – is a non-stretch, shock-absorbent material used for making bullet-proof vests and lumberjacks' trousers (as protection against the chain-saw). Braided around a carbon fibre core, it increases torsional strength (good for accurate long distance casting) and makes for a crisper action.

Rod length
It is possible to buy rods up to 17ft (5.2m) long but these are specialist tools and float

rods usually range from 11½-14ft (3.46-4.2m). Getting the right length of rod for the job is important. As a general guide the farther out you intend to fish the longer the rod needs to be.

Ultimately, choose the length of your rod to suit the actual swim you are fishing. If there are overhanging trees you may have to use a short rod. A longer rod will give you extra control when playing large fish over dense marginal weed or snags. If you intend to do all your float fishing with one rod then a rod of 13ft (3.9m) should cover most eventualities.

An 11½ft (3.46m) float rod is a good length for short range work – such as fishing the far bank of canals and lake margins with 2 or 3BB wagglers.

Rods of 12-13ft (3.6-3.9m) are a good length for medium to long range waggler work. A 12ft (3.6m) rod is useful when not casting too far on lakes or casting to the middle of rivers like the Warwickshire Avon or middle Severn. When fishing reservoirs or the far side of rivers, a 13ft (3.9m) rod will give you the leverage to achieve extra distance on the cast and pick up the line better when striking.

Rods of 14ft (4.2m) or more are useful when fishing a stick float. They give scope for extra float control such as holding the line clear of marginal weed or keeping the float on line in windy conditions.

Action and stiffness
Rods have a certain profile when a steady pressure is applied to the tip. This is the rod's action. Don't confuse rod action with rod stiffness – rods having similar actions may vary in stiffness.

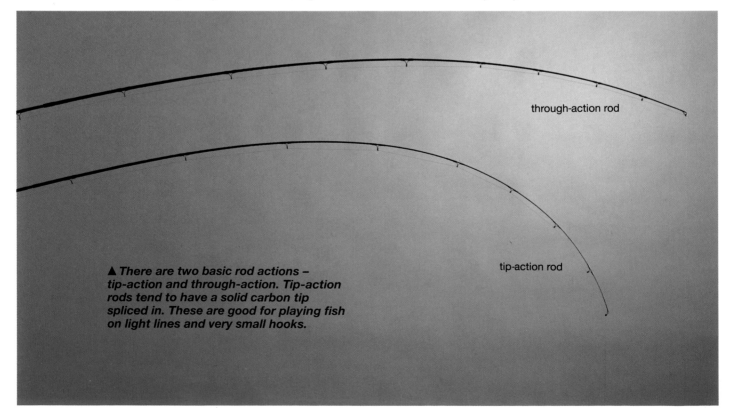

through-action rod

tip-action rod

▲ *There are two basic rod actions – tip-action and through-action. Tip-action rods tend to have a solid carbon tip spliced in. These are good for playing fish on light lines and very small hooks.*

▶ *For float fishing on rivers, Dave Harrell likes to use hard chrome rings. They do not wear as well as lined rings but they have a lower 'friction factor'. This helps when trotting a float because it means that the line can be paid out smoothly and the bait presented at exactly the same speed as the current.*

◀ *The most popular ring linings are made from either silicon carbide or a ceramic mixture of alumina oxide and titania oxide. Silicon carbide is a very hard, light, super smooth material but it is rather brittle and expensive. Ceramic linings are heavier and not as hard as silicon carbide linings but they tend to be more durable and are only a third of the price.*

Although there are two basic actions for float rods (tip-action and through-action) there are degrees of each. A recent trend is towards a rod which combines both actions. It is important to choose the right action for your fishing.

Through-action rods have a hollow, unspliced tip. With a through-action rod, the pliancy decreases steadily from the tip to the butt section. If you intend to do all your float work with one rod, a fairly soft, through-action carbon rod is a good choice. It will be sharp enough to hit quick bites, forgiving enough in the tip to handle fine hooklengths of 1lb (0.45kg), but also have enough power in the butt to handle heavier tackle and deal with fish like tench, carp and chub.

Through-action rods also have special applications. When fishing light wagglers of 2 or 3BB at short range for soft-mouthed skimmer bream or roach, a softish, through-action rod prevents fish from being bumped off or the hook working free.

For medium to long-range waggler work on lakes and rivers, a stiffer rod can punch the float out; and, when a long sweeping strike is needed to pick up the line and set the hook, it can absorb the shock.

Tip-action rods have nearly all their pliancy in the top section, making them very quick on the strike. Some tip-action rods have a fine, solid carbon top spliced into the top section which makes the rod even more 'tippy'.

✖ Clean rings

Many anglers never bother to clean their rods. Rings soon become clogged with mud and groundbait which dries to a rock hard consistency. This acts like sandpaper on the line and defeats the object of lining a ring with a low friction material. Your rods will benefit from an occasional wipe down with a cloth and soapy water. Worn or cracked rings should be replaced.

▶ *Your rod should have the correct number of properly spaced rings. Too few rings will make the line stick to the rod in wet weather and cause the line to depart from the rod's natural curve. Too many rings interfere with the rod's action. On a 13ft (3.9m) rod Dave Harrell likes to see two rings on the butt section, five on the middle and nine (including the tip ring) on the top section. He thinks a 12ft (3.6m) rod should have one ring less, a 14ft (4.2m) rod one more.*

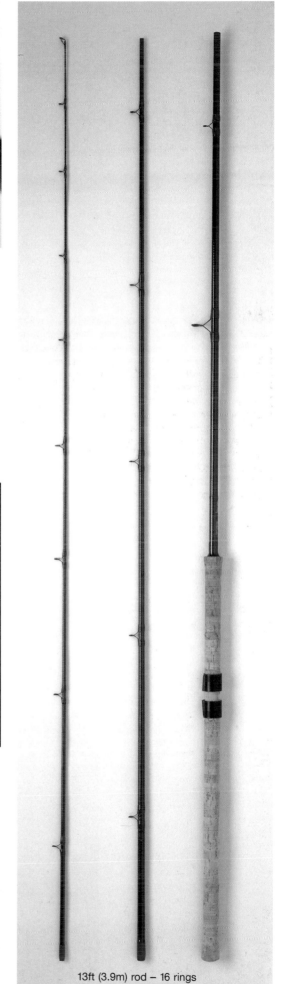
13ft (3.9m) rod – 16 rings

Tip-action rods are ideal for stick float and small balsa fishing on rivers like the Trent, Severn, Thames and Warwickshire Avon, where a fast rod is often essential for hitting quick biting roach, chub and dace.

A very fine tip will allow fish to be played out on hooklengths down to 12oz (0.34kg) and hooks as small as 24 or even 26. This is why some anglers prefer to do all their fishing with tip-action rods. However, some tip-action rods are too stiff in the middle and butt sections for certain kinds of fishing. If you expect to catch bream you should be particularly careful. A tip-action rod which 'locks up' on the strike will bump these soft-mouthed fish off.

A new action Recently the trend has been towards a rod having a 'hybrid' action. When light pressure is applied to the tip of these rods they behave as if they had a tip-action – making them suitable for stick work. As more pressure is applied to the tip, the middle and even the butt sections come into play, so that the rod is quite capable of waggler work, and able to handle larger fish too.

Fittings

Don't make the mistake of thinking that rod fittings are merely auxiliaries. The best blank won't make a good rod unless it is correctly ringed.

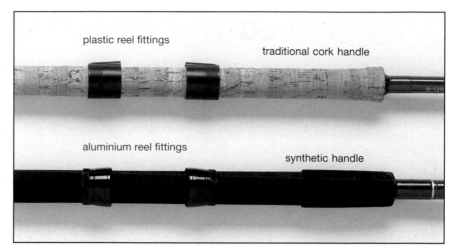

plastic reel fittings

traditional cork handle

aluminium reel fittings

synthetic handle

Rod rings The correct type, number and positioning of rod rings is crucial.

It is the job of the rings to guide the line smoothly, keeping it as close to the profile of the rod as possible. Good rings should keep friction to a minimum and be wear resistant. A wear-resistant material is less likely to damage the line.

There are only two types worth considering – hard chrome and lined rings. Hard chrome are good for trotting rods, where it is important to keep friction very low but they need changing every season. Lined rings are more wear resistant but not quite as smooth as chrome.

▲ A handle of 21-23in (53-58cm) is about right. Cork is traditionally the material for handles and it takes some beating. It is light and pleasant to the touch. Synthetic handles are easier to keep clean but choice of material really is a personal matter.

Aluminium is a common material for the reel fittings but new materials, such as plastic and carbon fibre, tend to be lighter and kinder on the hands in cold weather.

Using the rod

A float rod should not be thought of simply as a stick with which to cast the float out and bring fish in. Handled by a good angler, a rod can be used to encourage more bites. You can use it to sink the line in windy conditions, and to hold the line off the water on rivers so that the float is kept on course.

When playing big fish, a skilfully handled rod helps to keep the fish on the hook. Holding a rod high above the water will give you control over a fish that tries to dive for the cover of weed. If you are unlucky enough for a boat to pass through your swim as you are playing a big fish you may be able to avoid losing it by pushing your line deep into the water.

Playing a fish with the tip of the rod close to the surface of the water helps to prevent the fish from splashing about and disturbing the rest of the shoal.

Fixed-spool reels

Chosen with care, a reel should balance your tackle, suit your kind of fishing and, if it is good quality, last you a lifetime. But you must pick the right one for the type of fishing you do, says matchman Ken Collings.

There are three basic types of reel: fixed-spool, centrepin and multiplier. For coarse fishing the centrepin and multiplier are highly specialized and the fixed-spool is the most popular, all-purpose reel. Unlike centrepins and multipliers, the fixed-spool has its central axis parallel to the rod rather than at right angles to it. As the name 'fixed' suggests, the spool does not revolve when casting; the line leaves the spool by spilling over the lip instead.

Types of fixed-spool

There are two kinds of fixed-spool reel – open-face and closed-face.

Open-face On this design, the spool and bale arm are exposed. The bale arm is either disengaged with your free hand (the one not holding the rod) or, with automatic bale reels, by the hand holding the rod.

Closed-face These reels have the spool and pick-up pin enclosed in a housing. The pick-up pin is disengaged by pressing a button with the index or second finger of the hand holding the rod.

The choice between an open or closed-face reel depends on the type of fishing you want to do. Each has its good and bad points in particular situations and each is better suited to some techniques than others. Among the most important factors to think about before choosing are the line strength you'll be using and the spool capacity you want.

▼ *Effortless casting and smooth playing of big fish are tests that a good reel must pass with flying colours. Reel design has come on in leaps and bounds in recent years with the use of strong, light, corrosion-resistant materials. Graphite compounds are a typical choice for the body – as is the case with this open-face fixed-spool reel (inset).*

Line strength

The main disadvantage of the closed-face reel is that it has a narrow spool. Heavy line lies unevenly on the spool, causing casting problems and making the closed-face unsuitable for lines above 4lb (1.8kg) breaking strain.

If you intend to go for large, hard-fighting fish such as carp, pike, tench or barbel, you need an open-face reel. Its wider spool takes less coils to fill it and distributes the load over a greater area. This reduces pressure on the spool and, together with the reel's sturdy design, allows you to use lines of up to 20lb (9kg) b.s. At the other extreme , the open-face can handle lines as fine as 2lb (0.91kg) b.s. This capability makes it wonderfully versatile.

Spool capacity Most manufacturers provide tables telling you how many metres of a certain breaking strain will fill your spool to the correct level without backing. For most types of fishing 100-150m (109-164yd) of line is enough. Any more than this is a waste of money and leads to poor line-lay and `bedding-in'. Bedding-in is a condition where the surface coils of line (which would normally be free to leave the spool) become trapped between underlying coils. This causes the line to snatch as it comes off the spool, making it impossible to cast or trot properly.)

In general, open-face reels have a greater capacity than closed-face designs and good quality open-face models provide a wider range of interchangeable spools than closed-face models. Most closed-face models have only two spools: a shallow fine line (`match') spool which takes about 100m (109yd) of 2lb (0.9kg) line and a deep spool which takes about 100m (109yd) of 12lb (5.4kg) line.

▲ *The closed-face reel's push-button line-release makes it very fast but its trotting ability is often questioned on the grounds that it is prone to bedding-in. However, many Midlands matchmen do all their fishing with them.*

▼ *When trotting with an open-face reel, a manual bale is useful. It can be engaged with the free hand ready to play the fish.*

Casting and trotting

With an open-face reel the line peels effortlessly off the wider spool. This means that you can cast much farther, with less effort, more accurately than with a closed-face reel. This same smooth supply of line also makes the open-face reel a tempting choice for trotting on rivers. In this situation an open-face is better because pressure on the spool from big fish tends to make the line bed-in with closed-face reels.

Open-face problem

However, the open-face does have some disadvantages. The finger you use to control your line when trotting is in the way when the bale is engaged to play a fish. If you remove your finger from the lip of the spool the fish is briefly given slack line and may come off. Keeping your finger on while snapping the bale down on the line is not much of an answer: the line jolts the fish and it may be bumped off, or the hook hold loosened.

One solution is to have a manual bale so that it can be brought over with the free hand, and most modern reels have these. The alternative is to risk using a closed-face reel (whose pick-up pin is inside the housing away from the finger) and hope the line does not bed-in. Your choice finally depends on whether or not you think you will take big fish.

Closed-face advantages

When there is a facing wind, the open-face reel runs into serious problems. The line can blow back behind the bale arm and, if you don't notice this happening, you may snap or tangle it as you reel in. Having to

closed-face spool   open-face spool

look down at the reel all day to check the line is all right soon spoils your fishing. In this situation, closed-face reels are best as the spool is sheltered from the wind by its housing.

For speed fishing, too, the closed-face is a winner. Its push button line-release makes it fast to use and, even though some open-face models have automatic bails, the simplicity and convenience of the push button release is hard to beat and might give you the edge in a match.

Standard features

Different manufacturers' reels vary in over-all design but almost all have at least some of the following features.

Gearing All fixed-spool reels have a geared retrieval so that, for one turn of the handle, the bale or pin rotates more than once. The gear ratio varies from one design to another, but on fast retrieve open-face models the ratio is usually 5 or 6 to 1. Closed-face reels have a lower gearing; 3 or 4 to 1 is typical. In general, this means open-face reels have a quicker retrieve than closed-face reels.

Drag Nearly all reels are fitted with a pre-set drag system. This acts as a safeguard against the sudden rush of a big fish. On modern reels the drag is either at the back (stern drag) or, on closed-face reels, on the handle.

With a preset system, the line is put under pressure, and the drag set so that the spool begins to rotate and give line before it breaks. Good drags can be smoothly adjusted while playing a fish.

A characteristic of drags is that they can cause the line to twist as it comes off the spool, weakening it. One way to make sure

this does not happen is to screw the drag down tight and play big fish by back winding.

Anti-reverse Nearly all reels have an anti-reverse switch which stops the reel from back winding. This can be useful for getting just the right amount of tension in the line when you are quivertipping on fast rivers, where the flow makes the reel backwind.

Inter-changeable quick-release spools most reels have quick-release spools so you can remove them by simply pressing a button.

Reels which take spools of different line capacities are useful. It means that you can keep a spool of different breaking strain line for each type of fishing and need fill each spool with only 100m (109yd), say, of line. So, for example, in early summer, tench might be your quarry – and a spool taking

▲ On an open-face spool, line can peel freely from the wide spool. Tapered spools (like the one above right) reduce resistance at the front of the spool making casting even easier. Moulded concentric ribbing promotes even line-lay. Closed-face spools are narrower and suited to short-range work with lines below 4lb (1.8kg). The chenille trim at the front and back of the spool serves the same purpose as a skirt on the open-faced spool in stopping line from tangling round the inside of the reel.

When to use each type of reel

Open-face reels	Closed-face reels
Trotting when the fish want a bait presented at exactly the same speed as the current.	Trotting rivers when the fish are not particular about the bait being presented at the speed of the current.
When accurate casting is necessary.	Speed fishing with a medium-sized waggler (4 BB) when accurate casting is not important.
Fishing with light wagglers of about 2 or 3 BB.	Tangle-free casting when the wind blows line off the spool of your open-face reel.
When using heavy lines for big fish.	
Long range floatfishing with big wagglers of 2SSG or more.	

Bedding-in

You can reduce the effects of bedding-in on closed-face reels by loading them with as little line as possible. The late, great Clive Smith used to load his with just 25m (27yd) of line.

100 m (109yd) of 4lb (1.8kg) line would be ideal. But, in late autumn you may be after roach and need a shallower spool taking 100 m (109yd) of 2lb (0.9kg) line.

Automatic arm Some open-face reels have automatic bale arms for one-hand casting. These serve the same purpose as the push-button release on closed-face reels. The feature is useful when speed is important, as in match fishing, but on some the line is apt to tangle round the bale.

Bait runners These are found on some open-face models. They are useful for fishing for carp, pike, eels, or any other fish which runs with a bait. A bait runner allows the fish to take line freely while the bale arm is closed. By flicking a switch, you disengage the bait runner and you're ready to strike without having to worry about re-engaging the bale arm.

Buying a reel

Before buying a reel, think about the kind of fishing you'll be doing most. If in doubt, ask your tackle dealer to help you and check out the following points:
● As a general guide, go for the established brands as they provide the most efficient back-up service should anything go wrong or need replacing.
● The reel should be smooth running so that the handle continues to rotate a few times after a quick flick. Ball races promote smooth running and make reels particularly good for handling large fish. Manufacturers describe these as 'ballbearings' and some reels have up to three sets.
● Pay particular attention to the bale arm. It should open and close easily but positively. You shouldn't have to wind hard to get it to close over again. If it has a line roller make sure it rolls.
● Check to see that the drag gives out line smoothly.
● Try the reel on a rod. It should feel comfortable and you should be able to reach the lip of the spool easily with your fingertip.
● Check the spools carefully. Make sure they are of the right capacity for your kind of fishing. If they are open-face spools they are best if they have a skirt. This prevents the line from blowing inside the reel and tangling. Spools for closed-face reels should have a chenille trimming for the same reason. Make sure you can get spare spools and check to see if they are included in the initial price of the reel, or if you have to buy them as an extra.

▶ *Service your reel at least once a season. Major repairs should be left to your tackle dealer but if yours is a reel which can be reassembled easily it is best to strip it completely before cleaning.*

Remove the cover and pick out any sand or grit. Wash in warm soapy water. Use a good oil to lubricate the bearings and a light grease on the gears. A quick spray inside and out with moisture repellant will keep your reel in good order.

Open-face features

1. Adjustable (stern) drag
2. Bait runner setting
3. Bait runner switch
4. Anti-reverse
5. Push-button spool release
6. Manual bale option

The open-face design is probably the best choice for all round fishing.

Basic knots

A fish lost because the hook pulls out or because the fish gets into a snag is something that can't be helped. Fish lost because of knot failure is a result of poor angling.

There are no 'strong' knots – no matter how well-tied and reliable a knot is, it's still a weak link in the tackle. Unfortunately, even in the simplest rig you need at least one knot – to tie the hook on – so we're stuck with them. But by choosing the right knot for the job, tying it correctly and avoiding granny knots you can cut your losses.

A good knot

Two of the commonest ways in which knots fail are when the knot slips and comes undone and when the line breaks next to the knot as it is put under pressure. These can have several causes.

A slippery customer Nylon mono-filament isn't the easiest stuff to knot. Firstly it is extremely smooth so there is always a natural tendency for the knot to slip. (A slightly curly 'pig's tail' at the end of the line is a sure sign that this has happened.) Secondly, line damages easily. Surface abrasions, kinks, twists and general deformation of the cross-sectional profile all reduce line strength. In the higher breaking strains – above 10lb (4.5kg) – this may not be a significant reduction but light hooklengths can be weakened by 50% or more. Merely tying a knot and pulling it tight damages the line but some knots do more harm than others.

The old faithful It is surprising how many anglers pile one granny knot on top of another in the hope that the join won't yield. It only takes one encounter with a sizeable chub, carp, tench, pike or barbel to realize

that this faith is misplaced. Grannies are not designed to do any job in particular. They give a poor return in terms of knot strength – badly deforming the line so that it snaps well before its recommended breaking strain is reached.

Friction Easing a knot tight causes the line to slide against itself or another item of tackle, under considerable pressure. This generates heat. Excessive heat weakens the line and can even cause it to melt. It is essential to lubricate the knot **before** making it tight – you can do it with water or saliva – but it must be lubricated in some

▼ *Knots are the weak links in your tackle but there is no need to make them any worse by tying them badly. Make sure each knot is secure.*

▲ *There's a thin line between you and your fish. Don't ignore an unwanted knot in your hooklength – replace the hooklength.*

Six frequently used knots

1. Half blood knot

A simple knot for attaching swivels, legers, hooks etc. But do at least six turns to stop it from slipping.

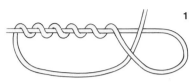

2. Tucked half blood

A variant on the blood knot, this knot has the same applications but is less likely to slip.

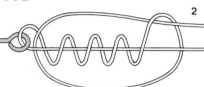

3. Double overhand loop

This is a reliable knot for making a loop in hooklengths or mainline – ideal for the loop-to-loop method.

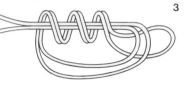

4. Loop-to-loop

A simple and popular method of attaching hooklengths to the mainline. Its only drawback is that it has a tendency to pick up weed.

5. Water knot

A small, neat versatile knot for joining line to line – good for attaching hooklengths and making paternosters.

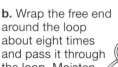

6. Whipping knot

a. This is for tying on spade end hooks. Make a loop and lay it against the hook shank leaving a 6cm (2 ½in) free end.

b. Wrap the free end around the loop about eight times and pass it through the loop. Moisten the knot.

c. Hold free end and apply steady pressure to the hooklength so the knot slides tight. The line should come off inside of spade.

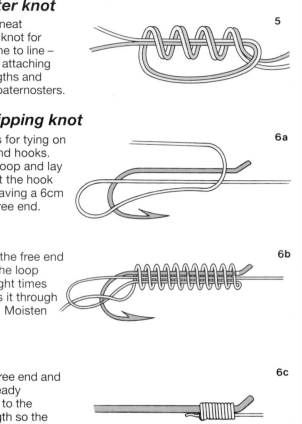

Stop knot

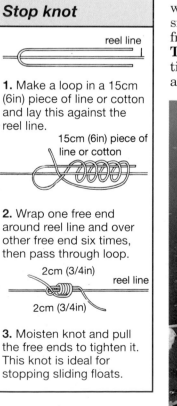

1. Make a loop in a 15cm (6in) piece of line or cotton and lay this against the reel line.

2. Wrap one free end around reel line and over other free end six times, then pass through loop.

3. Moisten knot and pull the free ends to tighten it. This knot is ideal for stopping sliding floats.

▶ **If you have trouble tying spade end hooks, then try using a hook tyer.**

way. Not only does this help the knot to snug down properly but it prevents the line from weakening.

Tightening the knot Don't pull a knot tight by tugging it. Line has a certain amount of elasticity but a sudden shock loading causes permanent deformation and weakens it. Ease it together slowly under an even pressure.

Twists and turns Give your knots a generous number of turns if this is appropriate. If you are advised to do at least half a dozen turns then make sure you do at least half a dozen or else the knot may slide undone when under pressure.

Knot gone wrong Most of the well-known knots look neat if they have been tied correctly. If the finished result looks untidy then it has probably gone wrong. Don't take chances – break the line off and start again. This may be a difficult task if your hands are wet or cold but it is worth it. A knot that has been badly tied doesn't function properly.

Trimming off When you've tied a knot you need to trim off any loose ends. Just how close you trim a knot depends on what it is being used for. Before trimming hook knots latch the hook on to something – such as scissor handles – and pull the knot tight. Use the scissors to trim within 1mm of the knot. With other knots – such as those used to tie on swivels – you can afford to leave 3-4mm. Always allow a little for slippage.

Keep knots to a minimum. Knotted line may be only 80% of its recommended breaking strain.

Mixing and using groundbait

Tackle shops sell bag after colourful bag of groundbaits, containing everything from pigeon droppings to molasses, but the real secret to successful groundbait is in the mixing.

▶ *A special groundbait catapult is essential for feeding bream swims a long way out on reservoirs and other large still-waters.*

At its simplest, groundbait is nothing more than dried and crushed bread. In recent years, however, so-called Continental groundbaits have become very popular. These contain all sorts of ingredients besides bread: binders such as ground peanuts; flavourings like vanilla; even laxatives (supposedly to make the fish hungrier!). The packaging of these groundbaits usually recommends what types of fish and waters they are for, and how best to use them, but it can still be very confusing to know where to start.

Mixing rules

Whether you use plain bread or a Continental groundbait, the basic rules of mixing and using are the same. Unless you understand these no amount of additives will help you to catch more fish.

The first thing to consider is the kind of container you mix your groundbait in. Many anglers use a bucket or such-like, which is a mistake because the deeper and narrower the container, the harder it is to get an even mix; the groundbait at the top tends to be over-wetted, while that at the bottom is too dry. Also, any maggots you put in tend to burrow down and accumulate in a mass at the bottom. The ideal con-

▼ *When fishing close-in you can throw your groundbait in by hand, but be sure to mix it properly or the balls will break up in mid-air and land all over the place, scattering your fish.*

Mixing groundbait

1. Put some groundbait into a large, shallow mixing bowl or tray, preferably one with rounded corners. Add the water a bit at a time, mixing vigorously and thoroughly with your fingers all the while to make sure the water is evenly absorbed.

2. With the right mix of water and dry crumb the groundbait feels light and fluffy. You will know it's just the right consistency when you can easily squeeze it into balls with gentle pressure yet break it up again without it forming stodgy lumps.

3. Mould your groundbait into orange-size balls for medium range breaming, tangerine-size balls for close-in fishing for skimmers and rudd. The harder you squeeze the balls, the farther you can throw them and the deeper they sink before breaking up.

4. If you have mixed your groundbait correctly you can add quite a few casters, maggots or sweetcorn or whatever, but don't overdo it or the balls will break up in mid-air and fly everywhere. Shown here are caster 'pies' – the downfall of many bream and tench.

tainer is wide and shallow, which allows a thorough and even mix.

Next, don't mix all your groundbait in one go at the start of the session. If you do it will dry out during the course of the day. Far better to make it up a small batch at a time, as you use it.

The same rule applies to adding bait samples, especially maggots. If you put a whole lot of maggots in at the start, as well as working their way to the bottom they absorb moisture and become floaters.

Different mixes

The most important quality of a groundbait is not its colour, smell, taste or ingredients, but its texture. The same bag of dry groundbait can be put to a wide range of uses simply by varying its texture when you mix it at the waterside.

Mix it very dry and squeeze it very gently so that the balls only just hold together, and you have a groundbait that breaks up into an attractive cloud as soon as it hits the water – ideal for fishing on-the-drop in still waters in summer.

The same, very dry, mix is also ideal for open-end swimfeedering on still waters, as the groundbait literally explodes out of the swimfeeder as it absorbs more water on the bed of your swim.

Mix groundbait so it is moist but not sloppy, and it will be just sticky enough to bind together with maggots or casters and hold together in mid-air. Yet it won't be so stodgy as to stop it breaking up as it sinks to form an attractive cloud in the bottom half of the water – ideal for still-water and slow-river bream.

Throwing groundbait

Most of the time you can comfortably reach your swim with your groundbait by throwing it in by hand, either overarm or underarm. Never struggle to get distance because, groundbait being relatively light, it is all too easy to strain a muscle in your arm or shoulder. It's much better to buy and learn to use a groundbait catapult.

When using a groundbait catapult, don't try to fire in balls bigger than about tangerine-size, and give each ball a 'glaze' with water to prevent it from sticking to the pouch.

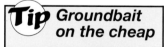

Tip Groundbait on the cheap

The cheapest way to buy ordinary groundbait is by the sackful. Store it in a plastic dustbin with a tight-fitting lid to keep it fresh and dry and out of the reach of rodents.

An even greater saving can be made by making your own groundbait. Ask your family and neighbours to save all their crusts and leftover bread. Dry the bread in an airing cupboard or similarly warm place, then grind it up in a food processor. Start this in the close season so you have some in reserve.

Fishing with wagglers

There is often confusion about what a waggler is. Is it a specific kind of float? Should it have a body? Why is it so special? Here are the answers.

▼ *After casting to the feed area, dip the rod in the water and give a few sharp turns of the reel to leave the line below the surface, away from any wind.*

S trictly speaking, waggler is a term that may be applied to any float attached bottom only. For this reason it comes in a variety of shapes, sizes and materials. It holds no mystery, but once you master waggler fishing you have at your disposal an extremely versatile technique and one that produces results when all else fails.

Types of waggler
There are basically two types: straight and bodied, both with or without inserts. The main stem of a waggler is usually made from peacock quill, sarkandas reed or plastic, with the body made from balsa or cork, and the insert from thinner quill, reed, cane or plastic. Some are fashioned entirely from one piece of balsa. Wagglers come in a range of sizes, from two BB (the lightest) to three SSG (the heaviest). Tackle shops stock these under different commercial names.

Why wagglers?
Without exception, you want to get the bait to where the fish are and keep it there. If the fish are a long way out you may have trouble casting to them. If the wind is strong you may be unable to keep the float over the feed. A waggler will help you to solve these problems.

Firstly, a float that is attached by its bottom, with the bulk of the shot around its base, acts like a dart as it flies through the air. It is possible to cast it a long way with great accuracy.

Secondly, because the line issues from the bottom of the float, you can keep the line (from float to rod) entirely beneath the water's surface, away from the wind.

However, there are times when you need to hold a bait back – when fishing medium and fast-flowing rivers, for example. If you use a waggler it will dive under each time you pull on the float; a float attached top and bottom – a stick float, for example – would be better than a waggler.

Which waggler?
Four things should be considered when choosing which waggler to use: location of the fish, wind strength, depth of water, and shyness of fish.

The location of the fish: as a rough guide,

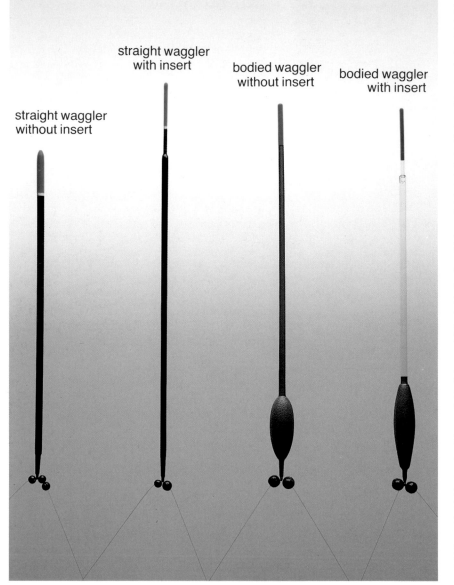

straight waggler
without insert

straight waggler
with insert

bodied waggler
without insert

bodied waggler
with insert

if the fish are three or four rod lengths out, you will need a lightish float taking only two, three or four BB. If the fish are further out choose a heavier float taking from two AAA to several SSG. When in doubt, it is almost always best to choose a float on the heavy side; this makes casting less of a strain.

Wind strength: a stronger wind demands a heavier float to get the bait out, especially if it is blowing in your face. On large, open expanses of water, where the wind is particularly strong, powerful surface drag and undertow tend to move the float out of position. Long wagglers – up to 45cm (18in) – help to counteract these effects, and using a bodied waggler increases stability.

Depth of water: the waggler's dart-like behaviour tends to make it pierce the water on entry. In shallow water a long float that dives too deeply may scare the fish away from the feed area. In this situation you can use a bodied float to good effect. With a body you can use a shorter float while retaining the shotting capacity of a straight waggler.

Shyness of fish: if the fish are biting shyly you may need an insert. Inserts are particularly useful for detecting bites on the drop. But make sure it is thick enough to see.

Attaching a waggler

The traditional method of attaching the waggler by its bottom eye makes float changing inconvenient. It is better to use ready-made, quick-change adaptors or – for small wagglers – a piece of silicone rubber tubing.

Silicone rubber is available in several diameters. Choose one to suit your wagglers. Keep a 15cm (6in) length in your tackle box and cut off pieces as you need them. Use

▲ *There are two basic types of waggler; the straight waggler and those with bodies. Both straight and bodied wagglers can have inserts which help detect shy bites. Most inserts are fixed though removable ones are available.*

 **Accurate casting**

It is hard to judge long distances over the water. When fishing at long range, Dave Berrow puts an elastic band on the spool. This enables him to cast to the same spot every time, ensuring that the hookbait is over the feed area. To do this, cast to the feed area then slip a small, flat elastic band over the spool, trapping the line at the required length.

DAVE BERROW'S FAVOURITE RIGS

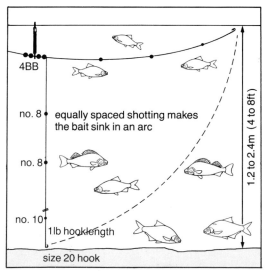

4BB

no. 8   equally spaced shotting makes the bait sink in an arc

no. 8

no. 10

1lb hooklength

size 20 hook

1.2 to 2.4m (4 to 8ft)

▲ *Lakes and rivers 'on the drop rig'. This rig will catch fish at all levels. The bulk of the shot goes round the base of the float. A fish taking the bait on the drop will cause the insert to lift or cause a slight delay in its settling.*

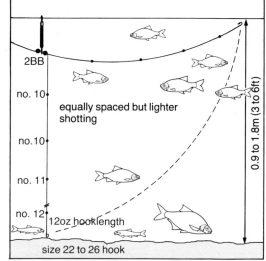

2BB

no. 10   equally spaced but lighter shotting

no.10

no. 11

no. 12

12oz hooklength

size 22 to 26 hook

0.9 to 1.8m (3 to 6ft)

▲ *Canals and ponds 'on the drop rig'. For shy canal fish use a lighter version of the lakes and rivers rig. A fish intercepting the bait causes a bite to be registered in the same way.*

scissors – this gives a cleaner cut and prevents the line from slicing through the rubber on the cast.

Float adaptors allow the float to swing more freely. When striking with a heavy waggler this is an advantage: the float is free to 'collapse' and direct contact is made between the angler and fish. To use a float adaptor simply thread it on to the line and insert the waggler.

Rods, reels and lines

To get the most from your wagglers your tackle needs to be balanced.

The rod should be powerful enough to pick up the line quickly when striking at distance but not so stiff that there is risk of snapping off, or bumping fish off on the strike.

Ideally you should use two rods. A 12 to 13ft (3.6 to 3.9m) through-actioned rod with a softish tip is perfect for handling pond and canal rigs. For waggler fishing lakes and rivers a 13ft (3.9m) rod with a similar action but with a bit of extra power in the butt is ideal.

If you only have one rod you will have to modify your striking and casting to suit the conditions.

Reel: an open-faced fixed-spool allows you to cast further than a closed-faced reel.

Line: remember that your line strength depends upon the size of fish you expect to catch and the size of float you use. Generally, for the size of float used on ponds and canals (2-4 BB) you can get away with a main line of about 1½lb (0.7kg). For the floats used on lakes and rivers (2 AAA-2 SSG) a heavier line is required; 2 to 2½lb (0.9-1.2kg) is about right.

▲ *Shop-bought wagglers come in a variety of shapes and sizes. The quality has been much better in recent years and it's no longer necessary to make your own.*

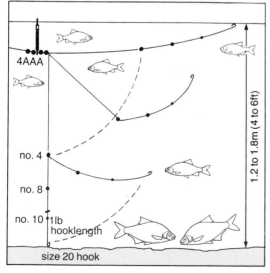

4AAA

no. 4

no. 8

no. 10 1lb hooklength

size 20 hook

1.2 to 1.8m (4 to 6ft)

▲ *Lakes and rivers 'on the bottom rig'. The no.4 makes the hookbait sink faster, getting it through to the better fish on the bottom. When feathering on the cast, the no.4 brings the hooklength over in a nice arc, preventing tangles.*

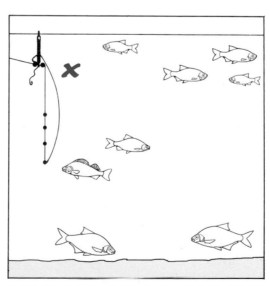

▲ *It is important to use the correct shotting pattern down the line because this directly affects bait presentation. Bunching too much weight too close together leads to tangles when casting and makes the bait behave unnaturally.*

⊗ Locking the float

Using most of the float's total shotting capacity to lock it in place is the simplest part of shotting a waggler and yet many people get it wrong by putting too much shot down the line. This makes casting impossible.

▶ *These beautiful specimen bream fell to a waggler rig. Whether you're long range fishing for bream on lakes or fishing for chub on the far river bank, using the waggler method is very effective.*

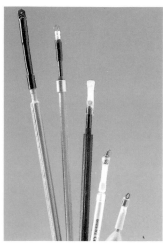

▲ *A selection of float adaptors. To use one, thread the line through the eye at the bottom, slide the adaptor up the line to the desired depth and push the bottom of the waggler firmly into the adaptor. Lock the float with shot placed on either side of the adaptor.*

More often than not you will want a sinking line. Some brands will sink of their own accord and it certainly helps to buy one of these, but you can treat a line to make it sink by soaking it in a solution of washing-up liquid.

Fishing the waggler

When you cast, let the rod and reel do the work for you. Unless fishing at an exceptional range, a smooth cast is all that is needed. If you have to lash the float out to reach the fish it could be because your float is too light for the job.

Feathering: an important trick to learn when fishing a waggler is feathering the line just as the float is about to land in the feed area. Do this by very gently increasing the pressure of your forefinger on the line as it spills over the spool's lip.

Feathering gives you extra control over where the float lands and reduces the float's impact. It allows the hook and shot to precede the float into the water and so prevents tangles. It is essential to good waggler fishing and takes a bit of practice to perfect.

Sinking the line: a light breeze is often enough to pull the float off your feed. If you are fishing a still water you will probably want to sink your line. To do this, cast a couple of yards beyond your feed area, submerge the rod tip and give a couple of sharp turns on your reel while at the same time jerking the rod to one side. Make sure all the line is submerged; even half a metre (2ft) left floating is enough to tow the float.

Float colour: choosing the correct colour for your float tip is important – get it wrong and you won't see the bites. Your choice should be determined by the surface colour of the water. Orange shows up well in broken (choppy) water. Black shows up well in areas of calm water where the sky is reflected. White is best when fishing in the dark reflections of trees or under the far bank of canals or rivers.

One transparent pattern of waggler uses interchangeable inserts so that quick changes of tip colour can be made to suit the conditions.

Striking: a hard, sharp strike may cause the fish to be bumped off or the hook hold to loosen – resulting in the fish being lost as you bring it in. A nice sweep to the side or a steady lift will set your hook sufficiently.

Feathering your line . . . . . . for the pinpoint cast

hooklength behind float

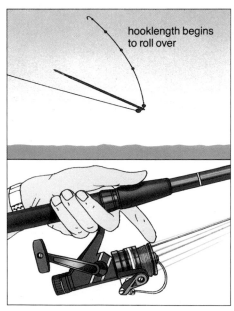

hooklength begins to roll over

hook in front of float

▲ *Release the line from under your forefinger to send the float zooming towards a target slightly beyond the feed area. Your forefinger is kept close to the spool's lip, ready to start feathering. At this stage the hooklength lags behind the float.*

▲ *As the float approaches the target area, slow the line by gently touching the spool's lip with your fingertip. Only with practice will you know just how much pressure to apply. The hooklength will begin to roll over and precede the float.*

▲ *Slightly increase the pressure to land the float spot on target (just beyond the feed area) with minimum disturbance. The terminal rig should land in a straight line with hook in front of float. Wind the float backwards over your feed, sinking the line.*

The basic leger kit

Roy Marlow, who has legered his way to hundreds of competition wins, gives his own choice of tackle for a basic leger kit.

In very simple terms legering means fishing on the bottom without a float, but using some form of bite indication.

Legering is by no means a new technique. It has been popular for hundreds of years. Yet in just the last decade there have been enormous developments.

A vast range of equipment is readily available – but to purchase every item would cost the earth. Fortunately it is not too expensive to buy a basic outfit that can do a little of everything and start you off on the right track.

Quivertips

Today the choice of rod and bite indicator is inseparable. Modern legering rods include provision for bite indicators as an integral part of the design.

The two main types of bite indicators are swingtips and quivertips. Swingtips have been around for 40 years and quivertips about 20 years. Most people use quivertips because they have many advantages as bite indicators – especially the fact that you can use them in fast-flowing waters where swingtips would be useless. If you are buying your first leger rod it should certainly be a quivertip.

Quivertip rods come in two forms, with either a screw-in end eye that will take a variety of bite indicators, or with quivers which can be pushed in and still be interchangeable. Quivertips that push in are preferable. They vary in sensitivity so it is important to choose the right one for your conditions.

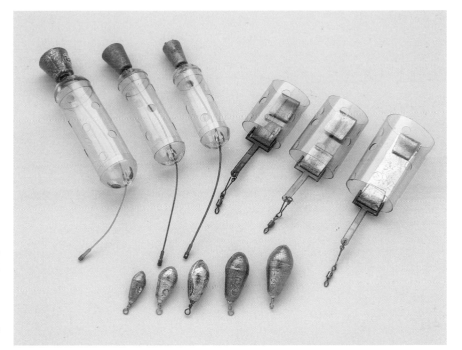

A selection of open and block-end swimfeeders, and a range of essential weights.

The basic kit

1. Target board – for easing bite identification.
2. Rod rest with multi-position head.
3. Sturdy fixed-spool reel with 3-4lb line.
4. Leger rod rest.
5. Leger rod butt – containing extra quivertips.
6. Leger rod – main section.
7. Leger rod – quivertip section.

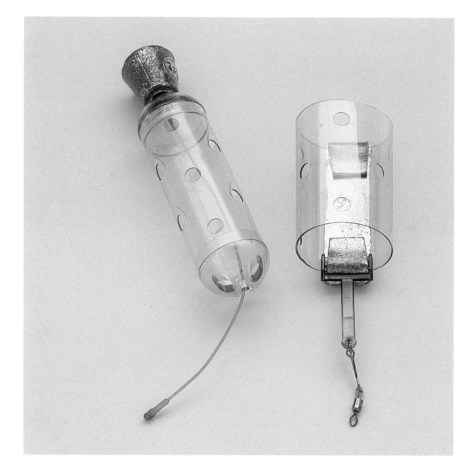

▲ *In action a block-end swimfeeder (left) releases the bait through holes in the feeder. To fish an open-end feeder (right), partially fill it with your hookbait and then plug the ends with groundbait. The bait is released through the holes and through the ends as the groundbait plugs dissolve.*

A basic mistake many beginners make is to buy a rod that is too short. If you buy one, say, 10ft (3m) long – including the quiver – then in effect you are fishing with a rod of only 8½ft (2.5m). This is too short. You need a rod with a total length of around 11ft (3.3m) – and if it comes with a variety of interchangeable tips, so much the better.

You should choose a rod made of carbon or a carbon composite – the difference in price between carbon and glass-fibre is negligible. Buy a rod manufactured by a top company, from the current catalogue. Ask your tackle dealer or local anglers for advice on which model to go for. It is a good idea to make sure you can get replacement joints for the rod in case you have an accident.

Reels and line

Your reel should be slightly bigger and stronger than a float-fishing reel. It needs to work harder – particularly if you use it for feeder-fishing. For most conditions a fixed-spool reel with at least 100yd (95m) of 3-4lb (1.4-1.8kg) line is strongly recommended. The reel should be filled to capacity, using old line as backing. Avoid the new 'super' lines – they may be excellent for float-fishing but most are rubbish for legering. It is important to remember that some lines sink and some lines float – you need a line that sinks.

Special equipment

You will also need a number of other items: one or more rod rests, a choice of swimfeeders – to attract fish to your patch – and a target board to show up bites on your quivertip more clearly. Target boards show up the shyest of bites, but allow you to concentrate when fish are slow to feed.

Leger rods

The length and stiffness of the rod is governed by the waters you are going to fish. For example, a rod ideal for fishing the lower Severn would not be ideal for use on a lake.

It would be nice if everyone could start out with a number of different rods, but since this is probably beyond most pockets you will have to accept a compromise with your first rod.

Tip Idleback

Rod rests were once nicknamed 'idleback' because it was thought they were used only by lazy fishermen eating their sandwiches! Now leger fishermen rely on them.

When fishing longer rods two adjustable rests can be used for support. A rest with a multi-position head means you can alter the rod angle with the minimum of fuss, or use two rods where permitted.

▶ *Quivering excitement – the sensitivity and robustness of a quivertip can be seen clearly here. An open-ended swimfeeder helped account for this roach. A wealth of species can be caught on basic leger tackle.*

Pole craft

Kevin Ashurst, the England team's most experienced member, maintains that when it comes to poles the simple things are important – and yet they are often overlooked.

▼ *This angler is using the long pole with a short line for perfect float control on the far side of the Kennet and Avon canal. The pole is excellent for this kind of fishing because you can drop the bait just where the fish want it and keep it there.*

Y ou may know the basic differences between whips and long poles but do you know about the limitations of each approach – where and when to use a whip and how to handle the long pole, for example? If you don't then you might run into problems. Since the pole is the most expensive item you'll ever buy, it pays to take care of it.

Fishing the whip

Whips are poles having very fine, flexible solid carbon fibre top sections – to which the line is attached.

Use the whip when there are small fish fairly close in – at about 3-5m (10-16ft) from the bank. It is most effective when there are a lot of fish because it is primarily a speed method.

It is faster than running line because the length of line from the top of the whip to the hook is kept constant – fish can be swung directly to hand every time. Although the long pole also uses a fixed length of line, the whip can be much faster because it does not involve elastic: it's a simpler, more direct method. Ideally the line should be about 30cm (1ft) shorter than the whip.

Control Whips are not exclusively for

▲ *Wielding a pole for the full five hours of a match takes a lot of effort, so it is important to be as comfortable as possible. This angler is using his knee as a pivot and taking the pole's weight with his left forearm – a method that Kevin recommends.*

✖ Breakages

"One thing that inexperienced pole anglers often do," says Kevin Ashurst, "is pick the pole up at the 3m point and try to hold up 10m behind them. Then they'll take it back to the shop and say it's broken. This isn't suprising because a pole isn't meant to take that kind of treatment. We've all done this kind of thing, though, and it is often the only way to learn."

▶ *In very windy conditions poles become difficult to manage and can break, so on days like this it is better to leave it to the experts.*

This angler is feeding the pole behind him to land a fish. You should do this smoothly so that you don't jerk the fish. Keep the tip of the pole out of the water so that you can see where the fish is.

speed. They are good for controlling rigs on slow rivers, canals and lakes with a slight pull. If a swim is not too deep – about 1.8m (6ft) at 4-5m (13-16ft) from the bank – then you might be able to run your float through about 2-3m (6-10ft). Within this region you'll have enough line out to control the float but if the flow is too strong you won't get a decent run through.

The float needs to be heavier than you would fish on a long pole but still light compared to those for running line – so you can cast it easily. When fishing at 5m (16ft) you need a float taking a minimum weight of 0.5g. If it's windy then you'll have to go even heavier.

Limitations It may sound obvious but the whip is only a fast method if you are catching. It is no use staying with it if you are missing bites. That's the time to try something else.

Big fish can present problems for the whip, too, because the flexibility of the flick tip is the only means of providing a running fish with line – and that may not be enough.

Long pole, short line

The term 'long pole' is misleading because you could use the top three sections of a 14m pole to fish a couple of metres out. More often than not, though, you'll be fishing at 7-8m (23-26ft) or beyond. It is usual for the length of line to be much less than the length of the pole. This means you have to dismantle – 'unship' – the pole to reach the hook.

The line is attached to elastic which runs through the top one or two sections of the pole. This serves a unique function – somewhere between that of a reel and rod top or flick tip – enabling a fish to take line but only up to a point and subject to increasing tension.

Buying a pole Poles are expensive and it pays to think carefully before parting with your money. You don't have to spend vast amounts – there are some very, very good poles for a perfectly reasonable price. It is up to you to go to a shop and haggle with your tackle dealer for a good price.

Materials Anything other than carbon fibre is not worth considering. Don't be tempted to get a glass-fibre pole. They are a thing of the past.

Length If you are at all serious about angling, you must buy one of at least 11m. Don't think: "Oh, I'll get a cheap one at 9 or 10m to learn with," because you'll see other anglers catching just a bit farther out and want a longer one. It is quite likely that any pole shorter than 11m will end up as nothing more than a landing net handle. There

Shipping-up

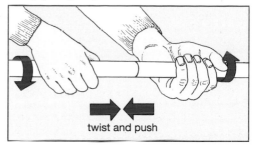

twist and push

When shipping-up, twist rather than push the sections together. This way you can control the amount of pressure and the sections are less likely to stick together.

is, nevertheless, a practical limit to the length of poles. Anything above 15.5m is difficult to handle.

Lightness and stiffness are related. Generally, an increase in lightness means a decrease in stiffness – though a good quality pole will be both light and fairly stiff.

Nevertheless, a good quality, light pole suffers when it is windy – bending, bouncing about and making good float control extremely difficult. (These kinds of conditions should in any case be left to the experts.) So to begin with it is a good idea to get a fairly light pole and to fish it when conditions are favourable. Only when you have mastered the basics should you think about fishing a heavier, stiffer pole in adverse conditions. One of between about 800-900g at 12.5m can be managed comfortably by the average angler.

Spare top sections Certainly for matches,

Pole rollers

Use a roller to take the weight of the pole and guide it when you are pushing it back. This removes the temptation for you to lift it by the end sections (something which you should never do) and prevents the end from getting damaged. A wide roller is easier to use because you don't have to keep looking to see where the end of the pole is.

Sometimes a hedge or fence behind you serves just as well as a roller.

it is essential that you have at least one, if not two spare sets of the top three sections to your pole. This enables you to set up several different rigs at the same time. So for example, you can change from a 0.5g float to a 1.0g float just by picking up other sections of your pole, or you might want to fish identical tackles with different size hooks so that you can try a bait change. With a spare you can do this in a matter of seconds. This makes the pole an exciting method; you can try many different things within a matter of half an hour or so – you can't do this with the running line.

Joints Most modern poles have put-over joints. They make shipping-up (putting the pole together) easier – you don't have to fiddle around, struggling with unwieldy lengths of pole, trying to find the hole. You can do it without looking.

Shipping-up When you piece your pole together make sure that it doesn't join up with a 'chunk', otherwise it will jam and you'll be taking it home in a 2m length. Twist – screw – the joints rather than pushing them directly together. If the joints are

▲ *When you are landing a fish, just where you take-off (unship) depends on the size of the fish. If it is big – above a couple of pounds, say – you'll need to unship a section closer to to the tip of your pole than you would without a fish on. This is so that you can draw the fish towards you.*

Be prepared to use your landing net on fish that are much smaller than you would net on rod and line. This is because a fish of only 6oz (170g) will stretch the elastic and make it extremely awkward, if not impossible, to swing in.

that loose sections of your pole aren't rattling about. If your pole does get damaged then whip over the damaged area to reinforce it – your tackle shop will probably be willing to help.

How to sit One method is to sit with your legs at a slight angle to the water, the pole resting across your knees and the end of it trapped firmly under your forearm. This way you don't need any pole behind you to balance it – you can use the full length of the pole for the job it was intended.

Casting is simple with a pole. All you need to do is push the tackle out with the pole and lay it on the water.

Striking A lot of anglers don't strike hard enough when fishing the pole. You need to pull it hard upwards. If you strike to one side then the float tends to 'clonk' out of the water like a stick float.

Pole on the water It isn't advisable to rest the pole on the water but it can be a help to sink the line when conditions are very windy by submerging the top two sections.

The only time that a pole seems to scare fish is on a clear water when you've got them feeding on rod and line. If you put a pole over them you'll stop getting bites – either because they move off or just stop feeding. At other times they'll come right under the pole and feed. There is a canal in Liverpool that is so clear you can actually see the fish doing this.

It takes practice to get used to fishing a pole. The change from using a rod of 3 or 4m to a pole of 10 or 11m is a big one, and at first you'll probably feel a bit awkward. But after a few good catches you'll soon feel more at ease.

supposed to overlap by 8cm (3in) make sure that they do overlap by that amount. If you lift a pole when the joints are not properly overlapping it will shatter.

The joints on the sections which are not unshipped should be tight so that they don't come apart when they are not meant to.

When you are catching fish and you are unshipping and shipping-up there is always a chance of picking up grit on the end of a section. If you try to push a pole together with grit between the joints you'll do irreparable damage to it. So always make sure the joints are clean.

Avoiding damage When handling a pole be careful not to knock it against rocks or stones. Although carbon fibre is strong for its weight it is also an extremely brittle material. Even the slightest nick in the pole's surface weakens it.

It is often the case that a pole shatters and the angler concerned insists that he wasn't mishandling it. The chances are that the damage had already been done and it was only a matter of time before the pole broke. Therefore, if it is windy make sure

▲▼ *Here are two methods of feeding while holding the pole. Gripping the catapult pouch with the hand holding the pole (above), and leaning on to the pole and trapping it under the belly to leave the hands free (below).*

COARSE FISHING

BAITS

Hooked on maggots

Maggots in their uncoloured, unflavoured form are often highly successful but a bright, enticingly flavoured bait will sometimes give you the edge.

special balance
hempseed
aniseed
super fruit
nut

I t's obviously important when fishing that the fish can see the bait and that they like what they see. For example, when fishing on murky waters a plain maggot may be hardly visible, whereas a bright red or yellow specimen may show up clearly. There are several things you can do to maggots to enhance their appeal.

Flavourings

Some anglers claim to have great success with flavoured maggots, arguing that fish prefer some tastes and smells to others. Whether true or not, unclean maggots have a strong smell of ammonia which certainly seems to put the fish off. This smell is greatly reduced by cleaning. Any remaining odour can be masked with flavourings. Handling maggots can also leave an off- putting smell, especially when handled by smokers who taint the bait with nicotine. These effects, too, can be reduced by using flavourings.

But how do you know which smells will be appealing to fish? Some anglers argue that sweet flavours – like vanilla – are best during the warm months and spicy ones – like turmeric – are best during the winter. The only way to find out which flavours suit your kind of fishing is to experiment.

Tackle shops stock a bewildering range of flavourings in little bottles and atomizers. On the whole these are used by carp anglers to flavour boilies but on

vanilla flavouring

bream attractor

bloodworm flavouring

roach attractor

waters where these flavourings have been introduced, anglers have found that other species (such as roach and bream, for example) sometimes show a preference for them. Flavourings in powder form that are specially formulated for adding to loose feed and groundbait are available. Popular ones are: vanilla, caramel, coriander and aniseed. Clean the bait,

▲ *All sorts of flavourings are available in liquid or powder form and some of them smell good enough to eat. But do the fish like them? There is only one way to find out which suits your fishing: experiment.*

◄ *Red, bronze, yellow and the humble white are all successful colours. A colour change often works when the going is tough. A catapult with a mesh pouch is ideal for firing out a few loose offerings each cast.*

Hooking maggots

The aim is to present a lively bait. To avoid bursting the maggot, choose a fine or medium wire, barbless or microbarb hook and gently nick the maggot just under the flap of skin at the blunt end. A crystal pattern hook is best as the maggot hangs directly beneath the point, helping you hook more fish. As a general principle, the choice of hook size depends on bait size, and the bait size depends on the size and species of fish you are hoping to catch.

Method for making maggots float

To make maggots float, the bait should be fresh – no more than three days old.

1 Put about 6mm (¼ in) water into a bait container to just cover the bottom.

2 Add a palmful of maggots. Then put the lid on so the maggots can't crawl out.

3 Leave them soaking for 20 minutes to absorb enough water to float.

then riddle off any maize or bran before sprinkling on the flavouring, or else the aroma and flavour will be absorbed by the cereal. Two teaspoonfuls are enough for a pint of maggots.

Colouring

Maggots can be dyed various colours. The most usual are yellow, bronze and red. Other maggots you may come across are green and blue, and the 'discos' in fluorescent orange, yellow and pink.

Anglers can dye their own maggots but the dye that is currently available does not 'take' so well and is easily washed off. It is better to buy ready coloured maggots. These have had the dye introduced during breeding, at the 'feed' stage, so the maggot is coloured internally.

Yellow and bronze During the Seventies, yellow and bronze were popular with matchmen (particularly on the Trent). It was then found that the particular dye used to colour these maggots causes cancer, so a ban was imposed on all such dyes. Safe alternatives have been found and yellow and bronze are widely used again.

Fish are able to differentiate between colours, and certain species do seem to prefer certain colours. Anglers have used yellow and bronze maggots to take large bags of roach, chub and dace.

Red One of the deadliest baits in the matchman's armoury is the bloodworm – the small red larvae of the midge. This highly effective, but controversial, bait has been banned at many venues. Anglers have tried to imitate it by using red squatts. Whether the fish are taken in by the substitution is doubtful, but the bait has certainly been used with considerable success for bream.

Large red maggots, red pinkies and red squatts are good for taking perch and carp, and tench sometimes show a preference for a red maggot.

Sinkers and floaters

The rate at which a maggot sinks through the water is an important factor in loose feeding. In some situations – when loose feeding on fast-flowing rivers, for example – you need to get the bait down quickly. At other times a slow sinking bait is best.

Whether your maggots are slow or fast sinkers will depend on their diet. Maggots which have been raised on meat sink quicker than those fed on fish (which have a higher water content). Most commercially bred maggots are fed meat offal, but it is worth asking your dealer what type he stocks.

Both fish-fed and meat-fed maggots can be made to float (see above right). Floating maggots can be fished on the surface to take surface feeding fish like carp, bleak, dace and chub.

Floaters can also be used to slow down the fall of the hookbait. When the bait is falling through the last foot or so of the water, it is important that it should look as natural as possible. The extra weight of even a small hook is enough to make a bait sink faster than your loose feed. You can counteract this by using a maggot that has been turned into a floater.

Bait, hook size and hooklength strength

Bait	Hooksize	Hooklength
Single large white	22 or 20	1-1½lb (0.45-0.68kg)
Two large whites	20 or 18	1-1½lb (0.45-0.68kg)
Three large whites	16 or 14	2-3lb (0.9-1.36kg)
Single pinkie	22	12oz-1lb (0.34-0.45kg)
Two pinkies	22 or 20	12oz-1lb (0.34-0.45kg)
Three pinkies	20 or 18	1-1½lb (0.45-0.68kg)
Single squatt	24 or 22	12oz-1lb (0.34-0.45kg)
Two squatts	22	12oz-1lb (0.34-0.45kg)
Three squatts	20	1-1½lb (0.45-0.68kg)

Tip Tangled hooklength?

With two or three maggots on the hook you sometimes find that the bait spins like a propeller on the retrieve, twisting and tangling the hooklength. This is especially common with fast-retrieve reels and on running water.

You might find you can solve this problem by simply winding in more slowly. Alternatively, some anglers find that hooking one maggot in the pointed end and the other in the blunt end can help to prevent twisting.

Experiment to see which works best for you.

Lobs, reds and brandlings

Worms are one of the most deadly, versatile and readily obtainable baits and yet they are often neglected in favour of more 'fashionable' baits.

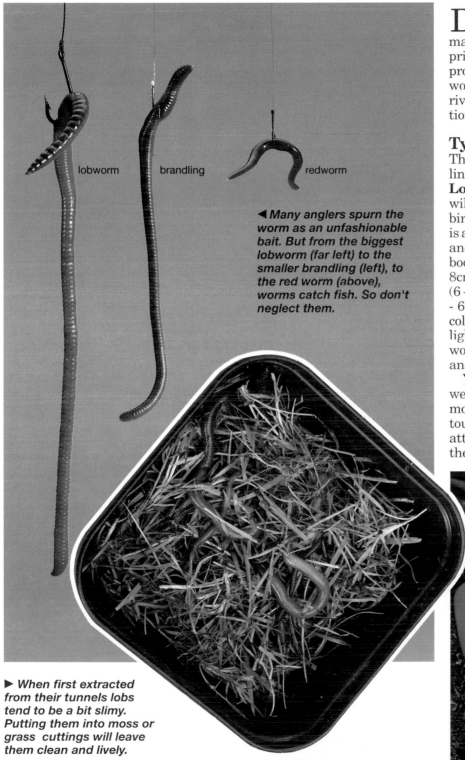

lobworm   brandling   redworm

◀ *Many anglers spurn the worm as an unfashionable bait. But from the biggest lobworm (far left) to the smaller brandling (left), to the red worm (above), worms catch fish. So don't neglect them.*

▶ *When first extracted from their tunnels lobs tend to be a bit slimy. Putting them into moss or grass cuttings will leave them clean and lively.*

▶ *Washing-up gloves are handy for easing lobs out of their holes. Hang on to the worm and wait until it contracts – it will pull itself out of the hole.*

During the summer months worms are a good bait for taking specimens; the matchman will often be pleasantly surprised by the bonus fish which a worm has produced. When the going gets tough, worms come into their own. On flooded rivers they often score when more conventional baits (such as maggots) have failed.

Types of worm

The three main types are: lobworms, brandlings and redworms.

Lobworms The big fat worm which you will have seen having a tug o' war with the bird in your back garden is the lobworm. It is a light reddish-brown and its tail is flatter and slightly broader than the rest of its body. These worms vary in length from 5 - 8cm (2 - 3in) to the real 'snakes' of 15 - 18cm (6 - 7in) but their average size is 13 - 15cm (5 - 6in). Lobs can be dug from the garden or collected from a wet lawn at night. Tread lightly, using a torch with a weak beam; lobworms are highly sensitive to bright light and vibrations.

You can keep lobs in the soil in which they were found or, better still, in sphagnum moss or grass cuttings. This cleans and toughens the worm's skin – making it more attractive to the fish – and helps it to stay on the hook better. Lobs can also be kept in

damp leafmould or damp newspaper.

Brandlings These have a red skin, which is softer than the lobworm's, and average 10 – 13cm (4 – 5in) in length with a series of yellow rings around the body. They are smaller than the lobworm.

When hooked, an unpleasant yellowish body fluid is released but this is only off-putting for the angler, not the fish.

Tackle shops sell pots of brandlings but they can be gathered quite easily from manure and compost heaps. Keep them in their original compost or manure and they'll stay lively for weeks.

Redworms These are deep red in colour – similar to the brandling but without the rings. They are the smallest of the three types of worm, growing up to about 5 – 8cm (2 – 3in), and are a favourite with the matchman. A single offering on a small hook, either by itself or as a 'cocktail' with caster or pinkie, is a most attractive bait for bream and perch.

This worm is fond of pig manure and can be found living alongside the brandling. Be sure to collect plenty – redworms make an excellent attractor when chopped and added to groundbait. Keep either in the substance in which they were found or in leafmould.

Storing the worms

All worms should be stored in a well ventilated box, in a cool place. Keep them damp but not wet (an atomizer is useful for applying a fine spray). Check them regularly and remove any dead or damaged worms to prevent contamination. Don't store them for longer than about two weeks.

Presentation

Worm will catch all species. Big tench, carp, chub and barbel are partial to a lob. These fish have big mouths so do not be afraid to use a big bait. Hook size depends on bait size. A bunch of two or three lobs on a size 4 or 6 hook, or a single offering on a 6, 8 or 10 is about right. Use a lob tail on a 14 or 16 to

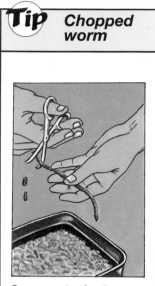

tempt roach, perch and eels.

Big bream can often be taken on a brandling or redworm when other baits have failed, and perch love these smaller worms. Present doubles on a size 14 or 16 and singles on an 18.

Hooking It is the worm's attractive wiggle and appealing scent that make it effective. Bear this in mind when hooking it. A common mistake is to try to 'staple' a worm to a hook that is too small by piercing it several times; this results in a lifeless lump of insipid looking 'worm meat'. After a couple of casts the bait tears as the hook pulls out, and soon becomes useless. Even if a fish is desperate enough to take a bait in this condition, it is likely that you will miss the bite because the hook will not be in the correct place.

Whether presenting whole baits, part baits or cocktails, hook the worm with great care, threading it on to the hook rather than piercing it.

◄ You might wonder whether a fish could swallow such a mouthful, but to large-mouthed fish such as barbel, carp and chub, baits like this are most appealing.

Tip — Chopped worm

Carry a pair of nail scissors for cutting up the worms. Chopped worms make an excellent attractor when added to groundbait.

▼ This big bream is typical of the kind of fish that often falls to a worm bait when other baits have failed. It always pays to take a few worms with you.

▲ Redworms are very lively, and when fished with a caster on a small hook, they make a good bait for skimmer and 'slab' bream – particularly during the winter months.

Succulent sweetcorn

Any bait that catches the record British carp can't be bad. Sweet and juicy, the bait in question is sweetcorn – don't leave home without it, says Andy Orme.

Sweetcorn is a superb bait. It's relatively cheap, requires little preparation and you can use it on a wide range of waters, both running and still, for a variety of fish. Roach, bream, tench, carp, chub and barbel are especially fond of it. They home in on its bright yellow colour and sweet smell and find its equally sweet taste very much to their liking.

Brightest and best

Tinned corn is more effective than the frozen or dried corn that you can buy in bulk – it's a much brighter yellow and comes ready-soaked in sugary juice.

▼ On hard-fished waters fish learn to associate yellow corn with danger. It can then pay to dye it different colours, such as red. You can even change its flavour by soaking it in one of the many concentrated flavourings available.

Sticky fingers

Sweetcorn is ready to use straight from the tin and indeed it's a simple enough matter to open a tin and tip the contents into a bait box. The drawback is that on the bank your fingers, rod and reel soon get covered in sticky juice, which in summer also attracts gnats and midges.

The way round this is to drain off the juice (not down the sink, but into a container, to keep for mixing groundbait), then rinse the corn in a sieve under a cold tap before putting it in the bait box. Before putting on the lid, cover the box with clingfilm to seal in the moisture and flavour of the now non-stick corn.

There's no reason, however, why you can't store a spare tin of corn in your tackle box, in case you forget to take some or run out

▼ Tinned corn – convenience food for the shopper, but more than just convenience bait for the angler. Barbel, chub, roach, bream, tench and carp all love it.

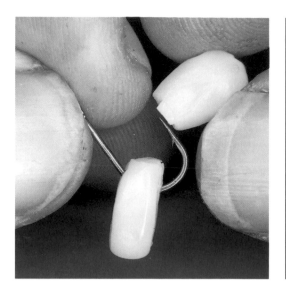

▲ *Two grains of corn fit snugly on a size 10 hook. For single corn, use a 14. For three or more grains, use an 8, 6 or 4. For carp and barbel you can use a hair rig to fish single or double corn on a big hook.*

▼ *Sweetcorn has seen the downfall of many a sweet-toothed specimen tench. Fish it under a float close to marginal weeds or at range with an open-end feeder.*

Tip **Sweetcorn soup**

Juice from a tin of corn adds flavour to groundbait but you can go further. All you need is access to a food processor.

Put equal amounts of water and tinned corn - juice and all – into the processor and liquidize. Take the resulting soup to the waterside in a vacuum flask (so it stays fresh) and use it instead of water to mix groundbait.

one time. And all is not lost if you don't remember the tin opener – simply punch a hole in the tin with a large bank stick then shake out the contents. But be sure to take the tin home with you at the end of the day. Don't discard it at the waterside – any litter is unsightly, and the jagged edges of a rusting tin are a danger to birds and animals.

Catching with corn

Small baits such as maggots attract all sizes of fish. Sweetcorn is large by comparison and small fish find it difficult to get their mouths round even a single grain. It's

therefore a selective bait, very good for when you're looking to pick out the bigger fish in a swim.

Rivers Loosefeeding a few grains of corn every cast and trotting or legering one or more grains is an excellent way of catching roach, chub and barbel. It pays to vary the depth when trotting because you often find that chub take the corn in mid-water while barbel and roach usually want it near the bottom.

Still waters Laying-on (floatfishing a bait on the bottom) close-in over a bed of corn, especially alongside weed beds, can be deadly for roach, bream and tench. If the fish are farther out, use an open-end feeder: pack it with corn and plug it with groundbait. There's nothing to stop you adding other baits such as hemp and casters to the groundbait, or trying cocktail hookbaits such as corn and breadflake.

Stalking Sweetcorn is a first class bait for stalking fish in clear, shallow water. Many a huge carp and chub has fallen for this method, but when feeding it's essential not to land the corn right on the noses of these wary fish.

Place it in their path or wait until they temporarily leave the swim. Being bright yellow, the grains shine like miniature underwater beacons, not only attracting the fish but making it easy for you to watch the bait being taken.

Using your loaf – flake, mash and crust

It never goes out of fashion. It's cheap, clean, easy to prepare and catches all species of coarse fish, apart from predators. John Bailey tells you about bread.

Bread's effectiveness as a bait is underestimated and it's a pity it is not used as widely as it was 20 years ago. Bread interests roach, rudd, bream, barbel, chub, tench or carp – even if they have never seen the bait before. It has no off-season and is as eagerly accepted in the winter frosts as it is in the dog days of summer. What is more, it tends to attract a better stamp of fish.

What makes bread good?
To us, a slice of bread tastes and smells rather bland and this is probably why we invented the sandwich spread, but to fish it is just this clean, natural taste that is so enticing. Maybe colour has something to do with it too. Unless the fish has its head buried in the mud, a white morsel lying on the bottom is likely to attract the attention of even the most heavily preoccupied tench or carp.

Our daily bread
Forget the baps, baguettes, cottage loaves and cobs. Humble, medium-sliced and unsliced loaves – fresh ones, mind – are the finest choice for bread baits. These two types of loaf are effectively half a dozen baits in one. Three of the simplest are flake, mash and crust.

Flake The advantage of flake is that it is light, fluffy, sinks slowly and rests on top of weed and mud rather than sinking into them.

Choice of hook size depends on bait size

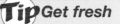

▼ *This fine tench fell to a big piece of flake fished hard on the bottom under a peacock quill – a method that has accounted for more tench than any other.*

▲ *Prebaiting with bread mash the night before you intend to fish is a good way of attracting tench and carp into a swim. Early morning feeders are caught quite close in, so don't throw your bait too far.*

which in turn depends on the species you expect to catch. Don't go too small – sizes 8-14 are about right for flake.

Simply pull a piece of bread from the middle of a slice – roughly round and 1-2.5cm (½-1in) in diameter. Push the hook through the middle and pinch the bread firmly around the hook's shank, leaving the bend and barb free. If the bread is fresh and the cast not too vigorous, flake stays hooked for at least 20 minutes.

A good place to try flake is a spot on a river, lake or canal where the ducks are regularly fed by the public. Big roach get used to mopping up pieces of bread which the ducks have missed and a piece of flake fished on the drop may get you a real beauty

(but make sure the ducks aren't around).

Mash Flake fished over a carpet of mashed bread is a good method for taking bream, tench and carp. Simply soak some bread thoroughly and mash it until the mix is firm enough to throw or catapult into the swim but sloppy enough to cloud the water.

Floating crust An uncut tin loaf provides one of the most effective surface baits for carp or rudd– floating crust. Use a fresh loaf – a dry crust cracks and comes off the hook.

Match the size of bait to the type of fish you expect to catch, and match size of hook to bait size. An 8lb (3.6kg) carp is quite capable of swallowing a piece of crust the size of a matchbox – a bait which easily hides a size 2 hook. A 1½lb (0.7kg) rudd has a comparatively small mouth, and a thumb-nail sized piece of crust on a 12 or 14 is perfect.

Flavourings

Often the subtlety of an unflavoured, uncoloured bait works perfectly but sometimes the fish prefer a souped-up bait.

Flavoured flake is excellent. You can use an atomizer containing liquid flavouring. Open the wrapper of a sliced loaf at both ends and spray with a few bursts from an atomizer. Reclose the wrapping, put the loaf in a polythene bag and store it in the freezer. On the bank the bread thaws and draws the flavour through the loaf. Liquid flavourings such as cream cheese, blue cheese and salmon are excellent but there are plenty more to experiment with.

▼ *A ragged piece of fresh flake pinched on to the shank of the hook is an attractive bait. White bread is the usual choice but brown can work just as well.*

▼ *A matchbox sized piece of crust, fished right on the edge of, or among, lilies is a traditional way of catching carp, but a scaled down version of the same method is excellent for specimen roach and rudd.*

Tip **Hooking crust**

John Bailey recommends that you push the hook, bend first, through from the soft side until it breaks through the crust and the point is just clear. Then wrap the line around the crust and pass it under the bend of the hook. Push the point firmly back into the crust in a different place from where it broke through, trapping the line under the bend. This ensures that the bait does not fly off when casting.

▲ *You can let water into a hollow plastic bubble float to vary its casting weight, making it ideal when fishing floating crust.*

Basic boilies

Boilies have helped transform carp fishing from a specialist pursuit to the fastest growing branch of coarse angling, says Peter Mohan.

Tip *Add flavour*

If you want to experiment with different flavours, but don't want to go to the trouble of making your own boilies, buy frozen 'neutral' boilies and bottles of concentrated liquid flavouring. Add about 30ml (about two tablespoons) of flavouring per 5lb (2.3kg) of boilies and reseal the bag. The boilies then absorb the flavouring as they begin to thaw out.

◄ *Boilies are the most popular bait for carp but can also catch big tench, bream, chub and barbel. Indeed, you can now buy mini-boilies, which are pea-sized to make it easier for these fish to take them.*

Twenty years ago carp fishing was the preserve of a dedicated few, and their successful baits were closely guarded secrets. Commercial carp baits as such didn't exist. Each carp angler had secret recipes for paste baits containing all sorts of weird and wonderful ingredients.

The trouble with paste baits was that while they caught carp, other, smaller fish could nibble away at them. To overcome this, carp anglers came up with the idea of binding their paste ingredients with raw egg, rolling the mixture into marble-sized balls, then boiling the balls in water for a few minutes to form a tough skin that would resist the attentions of nuisance fish. Thus was born the basic boilie.

Boilie power

By the early 1980s boilies fished on hair-rigs were proving so successful that people began to make and sell the bait commercially. For the first time, ordinary anglers could fish for carp with a bait and rig that gave them every chance of success. Ready-to-use, off-the-shelf boilies of every imaginable colour and flavour are now the most widely used bait in carp fishing.

On some heavily fished waters so many boilies are thrown in that they form the staple diet of the carp. In extreme cases

the amount of boilies thrown in is directly responsible for the carp steadily gaining weight from one season to the next.

On the minus side, boilies have been banned on some carp waters because so many have been thrown in that some lie uneaten on the bottom until they rot and contaminate the water.

Make or buy?

Dedicated carp anglers make their own boilies – a laborious task, but one that does let you make them cheaply and in

▼ *Together with the hair-rig, the development and commercial production of boilies in all sorts of colours and flavours has helped bring carp fishing within the reach of the ordinary coarse angler.*

Making floating boilies on the bankside

You can prepare floating boilies at home by cooking them in a microwave oven, or by grilling or baking them. But there's a quick and easy way at the bankside. Cut off

the top of the boilie with a sharp knife. Make a hole in the middle of the boilie with a drill bit (1). Put a small ball of polystyrene in the hole formed (2). Suitable polystyrene

balls are sold as bean-bag fillers. Stick the top of the boilie back on with a drop of instant glue (3). The result is a 'pop-up' – a bait that can outscore the ordinary boilie.

bulk. Moreover, you can experiment with new recipes, colours and flavours.

For the occasional carp angler, however, commercial boilies are more convenient and more than adequate. They are sold in sealed plastic packets. Unopened, they can be kept fresh for several months if stored in a cool place away from direct sunlight. Once the packet has been opened your best bet – if you want to save any boilies left over from a fishing trip – is to freeze them.

Boilie breakdown
The basic ingredients of boilies are egg, which binds everything together, and the bulk, which can be various mixtures of proteins, carbohydrates, fats, minerals and vitamins. The theory behind these bulk ingredients is that carp recognize their nutritional value. Whether this is

true is debatable. What is certain, though, is that it's the flavour of boilies – and to a lesser extent their colour – that entices carp to eat them in the first place.

Flavour seems to be more important than colour because boilies are usually fished on the bottom, where carp generally find food more by smell than sight. Strong meat, fish and fruit flavours are all proven carp-catchers, but to find out what works best in a particular water you have to ask around or use trial and error.

Using boilies
In waters where boilies are used a lot, the carp are used to eating them so you only need to throw in 20 or 30 free offerings around each hookbait. If boilies are not used very much on the water, or if you are trying to wean the carp on to a new flavour, you may need to throw in several hundred and wait longer to get results.

Each time you catch a carp, throw more boilies in – about 10 is usually enough unless you are fishing a heavily stocked, 'hungry' water, in which case it's worth putting in twice as many.

Boilies are best fished on a hair-rig rather than threaded on the hook. Partly this is because boilies are hard baits, but the main advantage of the hair-rig is that it increases the chance of a carp hooking itself. The carp sucks in the boilie and hook, feels the hook and tries to blow it out – and the point of the free hook catches in the carp's mouth.

To make it easier for carp to spot your boilie hookbait and suck it in, try a 'pop-up' – a floating boilie anchored over your bed of free offerings by shot on the hook-length. To make boilies float, cook in a microwave oven on full power for a few minutes, or gently grill or bake them.

▼ *When fishing at range you can use a boilie catapult to feed a swim. But for greater accuracy, especially at night, thread the boilies on to a piece of PVA string tied to the hook. The string dissolves, leaving the boilies around the hook.*

Say 'cheese' for chub

Apart from being a popular filling for anglers' sandwiches, cheese is a good bait for fish. It takes all species except predators like pike and perch, but the fish that loves cheese most is chub, reckons Graham Marsden.

Cheese is one of those baits that is often unfairly neglected. The advantage of cheese over other, more popular baits – such as maggots, for example – is that it tends to attract better quality fish. Cheese is fairly expensive but it is not an expensive bait – you don't need much for a day's fishing and a pound of Cheddar is cheaper than a pint of maggots. Cheddar, Gruyère, Camembert, Red Leicester, Stilton or Double Gloucester – there really are no bad cheeses when it comes to bait, but some are better than others.

Smelly cheeses make the best bait – so it's not suprising that Danish Blue and Stilton reign supreme. In winter, when rivers are in flood and the water is highly coloured, fish rely heavily on scent rather than sight. It is easy to imagine how cheesy smells trailing downstream from a legered bait can attract the attention of a 4lb (1.8kg) chub.

Firm cheeses such as Cheddar and Edam can be fished in cube form. Simply cut the cheese into cubes of a size to suit the hook size. A 6mm (¼in) cube sits nicely on a size 12 hook, a 12mm (½in) cube on size 10 and 8, and a 20mm (¾in) cube on size 6 and larger.

Crumbly cheeses such as Stilton and Danish Blue can be kneaded into paste form and then moulded around the hook.

Very soft cheeses are sold in tubs and tubes as sandwich spread. Mix them with powdered cheese – like Parmesan – or very fine groundbait to stiffen them up sufficiently for moulding.

Swine and cheese As an alternative to fishing plain cheese you can try a cocktail. Sit a cube of luncheon meat on the hook bend and then mould cheese around the shank. Both chub and barbel often respond to such a bait when neither bait on its own is enjoying a great deal of success.

Parmesan cheese is extremely smelly and when added to paste baits gives them a pungent aroma which the fish (and anybody else who might be standing in the vicinity) can't fail to notice.

Cheesy mixes It is always satisfying to catch fish on new baits – especially one you've discovered for yourself. If you are stuck for ideas then you might like to try Graham's potent, cheesy mix (see overleaf).

Cheesy tactics

If you are after specimen chub on a smallish, fast-flowing river – like Cheshire's River

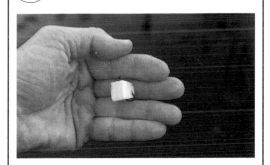

You can fish firm cheese in cube form but on hard-fished waters fish are often wise to this shape. Use your fingernails to rough up the corners of the bait, or try an unusual shape such as a pyramid.

▼ *Graham unhooks a 3lb (1.4kg) chub, taken on a legered cheese bait. Graham carries as little tackle as possible so that he can rove about searching for fish.*

Marsden's magic mix – it's good enough to eat

The ingredients are as follows: at least 4oz of Danish Blue, a bag of ground hempseed and a tub of grated Parmesan cheese. A microwave oven makes the job easier. You'll also need a microwave-proof bowl and a tablespoon.

Anglers are notorious for being messy. So for household harmony, keep a damp cloth at hand in case of spillages.

Put the cheese in the bowl and break it up with the spoon – this way it'll cook a bit quicker. Pop it in the microwave and give it about 30 seconds on full power. Be sure to take the spoon out of the bowl before putting it in the oven or else you'll get a firework display. If you've got it right the cheese should melt completely.

Stir in a tablespoon of ground hemp and a tablespoon of Parmesan. Hemp is a great attractor – chub, roach and barbel love it and it helps to bind the bait together so it stays on the hook. The Parmesan soups the bait up even more.

When the mix is cool put it in an air-tight tub. Don't refrigerate it, but allow it to mature – the smell can be foul.

Hair-rigged cheese baits

You may have fished boilies on a hair rig on still waters but have you ever thought of fishing cheese on the hair in a river? It works perfectly and leaves the hook free to do the job for which it was intended – hooking the fish.

Dane, for example – then you can't beat the leger for rolling a bait into likely looking holes. Any of the usual rigs – sliding link leger or fixed paternoster – are perfectly suitable for this.

Work the bait Cheese, because of its powerful smell and high visibility, tends to attract fish that are not already in the swim but you can improve your chances by taking your bait to the fish. Walk the banks quietly, keeping a sharp look out for likely spots where you can introduce your cheese.

In summer try dropping a cheese bait in the clear runs between streamer weed, in among the roots beneath trees and bushes, or in the fast water below weir pools. Sometimes you can tempt fish from right under the bank where the current has undercut the riverbank and formed a hollow where fish often like to hide.

In winter try the deeper pools and backwaters away from the full force of the flow. The bait really comes into its own at this time of the year. Even when there is snow on the ground and the line is frozen to the rod rings, you can still tempt fish on cheese. What better way to end a crisp December day's fishing than with a brace of 2lb (0.9kg) chub on cheese?

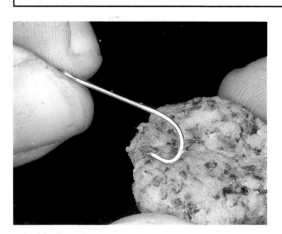

▲ When Graham is using his special mix on the hook, he uses a salmon worming bait holder hook (such as the Mustad 92641). This has two little barbs on the shank which help to keep the bait on when casting and as it rolls around in the current.

Tip Hard-to-swallow baits

Particularly in winter, cheese can go very hard on the hook when it's left in cold water for a long time. Don't worry about this putting the fish off – chub have very powerful pharyngeal (throat) teeth that can crush snails – but the hard bait can make hooking fish a problem.

Mould the bait around the shank of the hook but leave the point exposed. Then when you strike you won't pull the bait out of the fish's mouth.

Deadbaits

Many anglers believe livebaiting is no longer acceptable. You're just as likely to catch by deadbaiting – and it can account for bigger, better specimens.

▲ *Snap-tackle: at the end of a wire trace are two treble hooks (size 8 for pike), set a small distance apart. Push your bait firmly on to the hooks.*

▼ *Deadbaits such as this roach are too tempting for a hungry pike to leave alone.*

There are several species of fish whose main diet is other fish – dead or alive. Pike, zander, perch, eels and catfish all take legered deadbaits without a qualm.

It is a very effective way of catching **big** fish. The older and bigger a pike becomes, the less it wants to start chasing off after fast, healthy prey. It gives up 'fast-food' in favour of slow, wounded fish. If your deadbait is in view – either on the bottom, suspended or twitched to resemble a stricken fish – the pike and its fellow predators will go into action.

Differing deadbaits

Predatory fish take all types of available deadbaits. The following are the more popular baits.

Freshwater fish Bleak and bream are fished whole. Dace are a bait that will take perch, as well as the larger predators. Eels, fished in segments wherever they are naturally present, make good bait.

Minnows form a large part of the diet of predatory fish. As well as catching the usual species, they are an excellent bait for perch and even the occasional chub. They can be preserved in salt – which may well boost their taste and desirability.

Rainbow trout, if you have the money, are a good bait for pike. Another very successful fish is the roach – they're quite colourful, and therefore very visible. They form a large natural part of a predator's diet and are arguably the best of the freshwater fish.

Sea fish Herring, either used whole or cut

Paternostered deadbait

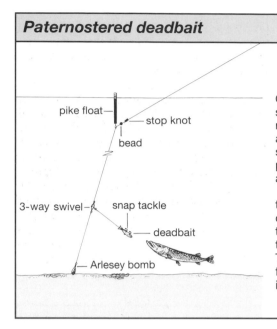

- pike float
- stop knot
- bead
- 3-way swivel
- snap tackle
- deadbait
- Arlesey bomb

One way of keeping small deadbaits such as roach or sprats visible above the river bed is to suspend them on a paternoster rig. The fish appears to swim slowly.

Use a swivel leading to an Arlesey bomb on one length and a wire trace with a snap-tackle rig on the other. The rig will suspend the fish invitingly – and hold it still.

▲ *A small herring on a classic snap-tackle rig. Pike bite through line so the snap-tackle must be attached to a wire trace.*

▼ *Well-known pike angler Ken Whitehead attaches a sprat to a snap-tackle rig. Ken believes in taking the deadbait to the fish, rather than hoping the pike finds his hook, so he likes to move his bait fairly often.*

in half, are a very popular bait. Though not normally part of a pike's staple diet, they are smelly and oily and can be detected from quite a distance. Bigger herring – cut in half – release more juices, which increases the pike's chances of locating them by following the potent smell trail.

Tip Hooked on pike

Anglers who have the welfare of the pike at heart prefer a rig with one treble hook and one single hook. This way deep-hooked pike are not caught on two sets of hooks – so improving their chances of survival.

Mackerel are another highly successful bait for pike. Fished whole, mackerel are more successful in certain waters than herring. They are good for long-range casting because they are firm and so stay on the hook easily. An advantage of casting with half a mackerel is that it is extremely aerodynamic in shape and slips through the air.

Smelt and sprat are both useful baits – sprats have the advantage of being easy to obtain from fishmongers. One last alternative is squid. Chopped into strips they make excellent bait for catfish.

Using deadbaits

Deadbaits are attached to the line by snap-tackle rigs and are frequently legered. As an alternative, you can sink-and-draw to make the bait imitate a sick fish swimming in an erratic way. Cast the bait in the water and raise the rod top – drawing the bait up through the water. Then lower the rod, reeling in a small amount of line. The bait will sink – wobbling towards the bottom. Keep repeating this sequence, re-casting and retrieving along the bank until you find a fish. You can cover lots of water this way.

Beans and peas for carp and tench

Although often regarded as only a reasonably successful change bait, beans and peas take large numbers of carp and tench every year. Peter Mohan shows how to use them properly.

Pulses (all kinds of beans and peas) are excellent baits for carp, and also catch other species such as tench. They can be introduced to a water in quite small quantities yet they often produce immediate results.

Their success may be due partly to their similarity to the natural foods of carp. Peas or beans thrown in as free offerings lie about in small groups, much like freshwater snails, for example, and are of a similar size. Carp are therefore likely to look on them as food straight away.

Cooking beans

Preparation is essential – you should never use pulses as bait or free offerings when they are dry. Unsoaked, uncooked beans

▼ *A handful of runner beans to tempt any carp. Lying around on the bottom, a group of colourful beans like this is quite visible and soon attracts the carp.*

and peas absorb water and swell up inside the stomach of the unfortunate fish which eats them. At best, this causes discomfort to the fish, but at worst it can be fatal.

All pulses must be soaked in cold water for at least three to four hours and then cooked. After soaking, put them on to boil for three or four minutes, and then allow them to simmer for another five to ten minutes. Some beans can be harmful even to large animals like humans if not prepared thoroughly. Kidney beans in particular should be soaked overnight and then well cooked. Even so, try to avoid overcooking or boiling for too long as this removes some of the nutrients, making them less attractive to the fish or too soft for effective use as hookbait.

Feeding and using

As with any new bait, pre-baiting can increase the effectiveness of pulses. Carp

▼ *Haricot beans fished singly or doubly can be deadly when fishing for big carp. The secret is not to overfeed, as pulses can be very filling. Just leave a small handful of free offerings on the bottom to attract the attention of any cruising fish, and top up with the same amount every time you catch.*

and tench sometimes need time to get used to the idea that a new object is edible. Often, however, the possible resemblance of pulses to natural food seems to ensure that fish take them from the start.

Very heavy pre-baiting, as with boilies on a new water, is not necessary, although you may need more on waters heavily stocked with other species. You'll find that on most waters, light pre-baiting is all that is necessary to switch the fish on to whichever pulse you want to use.

Beans to try include black-eye beans, tic beans, adzuki (aduki) beans, pinto beans, mung beans, lima beans, soya beans, coffee beans, butter beans, kidney beans and haricot beans. The larger ones – such as butter beans – are less successful as multiple, or particle baits. The carp seem to lose interest in them more quickly – perhaps because of their size.

Of the peas, chick peas are usually regarded as the best, and indeed they generally outfish all other pulses. Other peas to try include maple peas, gunga peas and dun peas. The smallest pulses, such as maple peas, are often successful with species other than carp and tench.

Bean shopping

Many tackle shops now sell beans and peas, particularly those which specialize in carp gear. They can also be bought in bulk from suppliers who advertise in the angling press. Other good sources include health food shops, delicatessens and food stores devoted to Asian foods, which often have a huge variety of pulses.

The advantage of pulses as baits, espe-

cially for carp, is that fish seem to take to them very quickly. On hard-fished waters where boilies and other large baits are mostly used, they are an excellent alternative. Their only real disadvantage is that it can be difficult to bait up with them at long range, even with a catapult. Chick peas, however, are quite hard and can be fired quite a distance.

If you are looking for a new bait to try for carp and other species, which doesn't require huge quantities of pre-baiting, try one of the pulses. They're comparatively cheap too!

Rigs for shy-biting carp and tench

1. Hair rig

1½lb bs line as 'hair'

2.5-5cm

boilie stop

The hair can be attached to either the bend or eye of the hook, or glued about 3cm up the line.

2. Balanced rig

pulse

pulse

pulse

2.5-5cm

1½lb bs line as 'hair'

A small polystyrene block glued to the hook shank balances the weight of the hook.

1. The standard rig for carp fishing with boilies can also be used with success for pulses. Mount the bean using a needle or simply tie it on. You can also fish multiple baits, using two hairs attached to different parts of the hook or line.

2. Since pulses are light, a frequently-caught fish may drop the bait because of the added weight of a hook, especially a large one. This is when a balanced rig is best. Glue a piece of polystyrene to the shank to balance the weight of the hook. A piece of cork on the hook eye has the same effect.

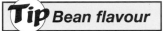

Tip Bean flavour

Only bait up with small numbers of pulses, and if the fish start to go off them, add flavour to the next batch while soaking, and a tablespoon of sugar during cooking. Maple syrup, paprika, oxtail soup and curry sauce work well, as do the commercial carp flavourings.

Hookbeans

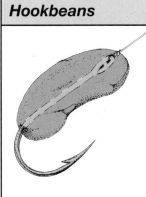

On waters where a hair rig is unneccessary, mount beans as shown. Push the bait over the eye of the hook, which helps keep it on, but don't let the bean impede the hookpoint.

▶ *In the early summer when most tench are hungry, some big specimens can be caught on beans. This trio of four pounders (1.8kg) fell to legered chick pea.*

A SPECIALIST
APPROACH

Tactics for barbel

The barbel is often regarded with something approaching awe – as a tremendous fighter caught by the lucky few. But catching one may be easier than you think. Martin Hooper tells you how.

▼ *Chris Yates plays a big barbel among the thistle-down. A centrepin reel is favoured by many anglers because it enables them to give line immediately.*

To catch barbel you have to be familiar with their nature and feeding habits. They are a specialized fish – streamlined and with an underslung mouth. The torpedo-shaped body enables them to swim with ease in the fastest currents. The four mouth barbels on the upper jaw – two at the leading edge and two at the trailing edge – are used to detect food lodged among stones and gravel on the river bed. It makes sense, then, to fish for them on the bottom of the river.

Feeding the swim

It may sound obvious but you can only catch barbel if they are in the swim. It is no use fishing blindly in the hope that one may eventually turn up – you might have to wait forever! By feeding a swim you greatly increase the chances of an encounter.

Shallow clear rivers make it easier to spot your quarry but you can still use the same tactics on deep, coloured waters.

To get the the fish interested, feed free offerings within a tight area on to the bed of the river.

The simplest way – if the flow and depth are not too great – is to throw in a few samples. If the flow is such that the bait is washed out of the swim before it reaches the bottom, it's best to try a baitdropper or swimfeeder.

Load the dropper with samples of the hookbait and swing it out into the feed area. When it reaches the bottom a plunger releases the bait. Droppers have a limitation, though. If you try to cast too far they have a nasty habit of opening in mid-air –

◄ *The business end of an eight-pounder (3.6kg). The fish's sensitive barbels are used to detect particles of food.*

dispersing both the loosefeed and the fish. This is the time you should start using a swimfeeder.

By baiting regularly on each visit to a water, you can 'brainwash' barbel so their appetites are tuned into your attractor. Hempseed is one of the cheapest and most effective. Liberally laced with a few choice hookbaits – such as sweetcorn or luncheon meat – it forms an enticing patch on the river bed. If there are any barbel around in feeding mood then it won't be long before they move into your swim.

If the stretch you have chosen sees a lot of a certain bait, then the barbel become accustomed to eating it. If not, then pre-baiting is essential. It can take a considerable time to introduce the fish to a new bait.

The hardware
Barbel are one of the most fickle of biters and the most powerful of fighters. So you need to get your tackle right.

A rod of around 1¼lb (0.56kg) TC with a through-action is fine. There's no need to break the bank – any mass-produced rod will do, provided it meets the basic requirements.

The reel A barbel specialist would probably choose a centrepin reel. This type enables you to respond immediately to the demands of an accelerating fish. Giving line with a fixed-spool reel is done through the gears and is therefore less direct – you have to anticipate what a barbel is going to do next, and that isn't easy!

Line of around 6lb (2.7kg) b.s. is about right. Use forged heavy wire hooks.

To complete the set-up you need a big landing net. One of about 1m (3ft) across with big mesh – so that it doesn't get caught by the current – is ideal.

End rigs and tactics
There are all kinds of leger rigs but one of the most versatile is a three-in-one rig which incorporates sliding stops.

With the stops pushed well up the line it's a free running rig; hard against the boom it becomes a bolt rig; just pushed away from the boom it is a variable-length confidence rig. Within a matter of seconds you can change the rig to suit the mood the barbel are in on the day – giving you a much

▲ *Where the current is strong a baitdropper like this is the answer. It is ideal for introducing samples of your hookbait directly on to the river bed – where the barbel are!*

Tip The edge

On heavily fished stretches, prebaiting with a less common bait can often give you the edge – helping you to catch more and bigger barbel.

The lazy man's rig

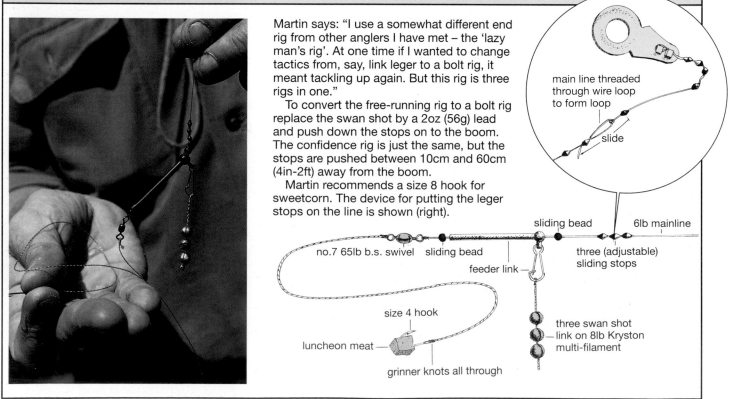

Martin says: "I use a somewhat different end rig from other anglers I have met – the 'lazy man's rig'. At one time if I wanted to change tactics from, say, link leger to a bolt rig, it meant tackling up again. But this rig is three rigs in one."

To convert the free-running rig to a bolt rig replace the swan shot by a 2oz (56g) lead and push down the stops on to the boom. The confidence rig is just the same, but the stops are pushed between 10cm and 60cm (4in-2ft) away from the boom.

Martin recommends a size 8 hook for sweetcorn. The device for putting the leger stops on the line is shown (right).

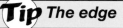

main line threaded through wire loop to form loop

slide

no.7 65lb b.s. swivel   sliding bead

sliding bead   6lb mainline

feeder link

three (adjustable) sliding stops

size 4 hook

luncheon meat

grinner knots all through

three swan shot link on 8lb Kryston multi-filament

Hooking luncheon meat

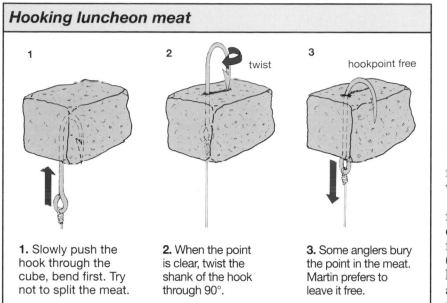

1. Slowly push the hook through the cube, bend first. Try not to split the meat.

2. When the point is clear, twist the shank of the hook through 90°.

3. Some anglers bury the point in the meat. Martin prefers to leave it free.

Tip A happy ending

Your end tackle is extremely important. Check your hook each time before you cast out. If there is any sign of damage then replace it. Hooklengths should be checked and dealt with just as ruthlessly. It's a horrible feeling when a fish is lost – even more so if the reason is through neglect.

greater chance of hitting bites.

A free running rig is the commonest choice when the barbel are their usual shy selves and you are fishing with one rod.

It's essential to hold the rod, feeling for bites with the line held between your finger and thumb. Bites are rarely savage, rod-wrenching affairs. This is particularly so with larger fish and on heavily fished waters. The bites are often tiny plucks – more akin to dace bites than anything else.

The bolt rig comes into play when fishing with two rods. Obviously, quick biting barbel are likely to be missed if you are trying to watch the ends of two rods at the same time. What's needed is a method where the

fish can take care of hooking itself. This is what a bolt rig does.

The bait is fished on a hair rig. When a fish picks it up it does one of two things. It either moves on to take the next piece of food, pricks itself then panics and bolts (hence the name of the rig) and, by doing so, hooks itself. Or it realizes its mistake and attempts to eject the bait – with the same result. This usually produces a fairly posi-

◄ *A simple, sturdy free-running centrepin such as this is ideal. Unlike fixed-spool reels, centrepins have no gears – making the contact between angler and fighting fish more direct.*

▼ *Martin Hooper stalking barbel on the Dorset Stour. Fish spotting in clear waters is made much simpler if you wear a pair of polarizing glasses and a hat to shade your eyes. It is easier to catch a barbel if you can see where it is.*

tive indication and gives you a chance to pull the hook home.

The confidence rig works on much the same principle as the bolt rig. The difference is that you should leave slack line to allow the fish to move away with the bait until it suddenly hits the stop. As its name suggests, this rig works best when the fish are feeding without a sense of caution. In clear water this is indicated by fish moving all over the swim trying to get as much food as possible before the others get it all. In coloured water if a lot of line bites are occurring without any fish being hooked, the chances are that they are feeding confidently too.

The advantage of this rig is that by the time a fish feels the hook it probably has it well inside its mouth. There is little chance of it ejecting the bait. With this method you should make no attempt to strike – if you do the likelihood of foul hooking is very high.

Picking swims

The more time you spend on the bank looking for fish, learning their habits, feeding patterns and preferred swims in times of low waters through to flood conditions, the greater are your chances of hooking up with a really big barbel. This is a much better general approach than feeding what merely looks like a good swim. If it looks good it was probably fished yesterday and may well be

Tip *Be prepared*

When touch-legering a rod rest should be used only for the purpose its name suggests – to rest the rod on while it is not in use.

Often barbel bites are extremely fast and shy. The angler who puts the rod on a rest misses nearly every bite before he has even cleared the rod rest.

Always hold on to the rod and be ready at any moment to respond to the slightest twitch.

▶ *An angler plays a barbel on the Royalty fishery on the Hampshire Avon. Barbel exhaust themselves during a fight. Return them to the water as soon as they have recovered.*

fished again tomorrow. The fish will be hard to catch – if they are there at all.

The farther you get from the car park, and all the other anglers, the better are your prospects of a good day's fishing – and possibly of connecting with that elusive double-figure specimen.

▼ *John Watson cradles a big Wensum barbel. With its bronze, streamlined body and large fins it is easy to see why the barbel is such a powerful and handsome adversary.*

The all-round roach

You can catch roach on the waggler, stickfloat, slider, swingtip, quivertip and all sorts of other methods from all kinds of waters – perhaps that's why they're so popular.

▲ *Plenty of waters hold two-pounders like this beautiful specimen – getting them out is another matter. But with light tackle, a quiet bankside manner and lots of patience you just might succeed.*

⊗ Softly, softly

Most big roach are very sensitive to vibrations and a heavy-footed angler clumping around the banks soon frightens them away. If you are to give yourself a chance of catching that magical two-pounder (0.9kg) you must tread lightly.

▼ *Few of our ponds, lakes, canals and rivers are without roach, but in spite of being found in most places these shy, handsome fish are a challenge – especially to young anglers.*

Think back to your first ever fish. The chances are that if it wasn't a perch then it was a roach – the species that has started a great many youngsters on the road to a lifetime's angling.

Small roach are much easier to catch than their bigger brethren, but they are fast biters and provide young anglers with a challenge that helps develop their skills. Really big roach are notoriously shy and most anglers never manage to capture one above the magical 2lb (0.9kg) barrier.

Roach respond to a variety of tactics and you'll find them in all types of waters from fairly fast flowing rivers to land drains, canals, lakes and small ponds.

Roach tackle

One of the more delicate, small-mouthed members of the carp family, the roach responds best to gossamer tackle.

Lines The trick is to strike the right balance between fishing light enough to get bites and heavy enough not to lose fish. In snag-free water, line of 1lb (0.45kg), b.s. is not too fine. If it is weedy and you are expecting roach above 1lb (0.45kg) then scale up slightly – 1½-1¾lb (0.68-0.79kg) b.s is about right. It is only necessary to go above 2lb (0.9kg) b.s if there is a chance of other species such as carp and tench, for example.

Hooks Roach are very particular about a bait behaving naturally, so avoid clumsy, heavy wire, eyed hooks. Go for a fine wire, spade end hook. (If you can't tie them your-

Hook size to bait size for roach	
Hook size	**Bait**
20	single maggot,
18	single maggot, single caster, hemp
16	double maggot, double caster, hemp, tares, bread paste
14	bread paste, bread flake
12	bread flake, sweetcorn

self then buy some quality hooks ready tied to a well known brand of line.)

Use the table above to match the size of hook to bait size.

Floats You don't necessarily have to use a light float for roach fishing – you can catch them on 2SSG wagglers. But the important thing is to dot the float well down so the fish feel the least resistance.

Leger indicators On some days quivertips tend to encourage fast bites from roach and in recent years there has been a trend back to swingtipping for them. A swingtip with a soft rubber allows bites to develop, making them easier to hit.

Favourite baits
Roach are not particular about what they eat but there are some good traditional baits.

Bread fished as flake, paste or punch is good for sorting out the better fish. Floating crust is normally associated with carp but small pieces fished in the margins are excellent for really big roach.

Casters Next time you are in the tackle shop and thinking of buying a pint of maggots for a session after the roach, try a pint of casters instead. Roach just love big, crunchy, golden casters and they tend to bring a better stamp of fish than maggots.

Hempseed has a pleasant nutty aroma which the roach find irresistible. Regular loose feeding of a few grains at a time often gets the fish queueing to intercept them on the drop. Fish a single grain on a size 18 or 16 hook. Push the bend of the hook into the seed slit – don't worry about the seed dropping off, it rarely does. The quality of big, hemp-caught roach has to be seen to be believed – the deep-bodied, brassy-scaled fish look almost like another species altogether. Hemp can produce very fast bites but if the fish are really turned on you should be able to hit them.

Tares are seeds sold originally in pet shops as pigeon food. They are now stocked by

▶ Roach are caught all the year round but the crisp, clear days of late autumn are traditionally the best. This is when big roach are fighting fit, with slightly brassy scales, deep creamy bellies and crimson fins.

most tackle shops. Boiled until soft enough to hook (but not split), tares make an excellent hookbait for roach when fished with loose-fed hemp. Hemp and tares work best during the summer and autumn. Compared to more conventional baits – maggots, for example – they look a bit unlikely and you need confidence to use them but once you've had a good catch you'll look for every opportunity to use them again.

Sweetcorn is a bait which the fish need to get used to but once you've got the roach turned on to it you can expect some big catches. Unlike hemp and tares it has the advantage of being a less selective hookbait, so you may get a suprise tench, carp or big bream among your roach.

Swims and tactics
There really is no such thing as a 'roach swim' or 'roach tactics' – that's the beauty of the all-round roach.

On rivers, medium flowing and even fast flowing swims yield roach to stick float and waggler tactics. A good catch of roach taken on the stick is a fair indication that you are on the way to mastering this method.

Still water roach can be taken on the drop with a waggler or on deep waters with a sliding float. A long pole can help you achieve perfect presentation – and it is useful for fishing the far bank of canals. Leger tactics often produce fish in the winter when the float has failed.

Tip *Just nicked*

If you are using single maggots on small hooks – size 20 or 18 for example – be careful to ensure that the bait is nicked by only the smallest amount of skin. Roach have a habit of wrapping a maggot around the hook bend as they take it. If it is hooked by too much skin it acts as a buffer and the fish comes off.

▲ Casters are an excellent alternative to maggots. They work well when loose-fed with hemp and tend to attract the bigger roach.

Guide to carp fishing

Carp are cunning, they grow big and fight furiously – it's not surprising they are so popular with anglers. But how do you catch a specimen? The successful specimen hunting family, Bryan, Jon and Stephen Culley, tells you how.

Mirrors and leathers are varieties of the common carp *(Cyprinus carpio)*. The crucian carp *(Carassius carassius)* is a separate species which is related to the carp family (as are roach, bream and tench) but does not reach the same enormous size as the common carp – which can often grow in excess of 50lb (23kg). Whatever the size, carp provide excellent sport.

Where to go

The beginner should try a water with a large head of carp – where bites (or 'runs') are not too scarce. This will increase the chance of getting to grips with a fish before patience wears out. You will find that tackle dealers and anglers are only too happy to tell you about the carp waters you can fish in your area.

The more experienced angler may prefer the challenge of a water with fewer carp but of a higher average weight. These fish will be wary and more difficult to hook. If you are to get one on the bank you must be prepared to put in the hours.

Lakes are generally best for really big fish. Canals and rivers are neglected and can be worth a try; few of the carp in these waters have been caught before so they often fall to less sophisticated baits and methods.

Locating the fish

Finding the fish is the secret to catching them. Walk around the water looking for tell-tale signs. Small clusters of bubbles or dark patches of muddy water indicate feeding carp. Look out for fish capering about – leaping clear of the water, for example.

During daylight carp retreat to the cover of islands, lily beds, weedbeds and overhanging or sunken trees. A bait cast tight up to these fish-holding areas will often produce runs.

On gravel pits it is worth trying a bait along the bottom of gravel bars. You can precisely pin down the location of these by careful plumbing with a float or by casting a lead and timing the drop.

◄ *Many carp-holding lakes are picturesque and tranquil – until a powerful fish grabs your bait and the action starts. Carp like the cover of heavy weed so look for them by features such as lily beds and reeds.*

Choosing the tackle

Before selecting your gear you should ask yourself a few questions. For instance, are you going to fish the margins or at long range, and is the water snaggy? And what size fish are you after? If in doubt, get advice from a tackle dealer or an experienced carp angler – especially one who knows the water you want to fish.

Rods You don't have to buy a special carp rod if you already have a through-action, 11 or 12ft (3.3 or 3.6m) rod with a 2lb (0.9kg) test curve. This is a good bet for most carp on most waters, especially at short to medium range. However, if you want, you can select a rod with a fast taper, tip action for fishing at longer range. Also, the further out you fish the heavier the weight needed to cast. So use a powerful rod, such as one with a 2½lb (1.1kg) test curve, when the weight is over 2oz (57g). Below that a 2lb (0.9kg) test curve rod will do and for close-in fishing with lighter weights use a rod with a 1¾lb (0.8kg) test curve.

Reels The reel should be of a sturdy, open-face design and have a spool with a line-holding capacity of at least 140m (153yd) of 8lb (3.6kg) line. It should lay the line evenly on the spool, so that a running fish is able to take line easily. A baitrunning feature is useful – it allows the fish to run without your needing to take the bail arm off.

Line Choose your line strength to suit the water – 8lb (3.6kg) is suitable for open waters but step up to 10 or 12lb (4.5 or 5.4kg) if there is heavy weed or snags.

Hooks A variety of carp hooks is available and choice is very much a personal matter. In any case hooks should be strong and sharp. Useful sizes range from 4s to 10s. Obviously, the bigger the fish, the bigger the hook.

▲ Effective carp baits include: dog biscuits (1) which you must soak before use or they swell inside the carp; cooked peanuts (2); flavoured boilies such as strawberry oil (3), oceanic oils (4) and tropicana oil (5); milk concentrate (6); sweetcorn (7); chick peas (8). Breadcrust (9), breadflake (10) and luncheon meat (11) can work on waters not often fished for carp.

◄ Whatever their size, carp are hard fighters and good fish for getting beginners interested. This fine specimen was caught in the margins on floating breadcrust bait.

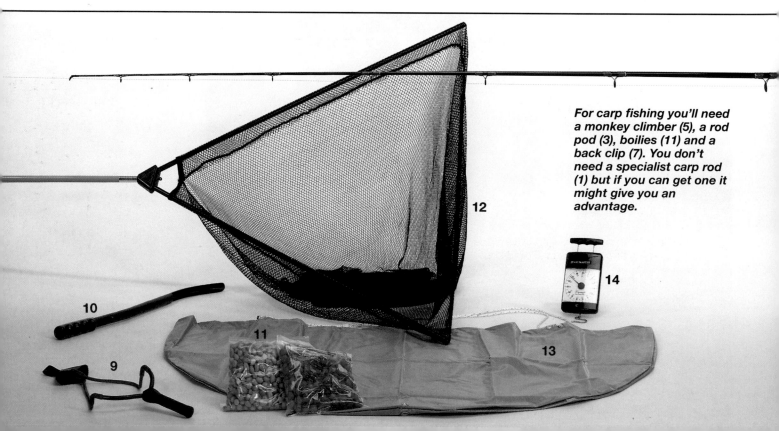

For carp fishing you'll need a monkey climber (5), a rod pod (3), boilies (11) and a back clip (7). You don't need a specialist carp rod (1) but if you can get one it might give you an advantage.

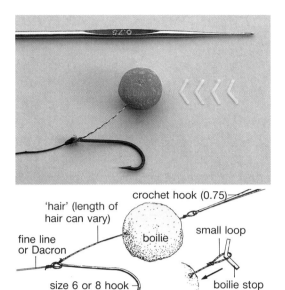

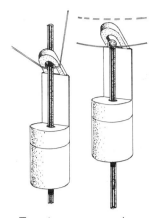

Bite indication

The monkey climber works on a simple principle: that of the old-fashioned dough bobbin. The 'monkey' is a plastic cylinder free to slide up and down a vertical metal needle. The top of the needle is usually enlarged to stop the monkey flying off. The line passes between the climber and the needle. On a run the monkey climbs the needle as the fish takes line. It drops if the fish runs at you. When you strike, the line is freed from the indicator. Monkeys can be fitted with glowing isotopes for night fishing, and fished together with electronic alarms.

Carp rigs

Rigs for carp divide into two categories: those for bottom-feeding fish and those for surface feeders.

Hair rigs Most carp are caught on the bottom, with the bait on the hook or on a 'hair' (a length of fine line). A hair rig is effective because it leaves the hook entirely free – so there is a much greater chance of it catching in the fish's mouth.

To set up your monkey climber, pass line between the loop and the needle. Leave the bail arm disengaged so that a running fish is free to take line. A run causes the monkey either to rise and hover on the needle or, if the fish runs towards you, to drop back.

▲ *To make a boilie hair rig push a size 0.75mm crochet hook through the boilie. Tie a loop in the hair and draw it through the boilie. Put a stop in the loop and pull hair to tighten stop against boilie.*

Carp baits

Boilies have an advantage over other baits in that smaller fish, such as bream and tench, are less likely to take them. You can buy boilies or make them at home. The range of flavours and colours is so wide that it is impossible to say which are best. You must experiment to find out which ones the carp on your water prefer.

Other good baits include breadflake and crust, luncheon meat, lobworms and sweetcorn (although the carp may be wary of these baits on hard-fished waters).

Dog and cat biscuits are good floating baits but soak them well before use.

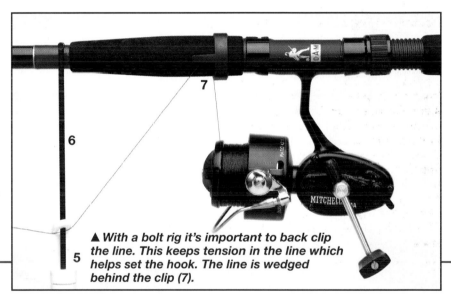

▲ *With a bolt rig it's important to back clip the line. This keeps tension in the line which helps set the hook. The line is wedged behind the clip (7).*

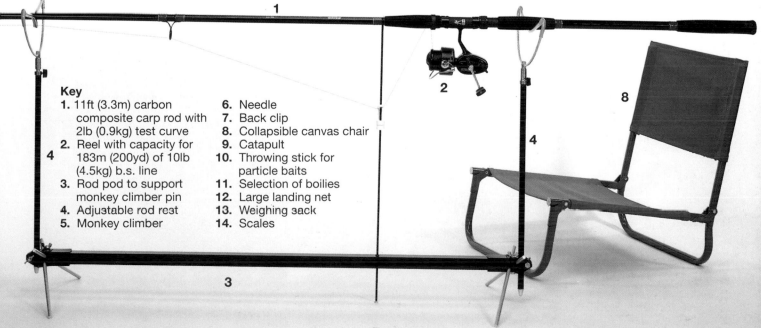

Key

1. 11ft (3.3m) carbon composite carp rod with 2lb (0.9kg) test curve
2. Reel with capacity for 183m (200yd) of 10lb (4.5kg) b.s. line
3. Rod pod to support monkey climber pin
4. Adjustable rod rest
5. Monkey climber
6. Needle
7. Back clip
8. Collapsible canvas chair
9. Catapult
10. Throwing stick for particle baits
11. Selection of boilies
12. Large landing net
13. Weighing sack
14. Scales

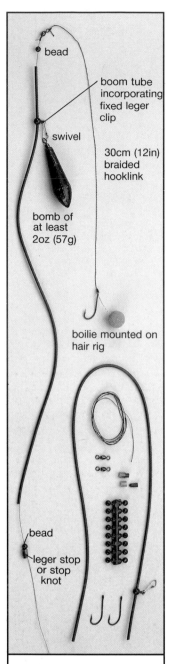

bead

boom tube incorporating fixed leger clip

swivel

30cm (12in) braided hooklink

bomb of at least 2oz (57g)

boilie mounted on hair rig

bead

leger stop or stop knot

Anti-tangle rig

Anti-tangle booms let you cast long distances without the line tangling and they help to keep the line off the fish's back as it is brought in. To prevent tangles, make sure that the length of the hooklink is shorter than the length of the boom. The boom can be either stiff or flexible.

▶ Bryan Culley's patience was rewarded with this double-figure common that fell to a simple hair rig. He took it from a river – an often neglected water for carp but worth a try if you are prepared to wait.

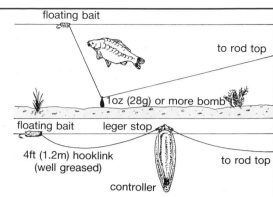

floating bait

to rod top

1oz (28g) or more bomb

floating bait   leger stop

4ft (1.2m) hooklink (well greased)

to rod top

controller

Rigs for surface feeders

The **running bomb rig** (right above) works on waters up to 1.8m (6ft) deep. The bomb anchors the rig. Use binoculars to watch the bait. A different coloured hookbait helps you to pick out your floater from the loose feed. On waters deeper than 1.8m (6ft) use the **controller rig** (right below). This acts as a casting aid rather than as a bite indicator. So, when spotting bites, watch your hookbait rather than the controller.

Bolt rigs A hair rig is normally used together with an anti-tangle bolt rig. Plastic booms with a fixed wire clip are available from tackle shops. A heavy bomb of about 2oz (57g) is clipped to the boom and the boom is free to slide on the line over a short distance.

It is in the nature of carp to suck in morsels of food and blow them out again before finally swallowing them. With the hair rig, a carp sucks in the bait along with the hook and as it blows it out again the hook pricks the inside of the fish's mouth, causing it to bolt. Line is pulled through the boom as the fish runs. The stop knot comes up hard against the boom and the fish hooks itself against the weight of the bomb. This self-hooking principle depends upon the hook being free from bait.

Running leger rigs Some baits have to be fished on the hook because it is not practical to put them on a hair. (For example, lobworms won't go on a hair and bread will go on but won't stay on.) These baits are normally fished on a running leger.

Surface rigs Fishing on the surface is one of the most exciting ways of taking carp and it always pays to throw in a few floating baits during the day to see if the fish are interested in feeding on the top.

Fishing for carp

Accurate casting and feeding is always important. Find a likely fish-holding spot and cast close to it. Encourage the fish to feed by using a catapult, throwing stick or bait dropper to present free offerings around your hookbait. Sometimes it is possible to intercept margin-feeding fish by dropping a bait right in the fish's path.

When carp fishing, patience is a virtue but if you are not getting results and you can see signs of fish in another part of the water, don't hang about – move on.

Caring for carp

It is important to use a large landing net with a soft mesh to protect the fish. Always unhook your carp on grass or an unhooking mat, weigh them in a net sling and then photograph them and get them back into the water as soon as possible.

Swingtipping for bream

Swingtipping is enjoying a deserved revival as more and more bream anglers realize its advantages over quivertipping – and nobody does it better than matchman Sid Meads.

The swingtip is the most sensitive bite indicator ever devised for legering, and the man we have to thank is the late Jack Clayton of Boston, Lincolnshire, who invented it back in the 1950s. Swingtipping as we know it today hasn't changed very much since then – Jack's ingenious invention has withstood the test of time.

Different links

Jack and fellow Fenland matchmen did a lot of experimenting in the early days, until finally they settled on swingtips with nylon links, which are stiff enough to prevent tangles at the rod tip when casting, yet are sensitive enough to show the slightest of bites.

You'll have to scout around to find such swingtips nowadays, because most modern

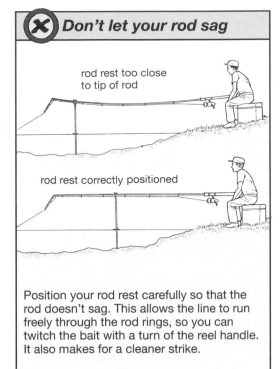

Don't let your rod sag

rod rest too close to tip of rod

rod rest correctly positioned

Position your rod rest carefully so that the rod doesn't sag. This allows the line to run freely through the rod rings, so you can twitch the bait with a turn of the reel handle. It also makes for a cleaner strike.

▼ *A bream angler waits expectantly for a bite on an Irish lough. Ireland is a mecca for anglers in search of a haul of bream, and one of the best methods there is to swingtip over a large carpet of feed. Sid Meads has won many Irish Festivals doing just that.*

ones have soft silicone rubber links that, though very sensitive, tend to make the swingtip flap about on the cast, causing tangles at the rod tip.

You can also get moulded rubber links, which make casting easier, but they aren't as sensitive as nylon ones.

Tip *Forget the swimfeeder*

Sid Meads prefers not to use a swimfeeder when swingtipping unless he really has to. The reason for this is that accurate groundbaiting is essential for success when legering for bream. Sid finds it easier to groundbait accurately by hand or by catapult, and easier to cast accurately with a bomb than a feeder.

With a feeder, one cast going astray can split your shoal, but if the odd cast goes astray with a bomb, no damage is done.

▼ *Ireland's rivers can be just as good for bream as her loughs. Here a happy angler returns a fighting fit Shannon bream. It fell to swingtipping, a method pioneered in England but used to devastating effect in Ireland over the years.*

Different lengths

Length of swingtip to use depends on the type of water you're fishing. The deeper the water and the stronger the flow or tow, the longer the swingtip needs to be. So carry a selection from 25-50cm (10-20in), to cover every eventuality.

The right balance

The key to success, as always, is balanced tackle, from rod to line, bomb, hooklength and hook.

Rods In the days before groundbait catapults you rarely swingtipped more than 30m (33yd) or so out because that was about as far as you could throw groundbait by hand. Swingtip rods then were usually 9-10ft (2.7-3m) long, which was fine. Nowadays, with groundbait catapults allowing you to fish twice as far out, you need a longer rod to pick up the line on the strike – one of around 11ft (3.3m) or so. Make sure it has a soft, through action, to absorb the shock of striking into soft-mouthed, deep-bodied bream.

Reel, line and bombs Choose a good fixed-spool reel with two spare spools. Fill the spools with 2½lb (1.1kg), 3lb (1.4kg) and 4lb (1.8kg) line. This is the start of getting the balance right. Generally, you want to use a ¼-½oz (7-14g) bomb to 2½lb (1.1kg) line,

Side-on or head-on?

Many anglers swingtip sitting side-on, with the rod almost parallel to the bank, saying this allows for a cleaner strike. But Sid Meads always sits facing the water with his rod almost straight out in front of him. This way he can spot rolling bream. As for striking, Sid points out that you usually strike upwards when you are floatfishing, so why not do the same when swingtipping?

a ½-¾oz (14-21g) bomb to 3lb (1.4kg) line, and a ¾-1oz (21-28g) bomb to 4lb (1.8kg) line. Weather and water conditions and distance to be cast dictate which combination to use. Always go for the lightest bomb you can get away with – but remember, it needs to be heavy enough to get your bait to the desired spot and hold its position when you tighten up.

End tackle For the bomb link, use a slightly heavier piece of line than your reel line, to take the shock of casting. Make the link about 40cm (15in) long, so that you can twitch the bait (to tempt a bite) without shifting the bomb.

Go for a longish tail – about 1.2m (4ft) – because a slow-sinking bait is more attractive to bream and the longer the tail, the slower the drop after the bomb hits bottom. Don't try to go any longer with the tail or you'll have too much line to pick up on the strike.

If you're fishing a water that's not had a hammering, a juicy bunch of redworms or a pinch of breadflake on a size 10 or 12 hook can work well, with a big weight on the cards. But you need to use a 14, 16, 18 or 20 on most of our hard-fished waters, with smaller baits to match – three pinkies on a 20, a caster on an 18, two or three maggots or casters on a 16, or a small redworm tipped with a maggot or caster on a 14.

Plan of attack

Now you're tackled up, you're ready to catch some bream. Mix a small amount of

A SELECTION OF SID'S SWINGTIPS

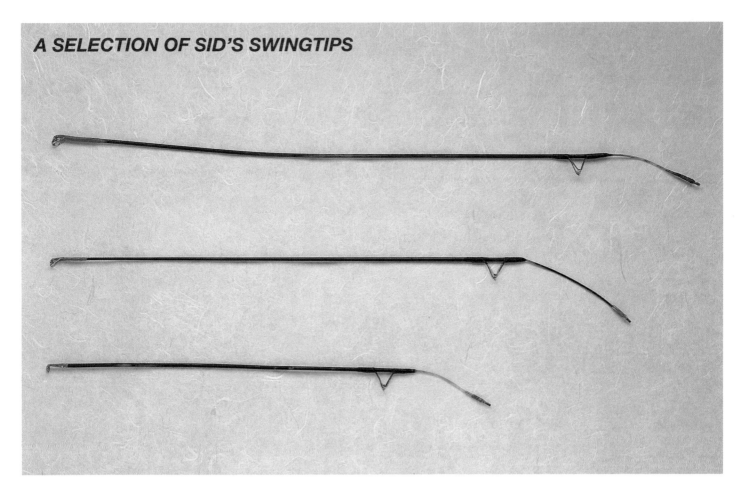

groundbait and add some squatts, casters and a few chopped worms – just enough so you can still squeeze the groundbait into balls that hold together in the air.

Let's assume you're fishing a Fen drain or slow river about 30m (33yd) wide and 2.5m (8ft) deep. Attach a shortish (25-30cm/10-12in) swingtip. Position the rod rests directly in front of you but angled slightly downstream or downwind so the rod is aligned with the bow of the line. Use a smooth overhead cast with the bomb hanging about 1m (3ft) below the rod tip and aim some 5m (5yd) short of the far bank.

Tighten the line so the swingtip hangs at a slight angle, just clear of the water. Then, if a bream swims towards you after taking the bait, you will be able to see the swingtip drop back.

Hang fire with the groundbait for a few minutes, just in case there's a shoal of bream out there already – you don't want to scare them away before you've even started.

If you haven't had any indication, put in five tangerine-sized balls – but not all down the same hole. Put the first three in a line across the back of your target area, then drop the next two slightly short, in a line towards you.

The idea is that when the bream move in they hang tight to the far bank. To keep them happy, let them stay there feeding on the first three balls of feed, while you take the odd fish from over the two balls you dropped short. These are the hungry ones that can't get into the main shoal and read-

ily accept your hookbait.

Only move into the main shoal once bites start to tail off. This is a crucial time. You must put more feed in to hold the shoal, but there's always the risk of frightening the bream away. So never overdo it at this stage. Try them with a single ball of groundbait only. If it doesn't spook them you've cracked it, and can put one in as and when you think they want it. If bites slow after you've put one in, leave it a bit longer before the next. Your main baiting area is the far side, on a three to one ratio – three to the

▲ *The swingtips at the top and bottom here were made for Sid by Jack Clayton himself. Needless to say, Sid still uses them to this day. The swingtip in the middle is one Sid made – from an old quivertip! The nylon strings of lawn edgers make good links, he says.*

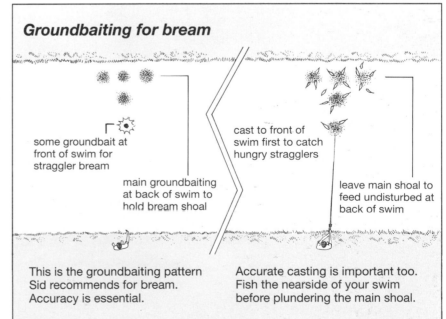

Groundbaiting for bream

some groundbait at front of swim for straggler bream

main groundbaiting at back of swim to hold bream shoal

cast to front of swim first to catch hungry stragglers

leave main shoal to feed undisturbed at back of swim

This is the groundbaiting pattern Sid recommends for bream. Accuracy is essential.

Accurate casting is important too. Fish the nearside of your swim before plundering the main shoal.

main area, one to the near side. But remember – only ever one ball at a time.

Once you get into the pack, expect a few line bites – big, sweeping bites from fish hitting your line and leaving your swingtip out straight. Only through experience can you learn to distinguish liners from real bites. Even then, you still only get it right about half of the time.

The problem of liners is not the fault of the swingtip, which has one big advantage over the quivertip. Those little half-inch taps of the quivertip on hard-fished waters often mean a bream taking the bait and moving just enough to tighten the line. On feeling this the fish drops the bait. These are the bites you can hit on the swingtip. Hold the rod in the rest and at the slightest movement, move the rod forward with the bite. Sometimes you'll be amazed how those tiny half-inch bites turn into big sailaways. When this happens you will be hooked on swingtips for life.

▶ *On an easy water it saves time, if the edge is shallow, to scoop each bream out by hand. On harder waters, where you have to work for your fish, take no chances and net every one.*

▼ *Slabs, lumps, lunkers...call them what you like, slimy-sided bream are the favourite fish of the many anglers who have fallen under the spell of the sensitive swingtip.*

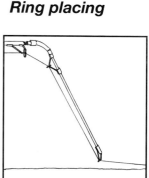

Ring placing

Sid likes swingtips with the top ring just below the link, to prevent tangles when casting.

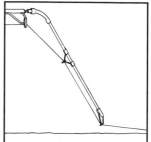

Other anglers prefer to have the top ring lower down, believing that it allows smoother casting.

Basic pike kit

Pike are Britain's supreme freshwater predatory fish. But – tough as they look – they can be easily killed or injured by inexperienced anglers, using incorrect tackle.

Piking is sometimes thought of by newcomers to the sport as an addition to a day's fishing. They take along an old boat rod and put a mackerel in the water 'to see what happens'.

This is exactly the **wrong** attitude to pike fishing. Pike frequently swallow hooks deeply and if your tackle is not up to the job and breaks – leaving the hook deep in the fish – they can suffer an agonising death. Always avoid deep-hooking pike.

There are three main ways of fishing for pike: livebaiting, spinning and deadbaiting. Arguably, anglers new to pike fishing find deadbaiting the easiest method of catching, but some specialist tackle is needed in even a simple deadbaiting kit.

The right rod
Your rod needs to be quite sturdy. Ideally you should choose a 2¼lb test curve rod. Most types of carp rod can be used, but

Basic pike kit key

1, 2. A 2¾lb TC Ryobi 'John Wilson' pike rod. This two-piece rod is 12ft (3.7m) long and is fine for 10-15lb line. Quality pike rods are not cheap – but can handle most conditions and most fish.
3. Specialist **fixed-spool reel**, designed to catch specimen fish. Get one with a good drag system to cope with the sudden rush of a large pike.
4. Pike slider float.
5. Pencil deadbait float.
6. Wire trace, complete with **snap-tackle.**
7. Treble hook guards – these reduce accidents.

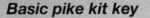

those with a soft action are inadequate for casting heavier baits long distances. A 10ft (3m) stepped-up carp rod is fine – but better still is a 10-12ft (3-3.7m) pike rod. The rod shown here has a 2¾lb test curve. This might sound about as responsive as a tree, but good pike rods, such as this, have an excellent tip action. They can handle casting big baits and landing large pike.

A robust reel
The pike fishing reel should be of a more robust, heavier design than those used for general coarse fishing. A fixed-spool reel, deep spooled and loaded with 10-12lb (4.5-5.4kg) line, is the easiest kind to use.

Open-faced reels are better than closed-face reels for piking – pressure from big fish makes the line bed-in with a closed-face reel. Specimen reels are a little more expensive than match and light float fishing reels, but offer greater flexibility and strength.

Specialist floats
If you intend to leger using a float, or to suspend your deadbait in the water, you need specialist pike floats. A sliding pike float is suitable for both a suspended rig and a bottom fished rig. When using large pieces of deadbait, such as herring or mackerel, make sure you get a sliding float big and buoyant enough to suspend your deadbait.

▲ *Pike are partial to smelt (shown here), roach, mackerel or half a herring. Try twitching your deadbait along the bottom to simulate a wounded fish. Pike prefer slow, easy targets.*

A pencil deadbait float – held in position by a stop knot and bead above the float – is also excellent for legering.

Line and snap-tackle

Your reel line should be 10-12lb (4.5-5.4kg) bs and must be connected by a swivel to an 18-20in (45-50cm) cable-laid wire trace of around 20lb (9kg) test. Pike bite through normal line, and are then left with treble hooks embedded in their bodies.

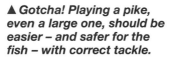

▲ *Gotcha! Playing a pike, even a large one, should be easier – and safer for the fish – with correct tackle.*

Attach the deadbait to the line by using two size 8 treble hooks connected together by 3in (7.5cm) of the wire trace. This is called snap-tackle. Attach the herring, mackerel or other chosen bait to the two hooks. To make doubly sure the bait is attached securely – if you are casting a long way – you can tie the fish to the snap-tackle rig around its tail.

Pike usually swallow whole fish head first, so keep the hooks as far back, near to the tail, as possible. This way the pike is less likely to swallow the hooks deeply. A deep-hooked pike is a dead pike unless you can get the hooks out very carefully.

Ideally, with barbed treble hooks, you should leave the barb on the point to which the deadbait is attached and file or squash the barbs on the two points that are to catch the pike. It makes them easier to hook, and they suffer less damage if they swallow the bait deeply. The occasional fish throwing your hooks is a small price to pay for these advantages.

Gags and forceps

Now you've hooked your first big pike – what do you do with it? A large, soft, knotless mesh landing net helps you bring the fish to the bank. To unhook it, 8in (20cm) straight artery forceps are best.

If you feel you must, you can use a pike gag to keep those powerful jaws open while you unhook your fish. Old pike gags are fairly barbaric instruments, but if you cover the sharp ends with rubber sleeves, cloth or cork they should not do too much damage to the pike's mouth.

◀ *Forceps are the ideal means of unhooking pike. Today's 'fish friendly' anglers, such as John Wilson, do not use a pike gag. A leather glove can protect your hands.*

Catching the mighty red-eye

Jim Gibbinson has been fishing for specimen tench for over 15 years with a variety of tackle and tactics. Here he passes on some of what he's discovered.

In the last 20 years or so there has been something of a revolution in tench fishing – the average and maximum size of tench has shot up. Until quite recently, a 5lb (2.3kg) tench would have been considered a specimen. Nowadays, in the 1990s, even a seven-pounder (3.2kg) is not that unusual.

No-one can be absolutely sure why this has happened, but it may be partly due to increasing water weed in British waters. Rivers, lakes, ponds, pits and reservoirs certainly have become much weedier, possibly because farmers have been using more artificial fertilizers to bump up the yield of their land.

Much of this fertilizer is washed into rivers and still waters where it encourages strong water plant growth. More plants mean more insects and a richer supply of the tench's natural food.

With more big tench around there has never been a better time to get to grips with a specimen. Unfortunately, the increase in weed means that these big fish are harder to get out of the water. There are few places left where it is possible to fish light lines and expect to land that huge tench.

All this means you need to take some fairly hefty tackle to many big tench waters. However, try to remain flexible in your approach so you can take advantage of any less weedy waters by fishing with lighter tackle. That way you'll enjoy your tenching more and get better results.

◄ *As waters have got weedier, so tackle has had to get heavier to cope with pulling big tench out of the weeds. Here the author poses with the end result.*

Big tench waters

● **Johnson's Lakes,** near Maidstone, Kent. Day/season tickets on bank.
● **Leisure Sport Pits,** Thames, Lea, Kennet and Darenth valleys. Permits from Leisure Sport, Thorpe Park, Staines Rd, Chertsey KT16 8PN.
● **Savay Lake,** near Denham, Bucks. Day tickets from some local newsagents, season tickets from the fishery manager, 309 Shirland Road, London W9.
● **Various other gravel pits** around Britain where big tench have grown unmolested and unsuspected. Check them out just before dawn in a spell of settled weather near the end of the close season. If tench are there in numbers you'll see them rolling. Don't fish a virgin water on spec.

Tip **Roll up**

Tench are quite territorial and remain in an area for several weeks before moving, often for no apparent reason. Don't flog away at a once-productive swim in the hope that it'll come good again. Look instead to see where the tench are rolling and fish there.

▲▼ *You need heavy tackle (like that above), fixed-lead rigs and particles or 16mm (⅝ in) boilies to have a realistic chance of landing a specimen tench from most waters.*

Fixed-lead rig

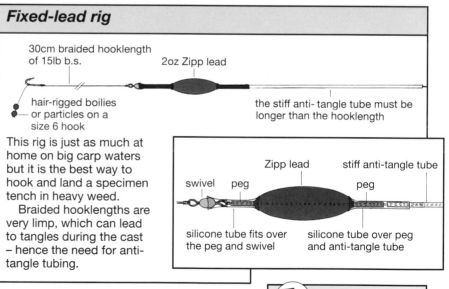

30cm braided hooklength of 15lb b.s.

2oz Zipp lead

hair-rigged boilies or particles on a size 6 hook

the stiff anti-tangle tube must be longer than the hooklength

Zipp lead

stiff anti-tangle tube

swivel   peg

peg

silicone tube fits over the peg and swivel

silicone tube over peg and anti-tangle tube

This rig is just as much at home on big carp waters but it is the best way to hook and land a specimen tench in heavy weed.

Braided hooklengths are very limp, which can lead to tangles during the cast – hence the need for anti-tangle tubing.

Tackling the weed

Many tench waters become heavily weeded, aquatic jungles in the summer and you must use appropriate gear. You need a 2¼lb (1kg) TC carp rod, coupled with about 200m (220yd) of 12lb (5.4kg) line on a sturdy fixed-spool reel.

Terminal tackle is a size 6 forged hook on a 15lb (6.8kg) braided hooklength. Fixed-lead, anti-tangle rigs are most effective in heavy weed. There's no getting away from it – you need carp tackle to get a big tench out of a weedy water.

Standard carp baits – boilies and particles – work best with carp gear. Tench seem particularly fond of fruity, creamy flavours such as Maple Creme and Strawberry Jam.

If you make your own baits, use a milk protein or bird seed base with these flavours. Tench also readily take fish flavoured boilies based on a fish meal mix.

The best of the particles are sweetcorn, black-eye beans, chick peas and maple peas. Fish both particles and boilies on a 2.5cm (1in) hair. Fish 16mm (⅝ in) boilies singly, but use particles and small boilies in tandem or as a trio on the hair.

An electronic bite indicator with monkey climber or swinging drop-off arm gives an accurate audible and visual signal of runs and drop-back bites. While not the most sensitive form of bite detection, if your rig and bait presentation are right you will only get sailaway bites.

Tip Times and places

The shallows are a good bet early in the season with lots of fish on the spawning grounds. Later many move into water up to 6m (20ft) deep.

Don't ignore the margins – you are just as likely to catch close in as at long range.

Don't fish the night and pack up at breakfast time. In pits the best time is often between 7am and noon with night time the worst.

A bit of subtlety

Where weed hasn't quite reached the horrendous proportions of the watery jungle, it's possible to be a little less brutish in approach.

Tackle can be lighter with 1¾lb (0.8kg) TC rods, 8lb (3.6kg) main line and a forged size 8 or 10 hook. A simple running leger with a ½-¾oz (14-21g) bomb works well with this particular set-up.

With an extending hooklength the leger becomes a fairly sophisticated rig. Devised by Ken Townley for carp fishing, it works equally well for tench in allowing the fish to take line without feeling resistance. This produces very confident takes.

Use the rig with a slack, drooping line. This gives a taking fish some low-resistance line and makes sure that the last few feet of line lie flat on the bottom – reducing line bites. Where drag caused by the wind or floating debris makes this impossible, use a small back-lead to avoid those liners.

Particle baits work well with this rig, as do mini-boilies. The best size for these is about 10mm (⅖in) across. Use them singly or, more commonly, in twos or threes.

▲ *Feed 2-3 pouches of hookbait samples. At short range loosefeed with hemp and casters but farther out use groundbait as a carrier.*

Crumbs before tench

Jim Gibbinson makes his own groundbait:
6 measures (by volume) of fresh white crumb
2 measures of layer's mash hen food
1 measure of roughly ground roast barley
1 measure of fish meal or finely ground trout pellets

▼ *Where weed allows, use 1¾lb (0.8kg) TC rods and a running leger. It's an enjoyable and effective way to take big tench.*

Concertina rig

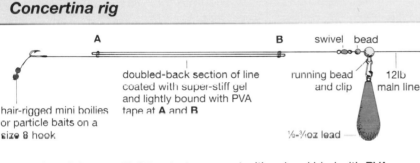

A
B   swivel   bead

doubled-back section of line coated with super-stiff gel and lightly bound with PVA tape at **A** and **B**

running bead and clip

12lb main line

hair-rigged mini boilies or particle baits on a size 8 hook

½-¾oz lead

This gives fish up to 2ft (60cm) of line without resistance. Fold 2-3ft (60-90cm) of Dacron into a Z-bend, coat with gel and bind with PVA tape. The gel and tape dissolve in water, leaving a folded hooklength.

Ultra-light

On a very few lightly weeded venues you can still fish very light – 1¼lb (0.6kg) TC rods, 4lb (1.8kg) line, fine-wire size 12 hooks and a feeder. Where this is possible, it is without doubt the most effective way to catch numbers of big fish.

A hooklength of at least 3ft (90cm) on a

Rotary feeder rig

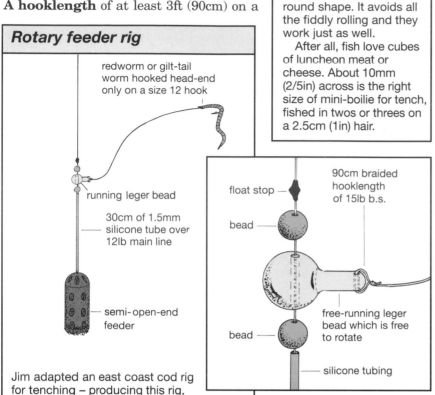

redworm or gilt-tail worm hooked head-end only on a size 12 hook

running leger bead

30cm of 1.5mm silicone tube over 12lb main line

semi-open-end feeder

Jim adapted an east coast cod rig for tenching – producing this rig, though carp anglers now commonly use variations on it. The feeder is filled with maggots and plugged with groundbait.

Tip A cubist approach

If you want to make your own mini-boilies, you'll find it easier to make cubes instead of the usual round shape. It avoids all the fiddly rolling and they work just as well.

After all, fish love cubes of luncheon meat or cheese. About 10mm (2/5in) across is the right size of mini-boilie for tench, fished in twos or threes on a 2.5cm (1in) hair.

float stop

bead

90cm braided hooklength of 15lb b.s.

free-running leger bead which is free to rotate

bead

silicone tubing

helicopter (rotary) rig works best. However, tench sometimes take delicately presented baits with such confidence that they become deep-hooked unless you use a shorter hooklength. With anti-tangle tubing above the feeder, this rig is as near tangle-free as a paternoster can be.

Feeding is easy – catapult two or three tangerine-sized balls of groundbait into the swim and cast your ready-loaded feeder rig into the centre of the spreading rings. Don't feed again until you've had a couple of runs or you'll put the big tench off.

The best bait for this type of tenching is a gilt-tail worm which looks like a redworm with a bright yellow tail. Look for them in the muck heap on a pig farm. You won't find many, but you will find lots of redworms which are a close second best.

Concentrate your efforts on the edges of the heap, where it's fairly cool. Near the middle of a muck heap it's too hot for redworms and gilt-tails – all you find are brandlings and these are greatly inferior as a tench bait.

If you do know of a virtually weed-free water that holds big tench – give light feeder tactics a try. The fishing is an absolute joy and well worth all that grovelling in pig heaps.

▼ *At waters without much weed you can land tench like this on light feeder gear. Give it a go and don't fish heavier than you need.*

Deadbaiting for pike

Deadbaiting is a highly successful way of catching pike because these fish, like many other predators, are active scavengers as well as hunters. Neville Fickling outlines the basics of this method for all seasons.

▼ *Neville Fickling, one of the most successful and respected pike anglers and authors in the country and a former British pike record holder, carefully returns a double-figure beauty to her watery home. The specimen fell to what is probably the most widely used method of all – deadbaiting. Correct handling and unhooking of pike is vital – put them back as soon as you can.*

Deadbaiting – using a dead fish, or part of one, as bait – is probably the most widely used method for catching pike and accounts for a great many double-figure specimens every year.

Sometimes pike can ambush live prey but often they have to give chase. Dead fish, however, are free pickings; there's no chase, which means the pike expends little energy in acquiring a meal.

To enable them to locate dead as well as live fish, pike have a highly developed sense of smell and keen eyesight. To be a successful deadbaiter, therefore, you must know how to exploit both of these senses by presenting a deadbait that is both encitingly smelly and highly visible.

Different deadbaits

A variety of dead fish, both freshwater and sea, are acceptable. The most popular sea species – because of their easy availability and high oil content – are herring and mackerel. Generally, use them whole up to about 15cm (6in) long, or as half-baits when larger. Sardines, pilchards, sprats and horse mackerel (scad) are also very popular. Less commonly used, but also very effective, are sandeels, garfish, whiting and red mullet.

Freshwater deadbaits can be any species easily caught on rod and line, but the most commonly used ones are roach, rudd, dace and eels (in sections). Also popular are smelt (a migratory fish) and rainbow trout.

Obtaining deadbaits

You can buy sea fish and rainbow trout from fishmongers and some tackle shops sell pre-packaged, ready frozen sea fish deadbaits. Frozen fish make just as good deadbaits as fresh ones, so have a ready supply in your freezer. Wrap and freeze them in polythene bags, individually or in small batches.

The same goes for freshwater fish baits. Rather than wasting time and even risking total failure trying to catch them on the day you go piking, have plenty in reserve at home in the freezer.

Choice of deadbaits

Your choice of deadbait on a particular venue depends on whether the pike there have been fished for extensively. Smelt and mackerel generally catch pike from any water, unless the pike have been caught many times on these baits. Then a change bait is well worth trying.

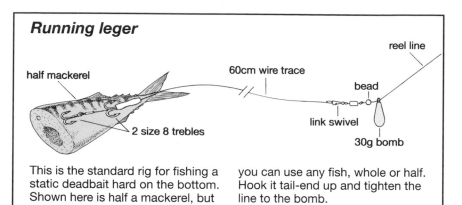

Running leger

half mackerel

60cm wire trace

reel line

bead

link swivel

2 size 8 trebles

30g bomb

This is the standard rig for fishing a static deadbait hard on the bottom. Shown here is half a mackerel, but you can use any fish, whole or half. Hook it tail-end up and tighten the line to the bomb.

To fool wary pike, you can modify the smell of a deadbait by injecting it with different flavours and fish oils. Likewise you can buy deadbaits dyed different colours, to ring the changes and tempt a cagey pike.

Tackle for deadbaiting

Deadbaiting requires tackle capable of handling baits weighing 100g (3½oz) or more. You need to use a rod with a 2-3lb (0.9-1.4kg) test curve and a good quality, robust fixed-spool reel loaded with 11-15lb (5-6.8kg) line.

Always use wire traces. Good quality

Wobbled deadbait

Put a bend in the deadbait before hooking it on (head-end up) to make it wobble on the retrieve like a sick or injured fish.

▲ *This set-up is one of the most effective means of bite indication when fishing a static deadbait. You cast out the bait, tighten the line, open the bail arm and trap the line in the white plastic clip. When a pike runs with the bait, the line pulls free of the clip and the orange ball drops – setting off the blue alarm.*

▶ *A small roach deadbait ready to be cast out. It's worth experimenting with different sizes of baits, but it doesn't necessarily follow that the bigger the bait, the bigger the pike. Small baits have proved the downfall of many big pike.*

Vaned float

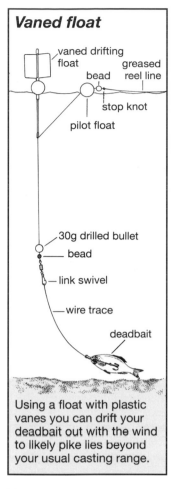

Using a float with plastic vanes you can drift your deadbait out with the wind to likely pike lies beyond your usual casting range.

▼ *Sea fish deadbaits can work very well for pike. It pays to stock your freezer with a variety of both sea and freshwater deadbaits, so that when one fails you can try another. On hard-fished waters, pike soon wise-up to baits.*

traces of about 60cm (24in) long, fitted with pairs of size 8 or 6 treble hooks, are readily obtainable from tackle shops (they are called 'snap tackles'). One hook from each treble holds the deadbait. You can slide the top treble up or down the trace, according to the size of the bait.

Last but not least, never go piking without a pair of long-nosed artery forceps for unhooking your catch, and a good-sized landing net.

Deadbaiting tactics

There are two successful deadbaiting techniques – static and mobile. Which one you use depends very much on the mood of the pike, and that is something you can only determine on the day. But once you have the tackle and know-how to fish the various basic static and mobile techniques, you are ready for every eventuality.

Static deadbaiting

Static deadbaits have caught many big pike over the years. Apart from its visibility, the big attraction of the static deadbait is the scent trail it gives off. This is why it can pay to try half a dead fish rather than a whole one – it greatly increases the scent trail. Alternatively, puncture a whole deadbait several times so that more body juices are released underwater.

The key to static deadbaiting is to have good bite indication so that the pike has no time to turn and swallow the bait and become deep-hooked. Plenty of weight – around 30g (1oz) – is needed to anchor the bait so a tight line can be kept to it.

Running leger This is the simplest static rig, with the bait held fast to the bottom (see *Running leger* diagram).

Popped-up deadbait This is a variant of the running leger rig. A foam stick is inserted into the deadbait to make it hang in the water off the bottom, where it is more easily seen by pike (see *Popped-up deadbait* diagram). It is especially effective over a weedy bottom or deep soft mud, both of which can hide a bait.

Suspended deadbait This is a more complicated but very effective rig. It uses a pilot float sub-surface to suspend the deadbait above the river or lake bed (see *Suspended deadbait* diagram). Again, this presents a highly visible bait and one that won't get lost in weed or mud.

Suspended deadbait

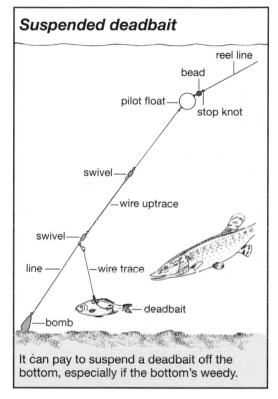

It can pay to suspend a deadbait off the bottom, especially if the bottom's weedy.

Popped-up deadbait

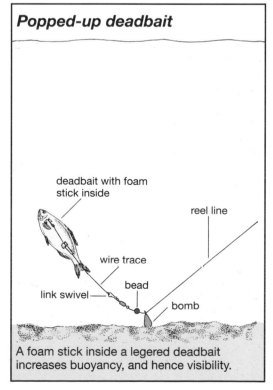

A foam stick inside a legered deadbait increases buoyancy, and hence visibility.

Drifted deadbait

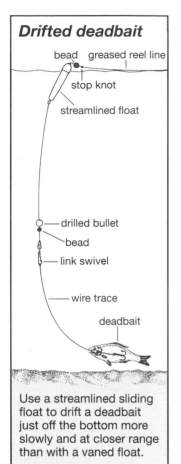

bead   greased reel line
stop knot
streamlined float
drilled bullet
bead
link swivel
wire trace
deadbait

Use a streamlined sliding float to drift a deadbait just off the bottom more slowly and at closer range than with a vaned float.

Static deadbaits can take time to work, but on a good day it is possible to get as many as a dozen runs from pike of all sizes. Only pike in waters where they are very well fed show little interest.

Mobile deadbaiting

With a moving bait you are playing not only on the pike's highly developed sense of smell and sight, but on the sensitivity of its lateral line to vibrations.

Mobile methods include wobbling a deadbait through the water, using a float to drift a deadbait out to likely looking lies, and trolling.

Wobbled deadbait For wobbling, the deadbait is mounted head up on the trace and retrieved in an enticing manner. The amount of bend you put in the body of the dead fish determines how much it wobbles through the water (see *Wobbled deadbait* diagram).

Drifted deadbait Sometimes it is impossible to cast your deadbait directly into the spot where you expect a pike to be lying, either because it is a little too far from the bank or because a reedbed or other obstacle is in the way. A drifting float can be the answer to the problem, provided the wind

▼ *The reward for picking the right swim, using the right tackle and presenting a deadbait correctly – a pike for the net.*

Handle with care!

If you want to inject deadbaits with oils and flavourings, remember that a syringe and needle is a potentially dangerous instrument. Use only purpose-made syringes sold in tackle shops, handle them with care and store them in a safe place with the points of the needles properly protected. Never leave them lying around when fishing.

direction is in your favour and the wind is not too strong (see *Drifted deadbait* diagram).

Drifting is useful anywhere when you want to search out likely looking areas of water rather than just fish your bait in one particular spot.

Vaned float A more difficult technique to master but one that allows you to fish a deadbait at extreme range – 100m (110yd) or more from the bank – uses a vaned float to 'sail' the bait through the water (see *Vaned float* diagram).

Trolling On very large waters you can often locate pike only by extensive searching. A proven method on such waters – Loch Lomond in Scotland, for example – is to troll (tow) a deadbait behind a boat. Like the vaned float, this is more a specialist technique than a beginner's method.

Legering still waters for specimens

The leger is one of the deadliest methods for trapping really big fish. A simple approach on a good water scores for the thoughtful angler, says Nigel Witham of the Perchfishers.

Margins for error

Don't cast over the fish – they're often closer than you think if you haven't scared them by blundering around the bank. Start close in and work outwards if that doesn't succeed, covering the likely spots methodically.

▼ *The author, Nigel Witham, lands a good roach at Haversham Lake in Linear Fisheries, Milton Keynes. It took lobworm legered in a deep hole in the lake bed about 40m (44yd) out from the bank.*

To many anglers there is nothing that quite beats the sight of a perfectly set float disappearing beneath the ripple. But perhaps these anglers have yet to experience the thrill as a bobbin twitches to life and creeps towards the rod butt.

And maybe they've never felt that missed heartbeat as their quivertip pulls round to the surge of a good fish. These are just some of the joys of legering, the first choice technique of most big fish anglers.

Over the last 30 years or so, legering in its many forms has developed greatly, becoming infinitely more sophisticated. Indeed, legering has progressed so much that you can now buy almost as many bits of tackle for it as you can for float fishing.

There are non-toxic weights in many shapes and sizes, beads of all descriptions, feeders, swing, spring and quivertips, rods lined up in racks and books full of varying opinions on the subject. It's no wonder that the novice can become confused. So let's look at a basic approach that will help you put a few better-sized fish on the bank.

Choose your water

Firstly, you can't catch a fish that isn't there, so you must fish the right sorts of waters. But where do you look? Local and national press reports and tackle shops are good sources of information. Tackle shops also sell permits for day ticket waters and some have contacts with local clubs and associations.

Some types of water are more likely to yield a monster to the right approach than others. For example, your chances of a 2lb (0.9kg) roach are much better in a big reservoir than in your local farm pond.

Estate lakes are well established lakes which form the backbone of traditional still-water fishing. They are called estate lakes because it was the fashion in the 18th and 19th centuries for wealthy landowners to dam streams and excavate lakes on their estates – and a good thing too!

This type of water contains some species to good size although others, such as roach, rudd and sometimes bream and crucians, become stunted and rarely grow to specimen proportions. Tench are also common and often reach good weights, with carp, perch, pike and other species very likely to be present .

Gravel pits are another common type of

big fish water. Whole books have been written about angling on pits; they are a complicated subject. In many pits the fish can grow very large, sometimes with record potential. In fact most stillwater records are pit fish.

Gravel pits are often difficult waters when it comes to fish finding. They are comparatively new, most having been dug since World War II. This means that they are rarely silted, sometimes have sparse weed growth and the species present can vary widely.

Reservoirs are also worthwhile. They come in a huge variety of shapes and sizes ranging from giant dammed valleys covering several thousands of acres to small concrete bowls but they can contain some very big fish.

Choosing your swim is your first task once you've found a good water. Nowadays it is common to cast long distances, but never cast farther than you need. In most estate

Your end gear

Terminal tackle is simple. You need a selection of swivel bombs **(1)** from ¼-2oz (7-56g), a few open-end swimfeeders **(2)**, leger beads **(3)**, leger stops **(4)**, swivels **(5)**, link swivels **(6)**, a selection of poly balls **(7)** or rig foam for buoyant legers and hooks **(8)** in sizes 4-16.

lakes the fish are likely to be near the edge.

In addition, long range fishing can cause difficulty with bite detection and undertow – you often need special equipment, such as weighted bobbins, to combat drag on the line. So don't worry if you can't cast far. You may catch more than those who can!

Look for areas of cover such as weed and all sorts of snags. Plumb carefully for abrupt depth changes and drop-offs and put your baits at various depths on these features. Try to fish facing the direction of the prevailing wind. It is said that food collects on the windward bank and it's certainly a good place to start looking for the fish.

Leger kit for all sorts of specimens

For carp and big tench, especially in weedy waters, you need (left) a 2¼lb (1kg) TC carp rod of about 12ft (3.65m), coupled with a fixed-spool reel that holds around 250m (275yd) of 12lb (5.4kg) line.

For smaller species and less snaggy waters, (right) a 1¼lb (0.6kg) TC fast taper leger rod coupled with a fixed-spool reel with a capacity of 350m (375yd) of 6lb (2.7kg) line, is about right.

You also need spare spools filled with lines of various breaking strains to cope with different conditions and fish.

▲ *Bryan Culley fishes the feeder for big rudd and tench. He's using a sweetcorn and maggot cocktail on the hook, fished over a bed of crumb, corn and maggot.*

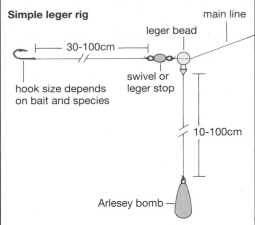

Nigel's stillwater leger rigs

Simple leger rig

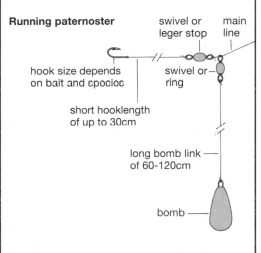

The **simple leger rig** is often the best for exploring a new water or where there are few complications. You may need to vary the lengths or change rig if you have trouble with finicky bites or with excessive weed.

▲ *This bite detection set-up looks complicated but it's pretty simple. Monkey climbers give visual indication of runs and drop-backs, while electronic buzzers alert the angler with an audible alarm.*

Tackling essentials

Always use tackle that's strong enough to land your fish – don't be afraid to try heavy gear in weedy or snaggy water when you're after big fish. You're going to need heavier, carp-type gear and up to 12lb (5.4kg) line for big carp and tench in weedy water whereas light Avon-type leger gear with 4lb (1.8kg) line is perfect for big perch in a snag-free swim.

Lighter tackle and smaller baits can produce some good roach, rudd or bream. Other species may surprise you. Perch can show up at any time and the big ones are not as rare as you might think.

Fish 'n' rigs

What should you try to catch? If your water is an estate lake, it may well be quite silted. Tench and carp don't mind a bit of mud – in fact there's little they like more than a good root around. But roach, rudd, bream and perch prefer a cleaner lake bed.

Nigel's running paternoster is ideal for small baits and smaller species as it is more sensitive than the running leger. The essential feature is that the bomb link is longer that the hooklength.

Tip How long a hooklength?

If you keep getting bites which never really develop, try a longer hooklength. This tends to give fish greater confidence. On the other hand, if you deep hook a fish, make the hooklength shorter and more sensitive, and remember to strike sooner.

▶ *A juicy lobworm wriggles enticingly – but you must make sure the hook point is exposed if you're fishing such a large, lively bait.*

▲ *Sweetcorn, maggot and worm are three fine baits for legering in still waters. Maggot is excellent in many cocktails, and other good things to put on your hook include breadflake, boilies and particle baits.*

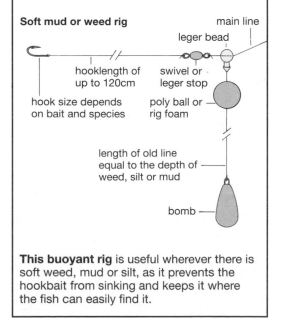

This **buoyant rig** is useful wherever there is soft weed, mud or silt, as it prevents the hookbait from sinking and keeps it where the fish can easily find it.

▲ *Baiting up at distance, as here, means you need to use groundbait to provide the weight and bulk. At close range, loosefeed is often better. Some species, such as bream, seem to prefer groundbait in the summer.*

Don't over-complicate things. Start with a simple leger rig and lobworm as bait. There is nothing quite as good as lobworm for helping you discover what species your lake contains. They all love them! If you find you're getting bites you can't hit, only then is it time to change your rig, or try varying hooklengths and bomb links.

If worm doesn't work or catches nothing but small eels, try breadflake or paste, sweetcorn, luncheon meat or boilies. Unless there aren't many small fish in the water, avoid maggots on the hook or you'll be plagued by twitches. Where there are still-water chub, try a deadbait quietly legered in the margins after dark.

The larger the bait, the more time the fish needs before you strike and the more freedom of movement you should build into your set-up. With a small bait like maggot or a single grain of corn, a swingtip or quivertip is best for spotting bites.

If you're using larger baits, a simple bobbin, such as a squeezy bottle top hung over the line at the rod butt, is usually better as they generally allow the fish more time to run. They work well with electronic bite indicators in many cases.

Groundbait lightly at first, or better still, loosefeed with samples of your hookbait, and perhaps some maggots or hemp as well. Only put in lots of feed when you're sure it's needed. You can afford to be more liberal with your free samples if you spot decent tench or carp rolling over your feed, or if you're getting plenty of bites.

A feeder can be a good idea. But don't try it in very shallow water as the splash can scare the fish. Make sure you cast accurately to the same spot each time.

With this basic approach and these few variations, you're well on your way to some highly productive stillwater fishing – and some excellent fish!

◄ *John Wilson displays the fruits of an intelligent approach to stillwater legering – a fine fat summer slab.*

Techniques for big perch

The Perchfishers is a club devoted entirely to the capture of specimen perch. Secretary Stewart Allum tells you about some of the techniques he uses for catching these beautiful fish.

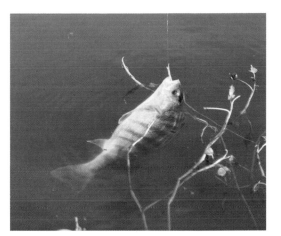

In the seventies and eighties, perch virtually disappeared from many of our waters because of disease. Now stocks are recovering and the bold, stripy predator is enjoying a comeback throughout the British Isles.

Time and place

Perch are aggressive and you can catch them on a wide variety of methods. Indeed, where small perch are numerous they can be a positive nuisance to the angler seeking bigger game. However, by carefully selecting the right waters, methods and time of the year, it is possible to locate larger specimens selectively.

Even tiny ponds hold very large perch – provided there is plenty of food for them. They are a fast-growing species and an abundance of tiny roach, rudd or gudgeon is just the sort of diet they thrive on. So if you don't live near one of the famous perch waters, don't despair – there is probably a neglected farm pond or derelict canal nearby which could contain that elusive three pounder (1.4kg).

Autumn is the best time to seek big perch. This is when they shoal up in large numbers in the deeper areas of lakes and gravel pits before migrating to the very deepest water for the winter. At this time of the year they are hungry and extremely

▲▼ Perch (above) rely on cover such as weed beds, sunken piles or tree roots at the edge of pools and rivers, from which they dart out and ambush their prey. In summer you can sometimes hear them as they chase fry around marginal weed close to the surface. (They produce a sharp click as their jaws snap shut.)

Here Nigel Witham of The Perchfishers strikes into a good fish (below). Fishing for big perch is no longer a hit or miss affair.

Simple waggler rig

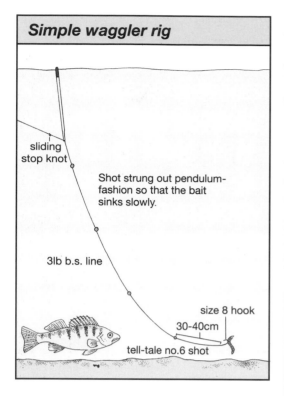

sliding stop knot

Shot strung out pendulum-fashion so that the bait sinks slowly.

3lb b.s. line

size 8 hook

30-40cm

tell-tale no.6 shot

▶ *This fish fell to a spinner tied directly to the line but it is best to use a trace – you never know when a pike might strike.*

aggressive and there is avid competition among shoals for any available food.

Baits and methods

In recent years – largely due to the formation of clubs such as The Perchfishers – techniques have become more refined. Traditional perch baits – such as worms, livebaits, deadbaits and spinners – are used together with state-of-the-art tackle and methods (usually associated with other species) so that big perch are now caught more by design than chance.

Worm and feeder Lobworms are a reliable winter bait and a great favourite with perch everywhere. You can floatfish or leger with them. On large, deep waters – such as gravel pits – where the fish are harder to find, try attracting the fish to your bait. One way is to leger a lob and use

▼ *A typical winter perch swim on the Berkshire Kennet – the trouble is that it looks pikey too! If you are livebaiting and think there may be pike about, then use a braided hooklength.*

Swimfeeder and worm rig

6lb b.s. reel line
free-running plastic bead

swivel with rig tube

4lb b.s. hooklength
50-75cm long

30-40cm link

link swivel

size 6 barbless hook

open-ended swimfeeder

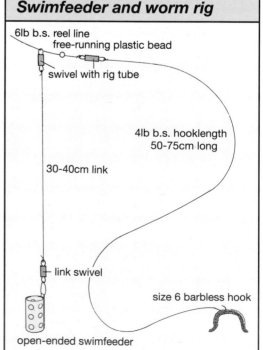

Paternoster rig

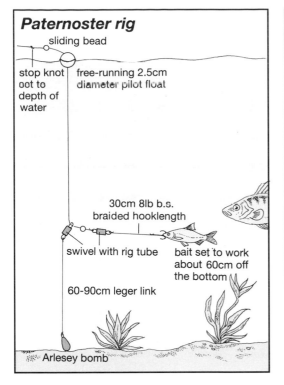

- sliding bead
- stop knot oot to depth of water
- free-running 2.5cm diameter pilot float
- 30cm 8lb b.s. braided hooklength
- swivel with rig tube
- bait set to work about 60cm off the bottom
- 60-90cm leger link
- Arlesey bomb

Air-injected bait rig

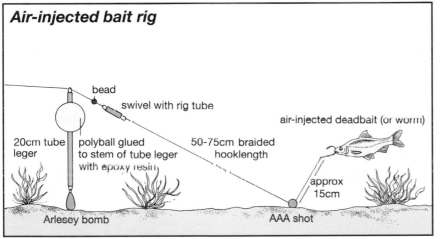

- bead
- swivel with rig tube
- air-injected deadbait (or worm)
- 20cm tube leger
- polyball glued to stem of tube leger with epoxy resin
- 50-75cm braided hooklength
- approx 15cm
- Arlesey bomb
- AAA shot

▲ *Small roach deadbaits are ideal for big perch but if there are pike about use a braided hooklength.*

an open-ended swimfeeder packed with maggots and flavoured groundbait. Try experimenting: additives such as dried blood, worm extract (which you can buy from tackle shops) and red dye (red is a favourite colour of perch!) often work. Maggots help to keep small fish interested and these in turn attract big perch into the area where your bait is.

Just worm On smaller lakes, ponds and canals, a swimfeeder can cause too much disturbance. Instead, try fishing a worm on a straightforward link leger or under a waggler type float.

When waggler fishing, loosefeed maggots to keep the swim alive. If no takes are forthcoming, try twitching the bait back towards you by giving a couple of quick turns of the reel handle every few minutes. This often brings an immediate response from an otherwise suspicious perch which may have

Top perch waters

● **The River Thames** Particularly in its lower reaches, the Thames holds vast shoals of perch – some of them well over 3lb (1.4kg). Perch appear to be on the increase in this river system with good fish being reported from tributaries such as the Mole and Wey.

● **The Oxford Canal** Just one of a number of canals nationwide now producing perch in good numbers. Many matches fished here in the latter part of the 1990-91 season were dominated by perch catches with some big individual specimens reported.

● **Linear Fisheries** is situated next to the M1 at Newport Pagnall. Run by well-known anglers Len Gurd and Bob Baldock, these gravel pits have produced many good perch in recent seasons. The fishing is well managed and, with the majority of regulars tending to specialize in the more popular carp, tench and pike,

there is plenty of scope for the enterprising perch angler.

● **Leisure Sport Angling** group probably controls more gravel pit fisheries than anyone else. Many of these contain perch which have scarcely ever been fished for.

● **The Yorkshire Ouse** above Acaster contains a great many perch which average around 12oz-1lb (0.34-0.45kg), with the possibility of bigger fish. Most of the fishing in the city of York is free to holders of a NRA Yorkshire region licence.

● **The Scottish lochs** Anglers who head north of the border to fish for pike are missing out on some great perch fishing. Loch Awe in Argyllshire, Loch Ken in Dumfriesshire and Lochs Tay and Tummell in Perthshire all provide excellent perch fishing. Most of the fishing is free, but check with local tackle shops and land owners first.

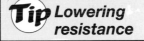 **Tip** **Lowering resistance**

Legering indicators such as swingtips, quivertips and monkey climbers either create too much resistance or don't allow enough freedom to a taking perch.

You can make a perfect lightweight indicator by cutting a 3mm strip of plastic from an empty shampoo bottle or similar container and forming it into a ring about 3.5cm (1½ in) in diameter.

Thread the ring on to the line when setting up the rod. It doesn't impede casting and, when the bail is off, allows fish to take line without feeling any resistance.

been eyeing the bait for some time, wondering whether to take it.

Spinning On large, deep waters spinning is a good alternative to the sit-and-wait approach – you can actively search the water for big fish. Patterns like the tried and tested ABU Toby, Atom and Reflex work well. It is important to retrieve the lure as slowly as possible – let it sink to the full depth before starting to retrieve.

Always use a wire trace. It doesn't put the perch off and is a good insurance against any unfortunate pike which might otherwise engulf the spinner and bite through monofilament line.

Live and dead fish baits catch their fair share of good perch. Unlike spinning – where an interested fish has to snap impulsively at a bait before it has gone – live and dead baiting allows an interested fish to inspect a bait thoroughly before deciding whether to take it. This means that you can't use a wire trace. If you are fairly certain there are no pike about, then you can get away with monofilament but if you aren't sure then use one of the new braided hooklength materials such as Kryston Silkworm, which is supple and reasonably resistant to a pike's teeth.

Livebaits should be lightly paternostered near a suitable ambush point – old lily roots, for example.

Deadbaits should, if possible, be freelined or lightly legered so as to minimize the resistance to a taking fish. Debris on the bottom such as dead leaves and twigs can

▶ *Perch populations rise and fall frequently – it is part of the natural cycle of these fish. This is why even famous perch fisheries – such as the private, record-producing lake in Kent – only hold the headlines for a couple of seasons before a new venue hits the news.*

cause the leger and bait to become buried. You can get round this by using a buoyant leger coupled with an air-injected bait. This helps to keep the bait and leger free of snags and prevents the bait from being obscured. (You can fish lobworms in exactly the same way.)

Deadbaits should always be freshly killed – small roach, rudd, perch or gudgeon of 3.5cm-5cm (1½-2in) are ideal. Never use a smelly old bait and avoid sea baits – perch do not like the taste of sea fish.

Hitting the bites

Perch have a habit of toying around with a bait – albeit in a fairly savage manner – which can make bites hard to hit. When floatfishing, for example, don't strike as soon as the float disappears. Allow the fish a couple of seconds to get the worm into its mouth, then take up any slack line and gently lift into the fish. Don't wait too long though, or else the fish may drop the bait or swallow the hook.

Tip No barbs

Some anglers don't like to use barbless hooks but Stewart says: "I always use a barbless hook when fishing for perch with worms. If a fish does take a bait deep down while you are waiting for a bite to develop, it makes the job of unhooking it much easier. I have lost very few fish as a result of barbless hooks."

▼ *If you miss a lot of bites when fishing worm, don't worry – this is probably caused by small perch tugging the end of the worm. A big perch has a mouth like a bucket and usually doesn't mess around for long.*

Advanced carp rigs

Peter Mohan's advice is to fish simply if you can. But in some circumstances you might need more complicated rigs to get the most out of your angling – so it's worth having a few variations up your sleeve just in case.

One of the greatest aids to success in modern carp fishing is knowing how to make up and use different rigs. In most carp waters, the standard running link leger method with a hair rig is all you need to catch bottom feeding carp.

However, in more difficult lakes where the fish are caught frequently and have become wary of baits on the bottom, experimenting with more advanced rigs can make

▲ *Dawn is one of the best times for carp fishing. This solitary angler stands a fair chance if his rigs are right for the water.*

all the difference between blanking and catching big fish.

Knowing when to switch

It's no good using complex rigs and then forgetting all the other skills which help you catch. However modern your rig, it won't work if you are fishing in areas where the fish are not feeding, or if you are using a bait the fish won't take.

But how do you know when to switch to a different rig?

If most anglers on your water are catching more than you, if you get a lot of small bite indications which don't produce proper takes, if you are frequently losing fish because they come off, or if the fish you catch are hooked just outside the mouth – then it's time to change.

If you get lots of twitches, slacken the line

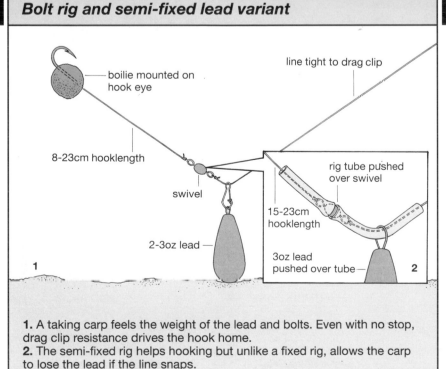

Bolt rig and semi-fixed lead variant

boilie mounted on hook eye

line tight to drag clip

8-23cm hooklength

swivel

rig tube pushed over swivel

15-23cm hooklength

2-3oz lead

3oz lead pushed over tube

1

2

1. A taking carp feels the weight of the lead and bolts. Even with no stop, drag clip resistance drives the hook home.
2. The semi-fixed rig helps hooking but unlike a fixed rig, allows the carp to lose the lead if the line snaps.

Tip Wallet wheeze

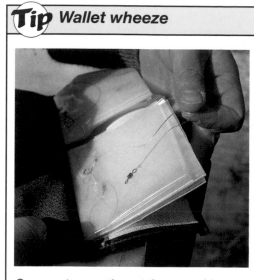

One way to save time at the waterside is to make up your rigs before going on a fishing trip. To keep them tidy and tangle-free a rig wallet is a fine idea.

so it lies along the bottom, making sure they're not line bites. If the twitches continue, try to make sure they're not caused by small fish (perhaps by trying a smaller bait – small fish often suck at a bait too large for them).

Bespoke rigging

When you're pretty sure you have a rig problem, you should think about trying a different set up.

Bolt rig For the original type of bolt rig use a fairly large long shank, down eye hook – a size 4 perhaps. Side-hook a boilie, leaving a gap of at least 3mm (⅛in) between the boilie and the hook point. If you don't do this the point will go into the bait when you strike

▶ *Is it a genuine rod-bender or a wad of weed? A helicopter rig often helps you to avoid snagging up in weedy waters.*

Lead free fish

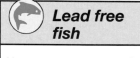

Never use a permanently fixed lead.

If the line breaks above the lead a fish might be swimming around for months with an unwanted weight attached. Worse still, a rogue lead getting dragged around could easily tangle up in a snag and tether a fish to one spot until it starves to death.

▶ *Almost there! Many carp anglers never adjust their rigs, and wonder why fish come off – it's often because they are only just hooked outside the mouth.*

and not into the fish.

Use a hooklength 8-23cm (3-9in) long and attach the 2-3oz (56-85g) lead to the line by a running link. Fish this on a tight line held on the rod by a drag clip.

Modern variation This variation of the bolt rig is the semi-fixed breakaway lead method. The lead is fixed as far as the fish is concerned, but if the line breaks the lead comes off with the tube so the fish doesn't end up dragging a heavy burden around.

Bolt hair rig If neither of these methods is successful, try a bolt hair rig. Mount the bait on a hair tied to the bend of the hook instead of on the hook eye.

Anti-tangle rig You're bound to get into tangles sometimes, whether you are using a bolt rig, a bolt hair rig or even a standard hair rig. When trying these methods for the first time it is worth retrieving your tackle quickly a few times after casting, to see if the rig is tangled. If it is, try an anti-tangle rig.

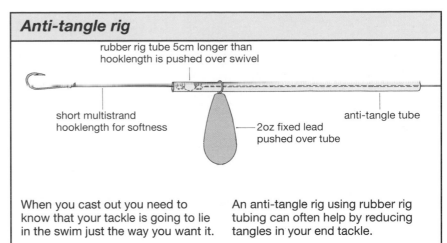

Anti-tangle rig

rubber rig tube 5cm longer than hooklength is pushed over swivel

short multistrand hooklength for softness

2oz fixed lead pushed over tube

anti-tangle tube

When you cast out you need to know that your tackle is going to lie in the swim just the way you want it.

An anti-tangle rig using rubber rig tubing can often help by reducing tangles in your end tackle.

▼ *If you land a decent fish like this one, make a note of the hook's position in the mouth – you may need to adjust your hooklength.*

Weed-free whirlybird

You may suspect that fish are rejecting your baits because the nylon line used for the hooklength in your rigs is too stiff, causing the fish to feel it over their lips. In this case try braided hooklengths or multistrand, which are much softer and can be used with all types of rigs. However, since they are so soft, these hooklengths are prone to tangling and you are likely to require an anti-tangle rig.

Helicopter rig Not all waters have clear bottoms. Some have a few inches of dense blanket weed in which the bait gets buried, and is hard for the fish to find. The helicopter rig – so called because the hooklength and bait revolve round the line during the cast – is especially good for this type of water. It is also a good anti-tangle rig.

A light hair rig type of hook is best for the helicopter rig and a soft multistrand hooklength goes some way towards preventing the bait being ejected by wary fish. The rig tubing helps to prevent tangles caused by the multistrand looping round the main line during the cast.

The hair rig can be tied to the bend or the eye of the hook. Better still, buy a hair rig fixing tube from a tackle shop and push it over the point of the hook. This enables you to have the hair coming from any part of the hook.

If you are fishing in snaggy areas or in heavy weed with a helicopter rig it's best to use light line on the bomb link. If the lead gets caught in a snag, the line breaks and the lead is lost, but you should be able to save the rest of your tackle and get any fish away from snags without difficulty.

Tip **Keep it simple**

Use the simplest rigs for as long as you can – even freelining can still work on some waters.

Only get into the more complex rigs when you are sure they are necessary on difficult waters.

Tip Moist method

Whatever carp rigs you decide to try, always check all knots very carefully and make sure you wet the line before pulling the knots tight – tying knots in dry line reduces the breaking strain by as much as 25%.

◀ *Top carp angler Ritchie MacDonald carefully displays a handsome thirteen pounder (6kg).*
Note the fish's grin – the carp's very sensitive, protractible lips are one reason why soft hooklengths are effective.

▼ *Advanced rigs are only effective if you combine them with sound angling methods.*

Helicopter rig

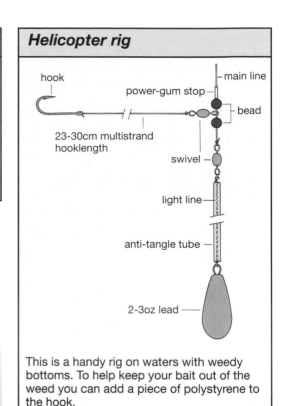

hook
power-gum stop
main line
bead
23-30cm multistrand hooklength
swivel
light line
anti-tangle tube
2-3oz lead

This is a handy rig on waters with weedy bottoms. To help keep your bait out of the weed you can add a piece of polystyrene to the hook.

Made-to-measure

Since advanced rigs are fairly complicated and include several attachments, make sure everything is secure before you cast, and that all the bits are in the right place.

Each time you catch a fish, note carefully where the hook is positioned in the mouth. If the fish is hooked just outside the mouth, you need to lengthen your hooklength by 2.5-5cm (1-2in) so that the hook will go further inside the carp's mouth.

Altering the length of the hooklength can also help you to get better takes from twitchers – these are often fish which have taken a hair-rigged bait inside their mouths leaving the hook still outside! Try shortening the hair as well.

Very short hairs On hard-fished waters many anglers now use rigs with hairs of only about 12mm (½in) between the edge of the boilie and the hook. They are often best for those wary fish that constantly mouth baits but don't take them.

This mouthing of baits happens quite a lot on most waters but when you can't see the fish you tend to forget what's happening. It's easy enough to see carp when they're taking every floater on the water except yours with the hook in it – and it's very frustrating. But at least you can see them doing it – you know what's happening and you can try to do something about it.

With legered baits all the action is underwater but it shouldn't stop you from trying different methods when you're not catching any fish. If you don't fancy donning a frogman suit to find out what the problem is at the business end of your line – a few rig adjustments might just do the trick.

Spinning for pike – the lure of success

Barrie Rickards, who began spinning forty years ago, and still catches many big pike, shares some of his secrets for successful piking.

Spinning's tops

Britains last two record pike were caught on lures. A 45lb 12oz (20.3kg) fish was landed on a bar spoon and one of 46lb 13oz (21.234kg) was caught on a plug – and in four years Barrie Rickards has caught 30 pike over 20lbs (9kg) by spinning.

Many anglers are unaware just how successful spinning for pike can be - possibly because of a few ingrained notions which are hard to budge. In particular it is necessary to dispense with two fallacies concerning lure fishing. First, while it is correct to say that the *average* size of lure-caught fish is smaller – about 7lb (3.1kg) – you do get plenty of big fish. By and large, you also get *more* fish.

Secondly, it is also true that spinning is more successful in summer and autumn than it is in the depths of winter. However, winter spinning can be very successful.

Choosing rods and reels

The rod you choose should be around 9ft (2.7m) for bank fishing. This is a good compromise since it overcomes two ever-present problems in pike fishing that create contradictory demands on the length of the rod. First, marginal reeds and rushes are a fact of life so a rod needs to be about 9ft (2.7m) long to reach over them. Secondly, overhanging trees also seem to be a year-round problem, so the rod can't be too long or it could well catch in the branches.

When boat fishing, or casting on small streams or drains, a 6ft (1.8m) rod may be ideal. Carbon rods are lighter if you intend to carry them all day, and a telescopic version – permanently fitted up with reel line – is invaluable.

Rod strength is important. You don't need a powerful deadbait throwing rod – nor do you need one with a through-action. A

▼ *Pike – when they are in a feeding mood – seem completely unable to resist a spinner. This pike has struck instinctively at a barspoon spinner.*

▲ *The term spinning is used to describe all forms of artificial lure fishing and not just fishing with revolving blade spinners. This is a plug – excellent for simulating a fish that is struggling in the water.*

they won't cast as far as a fixed-spool reel, but they are more accurate. A multiplier is not difficult to use and half an hour's practice serves to put a reasonably competent angler on the right road – with only a few tangles to follow.

If you are a right-handed angler – and therefore wish to hold your rod in your right hand while playing the fish – get a **left-hand wind** multiplier. Don't believe any one who says it doesn't matter. Using a left-hand wind outfit makes the whole action sweeter, smoother and much more efficient and keeps your right hand free for casting. Right-handed anglers cast better and more accurately using the right hand – you can't hold the rod *and* wind-in with just one hand!

One of the great advantages of using a multiplier is that the moment the lure hits the water you are in action, fishing smoothly, alert right from the start. Many pike strike the split second that the spinner hits the water – so be ready.

stiffish rod with a tip action and a 1¾-2lb test curve is excellent.

Anglers are spoilt for choice with fixed-spool reels. Almost any decent reel or brand suits perfectly well. There's no point in choosing a heavy reel – one that takes 100yd (90m) of 15lb (6.8kg) line is fine.

Multiplier reels are a pleasure to use –

▼ *A good selection of lures. On the top is a row of buzzers, the second row are spoons, while those on the round log nearest the bottom are spinners of various types.*

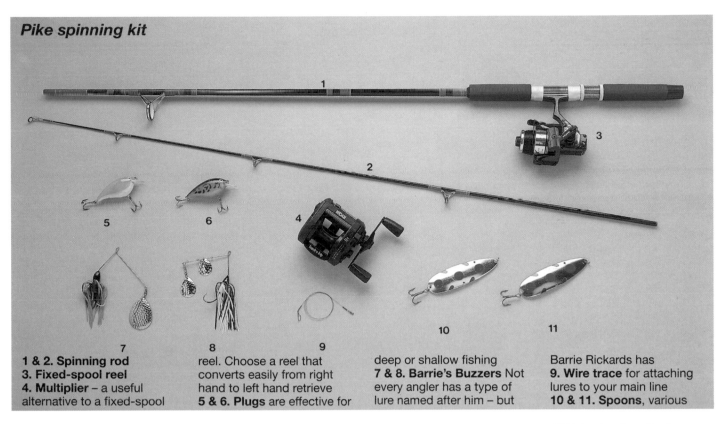

Pike spinning kit

1 & 2. Spinning rod
3. Fixed-spool reel
4. Multiplier – a useful alternative to a fixed-spool

reel. Choose a reel that converts easily from right hand to left hand retrieve
5 & 6. Plugs are effective for

deep or shallow fishing
7 & 8. Barrie's Buzzers Not every angler has a type of lure named after him – but

Barrie Rickards has
9. Wire trace for attaching lures to your main line
10 & 11. Spoons, various

Choosing line

Line for spinning can vary from 10 to 15lb (4.5 to 6.8kg) b.s. Wire traces should be 12in (30cm) long. Never use 6in (15cm) traces – a pike of 15lb (6.8kg) upwards can swallow lure and trace in one gulp. Choice of wire varies – try softer, supple varieties, but avoid very fine wires which tend to be stiff and difficult to twist by hand.

Put a swivel on one end and a link swivel on the other. Strengthen the exact point where the overlap of twisted wire ends with a blob of Epoxy resin Weed slides easily over the blob – but make sure it is a *blob* as a smear catches just as irritatingly as a knot.

Special extras

When you are spinning, line twisting can sometimes be a problem, particularly when using barspoons. However, you'll probably find that anti-kink vanes are rarely necessary. If you are using barspoons extensively, then fit a Wye lead at the top of the trace. This effectively stops the line spinning and as a bonus gives extra casting weight.

Landing nets are a vital piece of equipment for the keen pike spinner. Get a 75cm (30in) diameter round net. Avoid

micromesh nets – hooks get caught in them and may take up to half an hour to pull free, which is bad news for the poor fish. Try a knotless 12-25mm mesh net that is soft and knitted.

A backpack for carrying flask and food and warm clothes, including gloves in the winter, is also essential!

▼ *Spinning for pike is a particularly successful method during the summer months, when the water is clear. The shiny colours show plainly and the spinning action makes the lures strikingly obvious to hungry pike.*

Tip Buzzing along

Buzzers are the latest type of lure to reach the market, and they contrast strongly with more traditional lures in that they do not resemble wounded fish in any way. Pike can detect from some distance away the commotion buzzers create in the water when being cast and retrieved.

Tip Kinky devices

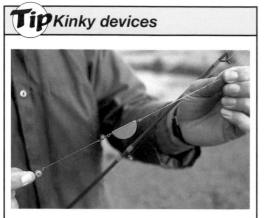

Barrie Rickards seldom uses anti-kink devices when spinning – except a Wye lead. But some pike anglers, such as Barrie's frequent fishing partner, Ken Whitehead, find an anti-kink vane is invaluable.

Pike spinning rig

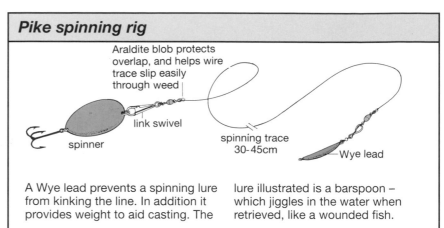

A Wye lead prevents a spinning lure from kinking the line. In addition it provides weight to aid casting. The lure illustrated is a barspoon – which jiggles in the water when retrieved, like a wounded fish.

▼ *This pike was fooled by the wobbling action of a typical spoon.*

Down to action

All the equipment mentioned is vital if the pike spinner is to enjoy piking. Good technique is worth nothing if the angler is uncomfortable and operating inefficiently.

The actual casting and retrieving is the least of your worries. Even so, there are a number of things to be wary of.

Don't get into the bad habit of 'casting round the clock'. Try to work out where the pike might be and cast accordingly. Just which lure you choose to use depends very much on the season and on the conditions you find in your swim. In many cases only experience will tell you what to try. You need to take into account water clarity, snags and weeds and the depth of water the fish may be feeding in. The lures themselves perform in various different ways – a spinner has a small blade that spins, a spoon wobbles on retrieve but has no blade and a plug closely resembles a fish and can do a variety of things on retrieve. Change lures frequently until you find the winning combination of style, size and colour for the day. This can be critical. The slightest change in depth, retrieve style or colour of lure can make a 'fishless' water productive.

In general, try a steady, slow retrieve, and in winter keep as deep as possible. During summer come up to the top with surface lures and try more varied depths as well. Vary the retrieve from steady to erratic only when the former fails.

Impossible swims?

Seek out seemingly impossible swims where no one has fished before – often a good fish lurks there. By using single hook buzzers you can fish among trees and in the middle of lily beds. If you suspect the location of a good fish, spend half a dozen casts nearby – but not actually too close to its lair. The pike will hear the repeated splashes and, by the time you throw the spoon to it, will be really curious and ready to strike.

In short, think before acting; be mobile; and be versatile. And above all, go spinning when you expect the pike to feed, not when other methods have failed.

GAME
FISHING

GAME FISHING

TACKLE

The basic fly kit

Trout fisheries are now so common in Britain that many die-hard coarse anglers are giving fly fishing a try. Peter Cockwill lists everything you need to enjoy some great sport.

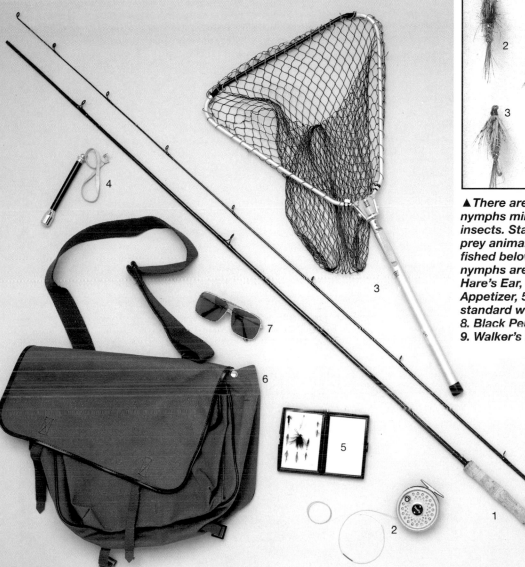

▲ *There are four types of fly. Dry flies and nymphs mimic the appearance of various insects. Standard wets and lures look like prey animals. All except dry flies are fished below the surface. Useful basic nymphs are: 1. Montana, 2. Gold Ribbed Hare's Ear, 3. Damsel. Lures include: 4. Appetizer, 5. Viva, 6. Whisky. Some standard wets are: 7. Mallard and Claret, 8. Black Pennell. Two reliable dry flies are: 9. Walker's Red Sedge, 10. Grey Duster.*

Key
1. Fly rod Two piece carbon fibre.
2. Fly reel, fly line, backing and leader.
3. Landing net This model folds away.
4. Priest Used to kill the fish quickly.
5. Fly box and flies This selection covers most situations.
6. Tackle bag to carry your equipment and catch.
7. Polarising sunglasses Essential to cut out reflected glare.

The fly fisherman is trying to tempt the fish into taking a hook dressed with fur, feathers and tinsel to represent its food. This is the fly and it is the only piece of terminal tackle used.

The fly weighs almost nothing and, because there are no other weights attached to the line, it is the line itself that is heavy. At the heart of fly fishing is the use of this special heavy line to cast the fly out into the water.

To start fly fishing you need a rod, a reel, fly line, some nylon, flies and a few accessories. As fly line is central to casting, you first need to know which type of line to choose.

Line and AFTM numbers

Line weights range from 1-15 (light lines have low numbers, whereas heavier lines, for long distance casting, have higher numbers) and this rating is referred to as the AFTM number. A number 7 is the most useful to the inexperienced angler.

In addition, lines come in a range of different densities – which allows them to float, or to sink at different rates. Lines also taper as an aid to casting – either from one end or from the middle towards both ends.

A floating double taper line is useful for most purposes and is marked DT7F (double taper 7 floating). A length of 27m (30yd) is all you need.

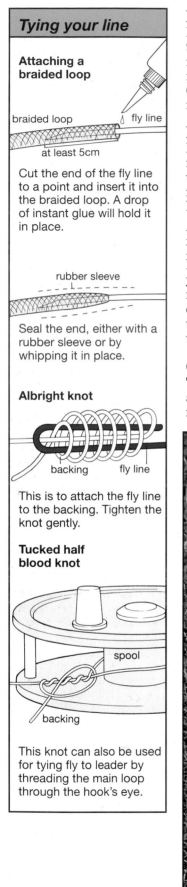

Tying your line

Attaching a braided loop

braided loop ··· fly line

at least 5cm

Cut the end of the fly line to a point and insert it into the braided loop. A drop of instant glue will hold it in place.

rubber sleeve

Seal the end, either with a rubber sleeve or by whipping it in place.

Albright knot

backing   fly line

This is to attach the fly line to the backing. Tighten the knot gently.

Tucked half blood knot

spool

backing

This knot can also be used for tying fly to leader by threading the main loop through the hook's eye.

Matching rod to line

For fishing small still waters you need a 9-9½ft (2.70-2.85m) rod, with a crisp action, rated for a number 6-7 line. The rod is marked with this rating, either as AFTM 6/7 or simply as number 6/7. Carbon fibre rods are light and good value for money.

Filling the reel

Fly reels are centrepins with a heavy ratchet and sometimes a drag mechanism to help slow down the flight of a running fish. Ask your tackle dealer for a simple lightweight reel that balances your rod.

Before you fill your reel with line, load at least 27m (30yd) of 25lb (11.3kg) backing line (nylon monofilament). This allows a large trout to run further without taking all your line. It also ensures that your fly line is not wound too tightly on the reel, which can cause casting problems. Tie the backing to the reel with a tucked half blood knot and to the fly line with an Albright knot.

Choosing flies

There are literally thousands of fly patterns and this can be very confusing at first. You need about ten to cover most situations on small trout lakes and you will quickly discover your own favourites. Ask other anglers which flies they have found effective on the waters you are going to fish. A small fly box keeps your flies safe and organized when you are not using them.

Because fly line is thick, which puts the fish off, the fly must be tied to a length of nylon, called a leader. This should be at least as long as the rod and about 5lb (2.3kg) breaking strain. It is tied to the main fly line by means of a loop. Any good tackle dealer will attach a short loop of 10lb (4.5kg) line to the fly line. You can also buy braided loops which you glue to the fly line. Tie the leader to the loop using a loop knot.

Accessories

Most waters require the use of a landing net. Stocked fisheries usually insist that you kill every trout you catch. A small cosh called a priest is best for this. You will need a bag to carry your tackle and a pair of polarising sunglasses to protect your eyes from glare and enable you to see where the fish are below the surface of the water. With all the correct tackle you are now equipped to try your hand at fly fishing.

▶ *Fly fishing for trout is often an active sport, involving a constant search for feeding fish. These two fine specimens fell for fly fishing tactics – the top fish is a brown trout, the bottom one a rainbow.*

Fly rods for trout

Tackle manufacturer and England International Bob Church recommends a selection of different fly rods for fishing brooks, streams, rivers and reservoirs.

◄ *Taking great care not to be rash or impatient, this angler gently persuades a fine lip-hooked rainbow into the net. This way the fish can be returned unharmed.*

There are three main materials for fly rods: split cane, glass-fibre and carbon fibre. Split cane, even though it is costly and rather heavy, has an enthusiastic following among stream and river anglers. Glass-fibre rods are now quite rare and virtually outdated.

Since its introduction in 1973, carbon fibre has revolutionized rod building. It is much stiffer and lighter than either split cane or glass-fibre. This means that a carbon blank can be much thinner than the alternatives, with more of a tip-action for distance casting. Other materials are often added to the carbon fibre, such as silicon carbide, kevlar and boron, which change the action of the finished rod.

Fly rods vary enormously in length – from a 6ft (1.8m) brook or small stream rod, through a 12ft (3.6m) loch style rod to a 18ft (5.5m) 'dapping' rod.

Just as a fly line is given an AFTMA rating according to the weight of the first 10.7m (35ft), so rods are rated by the line they are designed to cast. However, even rods of equal length with identical AFTMA ratings can feel quite different. This is because actions can vary. They range from all-through to tip-action.

There are many options in material, length, action and style to catch trout. Here Bob Church looks at the batch of rods he keeps for his own use. They cover all aspects of fly fishing in the UK.

Small stream rods

Bob's 6ft (1.8m) split cane rod is perfect with AFTMA 3 line. He uses it on small streams or chalk streams where long casting isn't necessary and where the fish aren't too big. The rod is a pleasure to use – and it can flip a tiny fly under an overhanging branch with great delicacy.

Short rods like this one are essential if you plan to fly fish streams with heavily overgrown banks where overhead casting might prove difficult. An all-through action lets you feel the fight of a small brownie more than a tip-action rod. Bob also has a crisp tip-actioned 8ft (2.4m) cane rod for dry fly fishing on chalk streams where accuracy and power are vital.

The AFTMA rating

AFTMA (the Association of Fishing Tackle Manufacturers of America) grades all fly lines in a scale from 1 to 15. The first 10.7m (35ft) of line is weighed, regardless of density or taper, and given a number. A number 1 line is the lightest and thinnest, a 15 the heaviest.

Fly rods at a glance

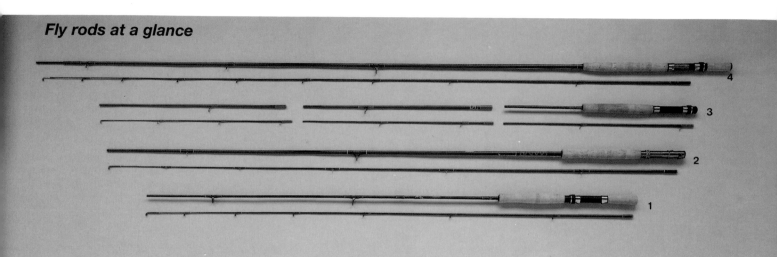

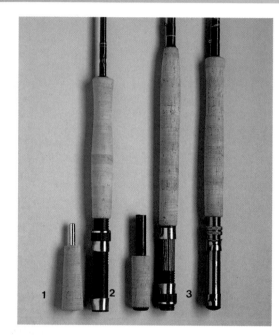

▲ *Most reel seats nowadays are screw fitting. They come in a variety of materials – mainly plastic (1), hardwood (2) or metal (3). Rod handles come in a variety of shapes such as the cigar (2) and half well (1 and 3). Some rods also have small extension butts to help keep the reel away from your body when playing large fish.*

River rods

A high modulus carbon rod of 8-9½ft (2.4-2.9m) with a middle-to-tip action (AFTMA 4-6) is suitable for many river situations. It is ideal for roll casting on a river lined with trees and bushes. It casts weighted nymphs very well and is good for various wet fly styles. An excellent all-round rod, it can be used at a pinch in any circumstances you are likely to encounter on the river.

When chest wading, working your way upstream, it can also be useful to have a 10½ft (3.2m) rod with a soft, all-through action. It is perfect for single Spey casting

▶ *Carbon fibre rods now dominate the scene as the best all-round rod material, but split cane rods like these are still held in high esteem although they are heavier than carbon.*

Look after it

All rods, no matter how well made, need to be looked after properly. Never put the rod away wet – wipe it down carefully before storing it. Keep the joints clean and rub them down occasionally with wax, and check the rod rings regularly for signs of wear.

▲ *A brook or stream rod (1) is usually between 6ft (1.8m) and 8ft (2.4m) in length. It needs to be short so that you can cast in very tight places along the bank.*

Small fishery and river rods (2 and 3) are generally from 8½-9½ft (2.6-2.9m) long. Small fishery rods are stiffer to handle the big fish and often include materials such as kevlar or boron in the blank. Multi-piece rods are convenient and easily stowed away.

Although long (up to 12ft/3.6m), reservoir boat rods (4) for fishing loch style often have a softish, all-through action. Shore anglers need a stiffer middle-to-tip action to punch the flies a long way out.

on wide rivers where there's not enough room to use the overhead cast or when it's necessary to handle long lines.

Small fishery scene

Generally, it's not necessary to cast a long way on small still waters, but often you need a powerful rod to cast heavily weighted flies and to fight very large fish which may be well over 10lb (4.5kg).

A middle-to-tip action with plenty of power in the butt is the preferred rod for fishing small fisheries, and here the high modulus carbons dominate because they are light, stiff and reasonably priced. Bob recommends a rod of about 9-9½ft (2.7-2.9m) – rated for AFTMA 5-8 line.

Big reservoirs

One of the most important aspects of reservoir rods is weight – the rod needs to be light enough so you aren't worn out after a few casts. Buy a light carbon rod if you plan casting at full bore for a whole day. For large reservoirs you need several rods to cover every eventuality.

Fishing from the bank or in a boat at anchor early in the year, you need to be able to cast great distances. Length, power and a stiffish action are essential. To handle the shooting head lines and large lures so often used for this, Bob suggests you use a rod about 10-11⅓ ft (3-3.5m) long with ratings of AFTMA 8 or 9.

Loch-style fishing (a team of three flies cast a fairly short distance and worked back to the drifting boat) is becoming more popular. Because distance casting is less important, an all-through action is common on rods for this type of fishing.

Rods with a stiffened mid section and a

▲ A semi-stiff 10-10½ft (3-3.2m) middle-to-tip action rod is ideal for many kinds of boat fishing since it allows you to cast a long way and to control hooked fish easily.

▲ **Rod rings are either wire snake rings (top) – or lined with a smooth, hard-wearing substance like aluminium oxide, silicon carbide or ceramics (centre and bottom). Snake rings are popular but wear out fast.**

soft tip are also gaining in popularity for fishing loch-style. They give you greater control over hooked fish, especially close to the boat. Whichever action you choose, the rod needs to be 11-12ft (3.4-3.6m) long, both to control the flies on the retrieve and to handle hooked fish.

You also need a long, powerful rod when using lead-core lines to fish at great depths. The rods need to be tremendously strong and stiff, quantities which tend to stifle the feel of a hooked fish. Nonetheless, they are essential for this style of fishing.

New style for old

One of the beauties of split cane is that its hexagonal cross-section structure resists twist and distortion. The round cross-section of carbon rods twists more easily.

But now some top of the range carbon rods simulate split cane in both looks and structure. The exterior of the blank is hexagonal and reinforced for extra strength – helping the rod resist twist and distortion.

Finally there is the art of dapping, in which a very long rod – as much as 18ft (5.5m) long – is needed to dangle or dap a natural or artificial fly on the water surface. The use of a special 'blowline' allows you to control the fly accurately in front of a drifting boat. A long rod and a light to moderate breeze are essential to float the flies out to where they're needed. Because this style does not involve casting, any long, light rod will do.

Right rod, right place

There are many different types of fly rod – each suitable for a particular fishing situation. You can't cover every situation properly with just one rod. Whatever type of fishing you do – whether casting 30m (33yd) or 3m (10ft), playing double-figure rainbows or small wild brownies – you need a rod to suit. Carbon is by far the best general choice because it offers better casting potential, helps you strike more effectively – and even the cheaper ones are excellent value.

◀ *Bob Church with a small-fishery rainbow. Use an AFTMA 5-8 rated rod at these waters.*

▼ *On a windy day at Coldingham Loch on the Scottish Borders, this angler has a stiff rod to power out his fly line. For shore fishing Bob Church recommends middle-to-tip action rods of about 10-11ft (3-3.4m) long with AFTMA rating from 8 to 10.*

Fly lines

Peter Cockwill – stillwater specialist and tackle dealer – sorts through the welter of colour and design to explain fly lines.

Since an artificial fly weighs so little, the main fly line must be heavy enough to allow the whole set-up to be cast out over the water. Lines come in a range of densities – some float, while others sink at any one of a wide variety of rates. There is also a complex range of tapers for specific types of fly fishing.

Originally made of silk dressed in oils, fly lines today are high-tech items. Modern lines consist of a braided Terylene core coated with PVC to repel water and give slickness for casting. Lines are now also being made of polymers over a core of Kevlar, or something similar. They offer improved slickness and lower stretch but some anglers prefer the slight stretchiness of the older, PVC-coated lines.

The AFTMA rating

All fly lines are graded in a range of 1-15 on a scale calculated by the Association of Fishing Tackle Manufacturers of America (AFTMA). The first 35ft (10.7m) of line is weighed, regardless of density or taper, and given a number on that basis. A number 1 line is the lightest and thinnest and a number 15 the heaviest. In Britain, the most

▲ *Floating line should be clearly visible to you on the surface – so you can spot bites. The colour does not usually deter the trout.*

commonly used lines are in the range AFTMA 5-8.

Fly rods are designed to work at their best with 35ft (10.7m) of a particular AFTMA-rated line out beyond the tip ring. The butt of each rod carries the rating of the line it is designed to cast. A number 7 rod would carry the mark AFTMA 7 or #7.

For casts of longer than 35ft (10.7m), this same length is aerialized (in the air beyond the top rod ring during the cast) and the

Tip **Daily stretch**

Before each fishing trip, stretch the line in short sections. This removes reel memory (those springy coils of line), making casting easier.

▼ *At a big reservoir – this is Fewston near Harrogate – you often need a long cast. This angler is using weight forward line and a style of casting known as double hauling to gain extra yards.*

A FLY LINE FOR EVERY SITUATION

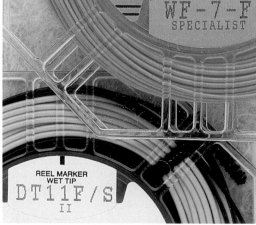

▲ *The codes for fly lines are common sense. Here, the top right line is marked WF-7-F and is a Weight Forward Floating line rated AFTMA 7. The other line (DT11F/S) is a Double Taper Floating line with a Sinking tip (F/S = floating/sinking) rated AFTMA 11.*

⊗ Even hand

It is not difficult to fill the reel evenly, yet many anglers still tend to forget. Every time you wind line on to the spool, avoid unevenness and loose coils or you'll have problems casting and playing fish. Also, at the end of a day's fishing, the finer nylon of the leader can fall between these loose turns of fly line, causing the reel to jam solidly the next time you come to use it.

rest of the line is pulled through the tip ring by the momentum of the 35ft (10.7m) used in the cast.

Which taper?
While it is still possible to buy fly line which is the same thickness along its whole length (known as level line), this has generally been replaced by line which tapers to help casting or presentation of the fly. Three main tapers are used in fly fishing although there are many variations on the basic themes.

A double taper line is thickest in the middle, tapering to a finer diameter at each end. It is generally the best line for delicate work at short range, such as dry fly fishing on running water or small still waters. It

▲ *Dry fly fishing on fast-flowing rivers is one of the most enjoyable ways to catch trout. Floating double taper line is the usual choice for this type of fishing. The taper allows you to cast a fly with great accuracy and to present it delicately.*

Tip Feet of clay

Try to keep your line as clean as possible while fishing, especially if the banks are clay based. The dirt your line picks up can wear through wire rod rings and reel fittings and can mess up your tackle. A line basket worn around your waist keeps it all cleaner. It also makes it impossible for you to stand on the line and helps to prevent it getting tangled – both of which can be disastrous when playing any fish of a decent size.

also has the advantage that you can reverse it if one end gets damaged at the waterside. This is an emergency measure only, because the undamaged end of the line tends to have a high reel memory. Replace any line which you're using like this as soon as you can.

A forward taper line (weight forward) has its main bulk concentrated in the first 35ft (10.7m). The rest of the line consists of a narrow, level section – so that it slips easily through the rod rings after the main section for casts of more than the 35ft (10.7m). It is used to gain greater distances than are usually possible with a double taper.

A shooting taper is essentially a weight forward line with nylon backing replacing the narrow section of fly line. The backing follows this shooting head even more easily – giving still more distance. However, using a shooting taper does involve a certain loss of accuracy and presentation.

Fly lines are commonly 27yd (25m) long though shooting heads are only about 35ft (10.7m) and some specialized makes and profiles can be up to 40yd (37m) long. In most cases it is best to learn to cast with a double taper, so that you gain good

control and presentation before moving on to forward and shooting tapers. The line you choose depends on the water you intend to fish, the distance you have to cast and how delicate your presentation needs to be.

To float or not to float

Fly lines not only taper to help casting, they also float or sink to get your fly right to the depth at which the fish are feeding. Lines which float are the obvious choice for dry fly fishing, but they are also useful when you want to fish your fly quite close under the surface. Using floating line, you can get your fly down as deep as the length of a sinking leader. This versatility makes floating line best for the beginner.

Floating lines come in a staggering range of colours, some of which seem guaranteed to drive fish screaming to the other end of any water. However, you must remember that fish see line that floats as a silhouette against the sky – a dark outline – rather than, for example, a shocking pink strand. The colours simply help you detect any movement that might mean a bite. Choose a line that is visible against both glare and dark water.

Sinking lines are usually a more sombre colour, such as green or brown. They have different densities, allowing you to search for fish at varying depths. On a small stillwater, an intermediate or slow sink line is often the most useful. If you want to fish deeper waters, such as reservoirs, lead-cored lines are often the order of the day to get the fly down deep enough.

Sink-tip lines are floating lines with an end section which sinks. These are popular with anglers fishing rivers for migratory fish (mainly salmon and sea trout). Once again, the density of the tip can vary enormously, allowing you to achieve the sinking rate you require.

Having learnt to cast competently you are then in a position to start thinking

---

Common line tapers

double taper

leader ——————————————— backing

forward taper

leader ——————————————— backing

shooting taper

leader ——————————————— backing

These are the three most common types of line taper or profile. The actual lengths of the various sections of line depend on the particular manufacturer.

about the presentation of the fly. Only then are you able to choose from the different lines available – and to use them to find the fish and tempt them into taking. A choice of lines at the bankside (on spare spools or different reels) can be invaluable to cope with varying conditions.

Care and maintainance

All PVC lines gradually deteriorate as the plasticizers used to keep them supple leak out of the coating. This leads to stiffness and eventually causes the line to crack. You can prolong the life of line by washing it in mildly soapy water and treating it with plasticizing agents. Keeping the spooled line out of strong sunlight and heat helps, but even so it won't last forever. A good floater lasts about two or three years.

Poor casting technique is the biggest single factor in line deterioration. It causes the line to flex excessively over a short length, hastening the cracking of the PVC. Stepping on your line is another short-cut on the road to ruin.

Fly lines vary widely in price and generally what you pay for is what you get. Expensive lines are more supple and slicker with smoother tapers – increasing casting efficiency. However, there is little point buying the best as a beginner,

because you won't be able to appreciate the difference. Move on to quality when you have command over the elements of casting. Whichever line you buy, make sure you choose the right AFTMA rating, taper and density for the type of fishing you plan to spend your time on.

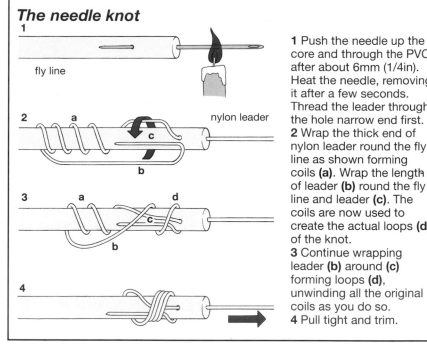

The needle knot

1 fly line

2 a   c   b   nylon leader

3 a   d   c   b

4

1 Push the needle up the core and through the PVC after about 6mm (1/4in). Heat the needle, removing it after a few seconds. Thread the leader through the hole narrow end first.
2 Wrap the thick end of nylon leader round the fly line as shown forming coils **(a)**. Wrap the length of leader **(b)** round the fly line and leader **(c)**. The coils are now used to create the actual loops **(d)** of the knot.
3 Continue wrapping leader **(b)** around **(c)** forming loops **(d)**, unwinding all the original coils as you do so.
4 Pull tight and trim.

▼ *Late in the season at Rutland Water, big rainbows like this one can be caught on fry-imitating lures. Lead-cored lines are often required to get your fly down to the depth at which the fish are feeding.*

Fly reels

Jon Beer, an enemy of unnecessary gear, discusses fly reels and boils down the unending list of accessories to the basics.

▼ *Reels with a wide spool of small diameter tend to store line in tight coils. The line needs a good stretch to remove 'memory' before you begin fishing.*

There is cheap tackle and there is expensive tackle. Nowhere is this price range wider than in fly reels – from under £15 to several thousand. However, pretty well all – even the cheapest reels – should do the job.

A word about bags

"My own choice," says Jon, "is practical – even if idiosyncratic. It is a leather tool pouch adapted to carry fly-box, clippers, spools of nylon, pliers, torch – and a folded landing net."

▼ *Stillwater fly fishing in Sussex. If he valued his eyes he would have added a pair of polarized sunglasses to his fishing equipment.*

A reservoir

A reel – an encumbrance on your rod – should be as small and light as possible, provided it can hold your line and backing without fouling the frame of the reel.

Fly lines are bulky. Reels are usually rated for the size of line they hold, but a low density floating line may be a size or two bulkier than an ordinary floater or a sinking line.

Spools can be narrow with a large diameter, or wide with a small diameter. The large diameter reels retrieve line quicker – each turn brings in more line – and the line is stored in looser coils, so it isn't stiff and full of 'memory'.

Giving out line

All reels have some form of brake or drag to stop the spool revolving freely. This prevents the spool from over-running as line is pulled off when you cast and when a fish runs. It also tires the fish. At its simplest, the drag is a spring-loaded pawl; at its most sophisticated it can be an adjustable thrust-bearing or disc brake. The value of such sophistication in trout fishing is debatable.

Retrieving line

Most British reels are simple winches. This has two advantages. First, there is little to go wrong in the reel itself, and second, an angler is in direct contact with the fish. The disadvantage is the slow speed of retrieve. It can take some time to wind loose line on to the reel. And *two* hands are needed to

A range of fly fishing equipment

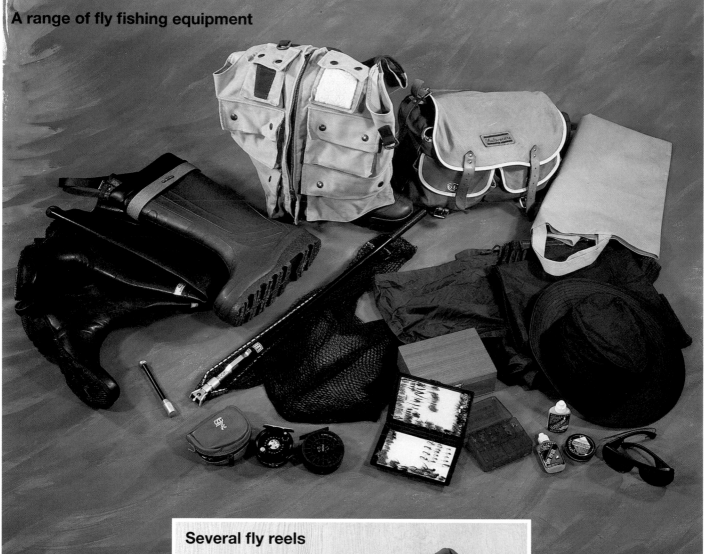

Several fly reels

Key to equipment

There are stacks of accessories with dozens of variations and myriad variations on these.

Above are a few pieces of suggested gear. But keep it simple.

Going clockwise, starting at about 9 o'clock, these items are: Thigh boots, wellies, a multi-pocket waistcoat, a trout bag, a bass bag for storing fish, waterproofs, a hat with a decent brim to shade your eyes from the sun, polarized sunglasses, floatants and a leader-sink agent, fly boxes, fly reels, a priest and a landing net.

▶ *The 'compleat' fisherman – with hat, waistcoat (with mounted scissors and fly patch), boots, net and River Avon brown trout.*

An array of reels

Some popular fly reels – going left to right, top row first, they are: System Two 56L (river), Silstar FG7 (river), an extra spool for the System Two 56L, Shakespeare Beaulite 2873 (still water), Shakespeare Fly 2629 (still water).

reel in the fish. In fact, you really need a *third* hand to hold the landing net. But there are ways round this.

Geared reels increase the speed of retrieve. Many Continental anglers use single-handed automatic reels which rewind by a clockwork spring or an electric motor. Inevitably, though, these reels are heavy.

A good compromise, rarely seen in Britain but found everywhere in Europe, is the semi-automatic. Line is wound on by pumping a lever with one finger of the rod hand. This reel is fast, very light and single-handed.

Other equipment

There is much innocent pleasure to be had in accumulating fishing tackle. But beware: when you buy yourself a super fly-fishing waistcoat with thirty-six pockets, you'll find thirty-six things to fill them. It's best to fish light.

Fly boxes Dry flies are best kept loose in small compartments to avoid distorting the hackles. If these compartments have separate lids a malicious wind cannot empty the whole box in one gust. Wet flies can be stuck into flat or ridged foam containers. Avoid using metal clips or springs: they can blunt the hook point. It is a good idea to have large boxes to stock and organize your collection – and a small box for a working selection at the water.

Floatants Dry floatants come in aerosols, powders, liquids and grease. To carry less gear when fishing, soak the dry flies in a permanent floatant for a couple days. Then they'll float all season long. Leaders can be treated to sink or float, to reduce their visibility or to keep a nymph just below the surface.

Clippers If your teeth won't do, you'll need something to trim excess nylon: small clips are safer than scissors, but it is easy to drop these. Attach them to your jacket on a spring-loaded reel. *Always* carry a small pair of side-cutting pliers. These can save a trip to the hospital if you get a fly embedded in some part of your anatomy. Push the barbed point through and out and snip it off: then withdraw the hook. You can also use the pliers to flatten hook barbs for catch-and-release.

A torch If you want to fish after dark or

▲ *A plump rainbow is returned to the water.*
Whether you're fishing on stillwaters or rivers, take a minimum amount of gear, so you can move around freely without encumbrance.

▶ *Extendible nets are used most on stillwaters. Some nets have ultra-fine mesh which, if returning trout, won't damage the fish.*

Tools to go?

For the self-confessed accessory addict, there is the portable 'match the hatch' kit – a set of fly-tying tools (usually enclosed in a compact folding pouch) which allows you to tie flies by the waterside. But hauling the feathers and fur is an unforeseen burden.

even into the dusk a small torch is invaluable. It can be clipped to the jacket, or you can hold it in your mouth to leave both hands free.

Nets To all but a boat fisherman a landing net is an inconvenience for most of the time. Occasionally it's an essential item for the river fisherman. The best river nets have a rim of collapsing spring steel and are housed in a holster to keep them away from brambles and barbed wire. Stillwater nets should have long handles and a wide, fixed rim.

Thigh boots and chest waders These are invaluable for the river fisherman. A wading angler can keep low and manoeuvre into the best positions to cast. Even ashore waders keep your legs dry from a dripping jacket and dew-covered foliage.

Whether you purchase chest or thigh waders depends on the depth of water you usually fish. The best investment in the long run is to get stocking waders of both sorts with separate wading boots. Underwater surfaces – rocks especially – can be very slippery: always buy either studded or felt-soled waders – or get a really good insurance policy.

Sunglasses These are eye-protectors first, fish-finders second. The lenses should be polarized to reduce reflected glare and as pale as possible to transmit maximum subsurface light.

Bags All this equipment must be carried in something. The traditional bag or creel is fine for the boat fisherman for whom weight is no object. For the river fisherman the

modern fly fishing waistcoat can carry everything you need in the numerous pockets and D-rings. But as with the traditional bag, the weight is carried on your shoulders which can tire you during a long day's fishing. A practical alternative is a fisherman's 'bum bag' which is worn around the waist.

So when boat fishing on stillwaters, you can take a mountain of gear. When you are river fishing, however, remember that it's best to carry as little equipment as possible – the minimalistic philosophy is of vital importance.

▲ *Deceived by a wet fly, a wild Lough Corrib (Republic of Ireland) brown trout lies in a standard, wide rimmed boat-fishing net.*

▼ *To some anglers trout bags are an unwelcome, extra weight to carry around. Others, however, make ample use of the space, packing sandwiches and a small flask for a mid-afternoon break.*

Fly leaders for trout

Charles Jardine explains what you need to know about the leader, the vital link between the fly line and fly. Success in deceiving a trout may depend upon choosing the correct type.

▼ *In the heart of the Yorkshire Dales, an angler fly fishes on the River Wharfe downstream of Bolton Abbey.*

Hot weather, bright conditions and low water all mean you'll need to use very light tippets of no more than 1½lb (0.68kg).

You can design a range of fly leaders simply by using various lengths of nylon in their many shapes, diameters and make-ups.

Balanced leaders

It's unwise to connect knotted lengths of monofilament which differ drastically in breaking strain (for example, 10lb/4.5kg line to 4lb/1.8kg). The step down from the heavier to the lighter line is too steep and unbalances the leader when you cast. As a result the fly lands abruptly. In short, an unbalanced leader hinders presentation – which affects a trout's response to your fly.

For proper 'turnover' – transferring the unfurling or unrolling motion of the fly line as you're casting to the leader and tippet – construct a tapered leader with staggered line weights (for example from 10lb/4.5kg to 8lb/3.6kg to 6lb/2.7kg to 4lb/1.8kg). Alternatively, buy a knotless tapered brand.

Types of nylon

The different kinds of nylon affect how both the leader and the fly behave. Nylon can be categorized into stiff, semi-stiff, limp and low diameter types.

Stiff nylons are a boon when it comes to making butt sections – the junction between fly line and the working leader. Stiff lines also help to hold droppers at right angles.

Semi-stiff nylons are the most useful, filling many leader functions from mid-sections to droppers.

Soft or limp nylons are best suited to making tippets. Soft nylon is pliable, allowing the fly to move freely in the current.

Low diameter (extra strength) nylons can be of enormous benefit if they are used correctly. The wariest of fish can be deceived.

Most of the nylons are shiny. It's a good idea to apply a liberal coating of sink mixture (fuller's earth and glycerine) to create a matt finish and also to help the line cut through the surface film.

Line colour

The colour of nylon (like fly lines) is a bone of contention among anglers. One thing, however, is certain: a clear line is less visible in a greater range of water conditions. Green nylon in green-tinged water works exceptionally well, as does brown line in the peat-stained water of Scottish lochs and spate rivers. If the colour is wrong, your catch rate may drop.

Fly size and line weight

Another factor concerning leaders in general is the importance of matching the fly

Some suggested leaders

Simple river rig

		standard knotless	
butt section		tapered leader 2.7m	renewable tippet
fly line	30-60cm of 18-22lb mono		60-45cm of 2-3lb soft mono

Complex river rig

		60cm of 10-12lb	8lb semi-stiff	6lb semi-stiff	60cm of 4lb	
butt section	stiff mono		mono	mono	mono	tippet
fly line	60-90cm of 18-22lb semi-stiff mono			←—— 1.2-1.8m ——→		60-120cm of 3-1½lb soft mono

Reservoir rig with droppers

	2.7m standard knotless tapered	90-180cm of
butt section	leader down to 6lb (2x)	3-5lb mono
fly line	60-120cm of 18-22lb mono		90-180cm of	15cm
	15cm dropper –	3-5lb mono	–dropper

Reservoir rig with optional dropper

		60cm tippet of
		4lb soft mono
butt section	3.7-4.8m standard knotless tapered leader (3x)	
fly line	60-180cm of 18-22lb mono	
	15cm dropper (optional) –	

Leader materials

This is a selection of different brands of braided leaders, lines and strike indicators. **1.** Braided leaders; **2.** Braided leaders; **3.** Shop-bought knotless tapered leaders; **4.** Monofilament leader spools; **5.** Strike indicators; **6.** Braided leaders.

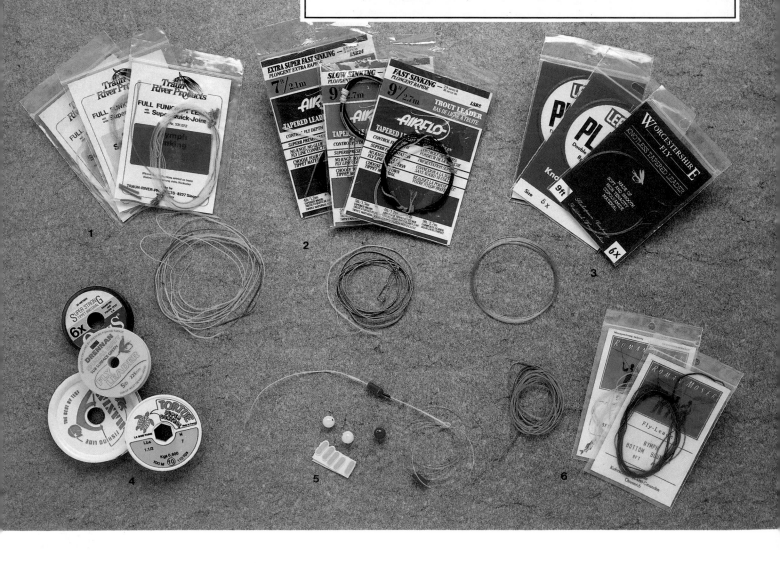

size to the correct diameter of line. A good match ensures that the artificial behaves as naturally as possible. A size 20 Black Gnat on a 5lb (2.3kg) point resembles a piece of thistledown tethered to a section of wire. As a general guide, hook sizes 18-20 require 1½-2lb (0.7-0.9kg) line. You may need 3-4lb (1.4-1.8kg) line for hook sizes 12-16.

Leaded patterns in sizes 4-10 need line of 5-10lb (2.3-4.5kg). Connecting a leaded pattern to a 3lb (1.4kg) tippet is asking for trouble. The hinging movement as you're casting creates leader fatigue, weakening the nylon. The fly simply doesn't fish well when retrieved.

River leaders

A combination of accuracy and delicacy is the criterion for fishing chalk streams or freestone rivers. The longer the leader is, the less accurate casting becomes. However, delicacy increases when the leader is lengthened, and a further advantage is that the potentially fish-scaring fly line is distanced from the fly.

A widely used type of leader is the 'Ritz' formula, created by Charles Ritz – in which as many as five or six nylon sections step down in decreasing breaking strains to the

> ### Tip Feeding zone
>
> The aim is to get your fly into the trout's feeding zone. There are various ways of doing this. One is to use a heavy fly so that it sinks quickly to the trout's level.
>
> Casting far enough upstream of the trout also allows the artificial to sink in time.
>
> In slow or medium currents casting upstream is practical, but if the water proves too fast, try a heavier fly, split shot or extra fast sinking braided leader.

▶ *Under the hand of a watchful angler, a brown trout is almost secure.*
A 10½ft (3.2m) leader with a 1½ft (45cm) tippet section of 2 or 3lb (0.9 or 1.3kg) is recommended for river fishing.

tippet. Using many double grinner or four-turn water knots may appear clumsy and unsound, but most river fly fishing is done 'dead drift'. Small knots along your leader can aid turnover when casting across or downwind. You also have the ease and economy of using large spools of various diameter nylons for knotting leaders yourself.

Alternatively, use standard 9ft (2.7m) knotless shop-bought tapered leaders. The weight or diameter is rated in 'x' numbers from 0x (9lb/4.1kg at the tip) to 8x (¾-1 ¾lb/0.34-0.79kg). You can extend their life by adding butt or tippet lengths. The added sections can be re-tied when they become either too short or damaged – proving to be an economical and practical move.

When you are fishing the dry fly, emerger and even the sub-surface nymph, the length of the leader need not be over 12ft (3.7m). A length of 9½-10ft (2.9-3m) is ideal for general fishing on medium or large rivers, and 8ft (2.4m) for brooks and streams. Using a leader any shorter is likely to lead to poor, splashy presentations. Sometimes when it's windy, however, you may need to shorten the leader. A longer leader length of 14-16ft (4.3-4.8m) is difficult to control and may cause tangles and inaccurate casts.

Tapered braided leaders (floating, sinking, extra fast sinking) are an effective alternative for river fishing. All you have to

◀ *The water seethes as a wild brown trout is brought to the surface.*
Long leaders are a must when fishing in flat, calm water.

Tip Greasing your fly line

Apply grease to your fly line and first few feet of leader every ten or so casts, so they float. This is important on fast water, where they need help to stay on the water's surface.

▼ *A plump, fully finned and beautifully marked 7lb (3.2kg) brown trout like this one can make up for those occasional fishless sessions.*

do is increase or decrease the tippet diameter and length to suit the various conditions.

Because they are supple, braided leaders help to transfer energy from the fly line to the leader to the tippet better than straight mono. This aids presentation. They aren't recommended for casting long distances, though, because they don't cut through the air well.

When nymph fishing from mid-water down to the river bed, ensure that your leader is over depth, and make allowances for your angle of entry and the river's rate of flow.

Problems arise, however, when trout are feeding in fast currents or deep water. Try attaching a fast or extra fast sinking braided leader, weighted pattern and suitable tippet.

Leaders for stillwaters

A long leader is crucial in stillwater fly fishing since it separates the fly line from

The nail knot

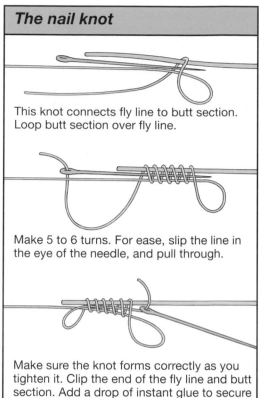

This knot connects fly line to butt section. Loop butt section over fly line.

Make 5 to 6 turns. For ease, slip the line in the eye of the needle, and pull through.

Make sure the knot forms correctly as you tighten it. Clip the end of the fly line and butt section. Add a drop of instant glue to secure the knot.

the fly. Bulky flies and a floating fly line tend to create wake when retrieved – especially in flat conditions. On days where there are waves, this isn't as important.

On many occasions when using a floating line, the depths you want to reach may be more than 9-10½ft (2.7-3.2m), the length of the standard leader with a tippet section added on. In order to fish a depth of 12ft (3.6m), for example, you need an 18ft (5.4m) leader. There comes a point (over 24ft/7m) where a leader simply becomes unmanageable. Consider alternative solutions such as using a sinking fly line.

You can buy a 12ft (3.6m) knotless tapered leader and add on a tippet or butt section. There are even 15-16ft (4.6-4.9m) lengths available, perfect for stillwater nymph and lure fishing.

The knots in the Ritz formula for river fishing can be detrimental on stillwaters, creating disturbances when using a floating line as you pull the line over the surface of the water.

Experiment with the distance between the droppers. In general, spacing nymphs or lures 3-4ft (1-1.2m) apart is appropriate. Dropper lengths should never be much longer than 6in (15cm).

Even level leaders (straight 6lb/2.7kg mono, for instance) have a purpose, for example when loch-style fishing or using large lures, tandems or tubes for fry-feeding trout. It is rare to use line much lighter than 6lb (2.7kg) when casting with lures.

There is without question still a world of exploration in leaders!

Selecting flies for stillwater trout

Understanding what a trout is feeding on can help the boat and bank angler catch more fish. Taff Price looks at some insects which are major food items for stillwater trout, and he also recommends how and when to fish imitations.

Too many game anglers dismiss the study of insects as being too complicated and not that important when fly fishing. This is simply not true.

Six stillwater giants
The following are some of the most important groups of insects and crustaceans for trout.

Midges Because of their sheer numbers, midges (chironomids) are one of the most important insect groups for stillwater trout. Like most other insects, a midge has four stages of growth: egg, larva, pupa and adult. The colours of the immature insects range from black to olive, brown, orange, green and red.

The fly fisherman is concerned mainly with only two stages of this insect – the larva and the pupa, both of which can move around. An adult imitation is only important when mated females return to lay their eggs on the surface of the water.

Midge larvae, known as bloodworms, can grow up to 19mm (¾in) long. They live in the silt at the bottom of lakes. To fish a bloodworm imitation, slowly retrieve it directly along the bottom.

Midge pupae or 'buzzers' grow by moulting their outer skin. In the pupal stage they can be found at all depths of water.

▼ *Mid-season tactics on big stillwaters wouldn't be complete without using sedge pupa imitations fished in deep water.*

Some patterns

● **Marabou Bloodworm**
Hook: 12-14 long shank
Head: peacock herl
Body: red floss ribbed with fluorescent red floss
Tail: long red marabou.
Head: black

● **Midge Pupa**
Hook: 8-14
Head: peacock herl or black hare's fur
Body: black silk ribbed with gold or copper wire
Thread: black

● **Damsel Nymph**
Hook: 6-12 long shank
Body: dubbed green marabou or wool
Thorax: dark olive marabou
Wing case: light green feather
Tail: olive hackle fibres
Rib: copper wire
Thread: green

● **Little Red Sedge**
Hook: 12-16
Body: hare's fur, palmered red cock hackle
Rib: fine gold wire
Wing: partridge tail

▲ *A ravenous predator of other insects, the damsel nymph is found mainly in stillwaters – from huge reservoirs to tiny ponds.*

Tip *Into the wind*

Why fish into the wind and put up with casting and presentation difficulties? The answer is simply because the wind blows surface food (weak-flying hatching insects such as midges) into a corner. All that concentrated food means hungry trout won't be too far away.

▲ *This well-tied damselfly imitates a mature nymph. It is fished in weedy margins or along the bottom of the reservoir.*

In still conditions when dust and other particles – combined with the surface tension of the water – make it difficult for the hatching pupae to break through, trout go on a feeding spree, and midges are picked off by the thousand.

Most major hatches occur in spring and summer, during the early morning and evening. These are prime times to fish a midge pupa imitation. Fish an artificial

▼ *The midge pupa, a staple diet of stillwater trout, has problems breaking through the water's surface tension. A build-up of dust in calm conditions may also hinder midges.*

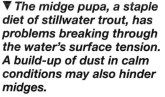

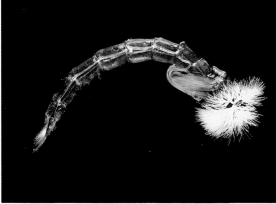

▶ *This is an artificial midge pupa (size 8), also known as a buzzer, pupa buzzer or buzzer nymph.*
A slow, constant retrieve often proves successful when using this ever-popular fly.

▲ *Stillwater trout depend upon freshwater hoglice (above) and shrimps in the early months of the year. Unlike shrimps, hoglice rarely leave the safe haven of weeds in summer.*

▼ *Corixas are generally found near weedy lake margins. They can survive in waters with low levels of oxygen. You can sometimes see them rising to the surface to take in air and then darting back down to hide.*

▲ *Though daphnia are too tiny to imitate properly, many anglers claim a small orange nymph (14-18) attracts daphnia-feeding trout.*

emerger – this has a polystyrene ball located near the eye of the hook – in the surface film, giving it an occasional twitch to imitate a struggling pupa in the process of hatching.

Darting damselflies Damselfly nymphs make up a large proportion of a trout's diet in summer. They are usually brown or green, blending in perfectly with their weedy or reedy environment. Damselfly nymphs are capable of short bursts of speed.

The nymph stage lasts about a year – though some species take up to five years to develop into an adult.

Fish a damselfly imitation in weed beds along the bottom or just under the surface in shallow lake margins. Experiment with different retrieves such as slow and steady along the bottom or short, fast strips near the surface.

Margin-loving corixas These brown beetle-like insects – known as lesser water boatmen – are found on most stillwaters near shallow weedy margins. They thrive on algae and other plant debris. Varying in length from 4mm to about 10mm, they have a remarkable ability to live in water with a low oxygen content. You can often see them rising to the surface and then quickly sinking to the bottom like a small stone. Corixas carry their air supply in a bubble between their wings and back. When the air is used up, they must leave the security of their weed or root and make a dangerous journey to collect more.

Fish the fly in shallow, weedy areas, suggesting the insect's natural habit of sinking from the surface to the bottom.

Caddis (sedge) flies Some species of caddis larvae make shelters from sand, small stones

Using a marrow spoon

Once you have caught a trout, you can examine its stomach contents with a marrow spoon to see what else it has been feeding on (in addition, of course, to your fly!).

Put the spoon into the trout's mouth and ease it back until the fish deposits its meal. You may have to look closely to discover what the trout has been feeding on.

Sometimes you may not need to use a marrow spoon: some trout still have half their meal in their mouths!

Tip Acting real

To catch a trout with an imitation involves everything from how a fly or lure *looks* to how it *acts*. Looks alone won't always convince wary trout. Nymphs must be fished to act like real-life nymphs, and not like lures.

▼ *Five medium-sized stillwater rainbows display their bright silver sheen. The importance of having an intimate knowledge of a trout's favourite food items can't be overstressed.*

and plant debris. Others rely solely upon camouflage. During the larval and pupal stages the insects develop under water.

Even though the pupa is fast-swimming, it is no match for a trout. At the point when the insect is about to break its sheath and hatch into an adult on the surface of the water, it is virtually immobile for a few seconds and vulnerable to hungry fish.

To imitate the caddis larva, fish a pattern such as a Stickfly slowly along the bottom. To imitate the quick and ever-popular pupa, fish an imitation such as Goddard's Sedge Pupa near the surface of the water – particularly at dusk when major hatches of caddis flies take place. Remember, the pupa can swim quite fast, so you should retrieve quite quickly.

Fish an adult sedge imitation (such as a Little Red Sedge) static on the surface, giving it an occasional twitch to suggest life.

Crustacean magic Water fleas, freshwater shrimps and hoglice are an important year-round food source for trout. Recently hatched trout often feed on daphnia until they are large enough to tackle bigger mouthfuls. Since daphnia are so small, proper imitation is difficult.

Stillwater trout may feed exclusively on shrimps and hoglice during the lean months in spring when insect life is low and competition between recently stocked fish and overwintered trout is high. Freshwater shrimps and hoglice are much more common around weeds where they have cover. In April and early May, fish an imitation slowly right along the bottom.

Terrestrials Land insects such as hawthorn flies, daddy-long-legs, black gnats and flying ants can be blown on to stillwaters in late summer and early autumn when they are numerous. Terrestrials are in an alien environment as soon as they touch water. Many become trapped in the water's surface and then waterlogged – an easy meal for trout. Use floating line and long leaders of at least 6lb (2.7kg) breaking strain.

Dry flies for rivers

Fly fishing on moving water has many challenges – fly selection is one of them. Here are a few suggestions to get you started or to add to your collection.

The following flies – twelve of the best – are well-established, some for over a hundred years. They will certainly meet almost every dry fly river situation you may encounter, forming a nucleus of both imitative and suggestive patterns which no serious fly fishermen should be without.

1. Adams This is a fly which has many devoted enthusiasts – especially those who fish on southern chalk streams.

Ray Bergman created the Adams in the late 1920s or early 1930s, the exact date being difficult to pinpoint. With its blue-grey body and light brown hackle, it can pass as an iron-blue (upwinged fly) – though it wasn't created to be an exact representation of a particular species. Some anglers claim the grizzle-point wings are one key to its long-lived success.

2. Pheasant Tail First invented by Payne Collier in the early 1900s, this is another general, nondescript fly that has accounted for many trout. Its body is made of pheasant tail fibres, ribbed with copper wire, with a honey dun or natural red cock feather for the hackle.

▲ One of the best times to fish rivers such as the Upper Nidd in Yorkshire is early May – when the mayflies abound, and trout are keyed up and rising readily. A Grey Duster or Grey Wulff is a good pattern for these conditions.

Variants

Famous patterns have almost always produced a number of 'offspring'. If the patterns don't follow the creators' designs and use their ingredients, then call them variants.

Sometimes, however, variants go on to become more popular than the original flies.

Twelve dries

The following suggested flies should see you through the season quite well.
1. **Adams** (hook sizes 12-20)
2. **Pheasant Tail** (12-18)
3. **Iron Blue Dun** (14-16)
4. **Red Tag (variant)** (14-18)
5. **Grey Wulff** (0-14)
6. **Walker's Red Sedge** (10)
7. **Terry's Terror (variant)** (12-16)
8. **Wickham's Fancy** (14-18)
9. **Coachman** (12-16)
10. **Black Midge** (20-22)
11. **Beacon Beige** (14-16)
12. **Grey Duster** (12-16)

3. Iron Blue Dun Named after the natural, it is an imitative pattern which is useful from May to October. The natural iron blue nymph emerges during the daytime and is commonly found in most unpolluted, weedy, alkaline rivers. The Iron Blue's red tag gives it an extra flair that attracts a fair share of trout every season.

4. Red Tag (variant) An excellent fly which doesn't look like any natural, the Red Tag has taken thousands of grayling since its creation in 1850. To limit it strictly to grayling, however, would be a mistake: it catches many trout, too.

5. Grey Wulff This pattern is known world-wide and can easily pass for spinners of upwinged species. Lee Wulff devised a whole series of patterns with thick, beefy bodies and wings and tails made from hair (bucktail, calftail or goat hair) rather than feather fibres. He claimed the chunky flies offered trout more of a mouthful, compared with the quill-bodied flies which were being used.

6. Walker's Red Sedge Created by Richard Walker, this represents not only red sedges but also many other species. The naturals are on the water from May to the end of July. Because sedges hatch during the day, use the Red Sedge as a searching pattern if nothing is rising. The artificial's orange tag represents an egg sac on a mature female. When females lay their eggs on the top of the water, some remain motionless, while others skitter about the surface. Fish this fly according to the circumstances. Cast it upstream, and allow it to drift back drag free. If that fails, cast upstream again and when the fly is across from you, lift up the rod, skating the fly across the surface.

7. Terry's Terror (variant) Though it seems that it wasn't created to imitate a particular natural, this fly can pass for many upwinged and sedge species. The

▲ *An angler returns a dry-fly caught brown trout to its weedy, chalk stream home.*

Up or down?

It's often said that if trout are refusing your imitiation, go down in hook size. Some anglers, however, say that the opposite is true: attach a **larger** fly. This might provoke a take. Try it and see what happens.

▼ *This small wild brown trout fell for a dry fly – a Pheasant Tail, in fact. For wild trout it's important to use small hooks – sizes 18-20.*

original called for a hackle of a natural red cock; this pattern varies slightly in that the hackle is a dark red cock.

8. Wickham's Fancy is over a hundred years old. Veteran fly fishermen swear by it. Even its wingless derivative has many followers. As the name implies, the fly is impressive with its gold tinsel body, starling wings and palmered ginger cock hackle – though it's not overly ornate. In smaller sizes it works well as a general searching pattern; the gold flash helps to tempt fish up from below.

9. Coachman Another general utility fly that has caught hordes of trout and grayling is the Coachman. Though the fly won't pass for most naturals (except possibly a moth), many river-fishing experts agree that the white wings and the bulbous peacock herl body provide the stimulating combination which few trout can allow to drift past untouched.

10. Black Midge On occasions you need the smallest of flies to convince stream-wise trout. Enter the Black Midge. When the naturals are hatching, or when the adult female flies return to the water to lay their eggs, this pattern – fished in the surface film – is the standard choice. The naturals often hatch throughout the trout season. With small flies such as this, use a very light, pliable tippet.

11. Beacon Beige One of the all time classics, this fly is highly regarded for freestone rivers – though on chalk streams it is even more acclaimed.

The Beige was created during World War I in the West Country as an imitation of upwinged flies (especially olive duns, which abound throughout the trout season). It was later renamed Beacon Beige.

12. Grey Duster In various sizes this Welsh fly imitates midges, olives and even mayflies. It's also one of the easiest flies to tie. Blue-grey rabbit fur for the body and a badger cock for the hackle are a simple yet deadly combination.

Stillwater trout lures

Over the past twenty years the popularity of stillwater trout fishing has soared, and the range of lures mirrors this boom. Peter Gathercole describes twelve top trout lures.

Tip *Smash takes & floating fry*

If you see a trout surface next to your imitation, don't strike right away. Wait until the fish has taken the lure and gone under before striking.
As is the case when using a daddy-long-legs in autumn, use at least 6lb (2.7kg) mono to guard against smash takes when using a floating fry.

▼ *Fly fishing on Tal-y-llyn in Wales. Brown trout such as this one in the net often fall for lures, especially Goldies.*

Defining what makes a lure a lure is not an easy matter. At first glance it appears simple enough to the beginner: a lure is a large artificial fly which does not imitate or suggest a living creature.

This statement is perfectly correct for most patterns, but there are notable exceptions. Some lures are specifically designed to imitate the fry of roach and perch.

Two explanations

Why does a trout take a non-imitative lure if it isn't trying to eat it? Although no one has yet managed to obtain an answer from a fish, the two most plausible explanations are aggression and curiosity. Of the two the 'curiosity theory' is more convincing. When a trout sees something different, the only way to find out if the object is edible or not is to take it into its mouth.

Whatever the reason, the important point is that trout do take lures. On most stillwaters lures catch the largest number of fish, compared to other flies.

Types, sizes and colours

Lures range from sombre-coloured Muddler Minnows to bright orange Dog Nobblers. Sizes vary too – from ½in (13mm) to the giant 4in (10cm) long Tandem or Tube Fly. Most lures, however, fall somewhere in between. They are usually tied on long-shank hooks ranging from size 6 to size 10 and are made from a wide variety of materials including hair, feather, chenille, wool and tinsel.

Two main types of lure are hairwings and streamers. Wings of feather (cock hackles or the extremely popular marabou) are used in streamers. Marabou is the soft downy feather of the domestic turkey. The feathers are sold in many dyed colours.

You only have to see marabou work in the water to understand why it's so effective. On every twitch of the retrieve it pulses in the most enticing manner – one which trout often find irresistible.

Here are 12 modern trout lures. Each one has proved its worth on British stillwaters over the years.

Goldie Devised by Bob Church, this hairwing lure combines two colours which work particularly well for brown trout – yellow and black. The pattern fishes well regardless of depth. It is effective dressed either on a single long shank hook or as a tandem.

Viva Black and fluorescent green are perhaps the most killing combination available

to the trout angler. Although the Viva works particularly well when it's fished slow and deep during the early season, it takes trout throughout the year. The lure also catches well at a variety of depths and retrieval speeds. This is truly a lure for all seasons.

Cat's Whisker Any lure that contains marabou, either as a tail or a wing, is usually effective. David Train's Cat's Whisker goes one better: it has both! The combination of white marabou wing and fluorescent green chenille body is a deadly alternative to the black and green Viva.

Floating Fry Allowed simply to drift, this is an imitative lure which mimics a small dying coarse fish floating on the surface. During the months of August to October trout (usually really big browns) go mad feeding on shoals of small fish in preparation for the lean winter months to come. Trout rip through the shoals of fry, stunning and killing many fish. The hungry trout then return to their easy meal.

Muddler Minnow Don Gapen of the USA created this pattern in the 1950s. The Muddler has since spawned a vast range of variations. The original imitated a small

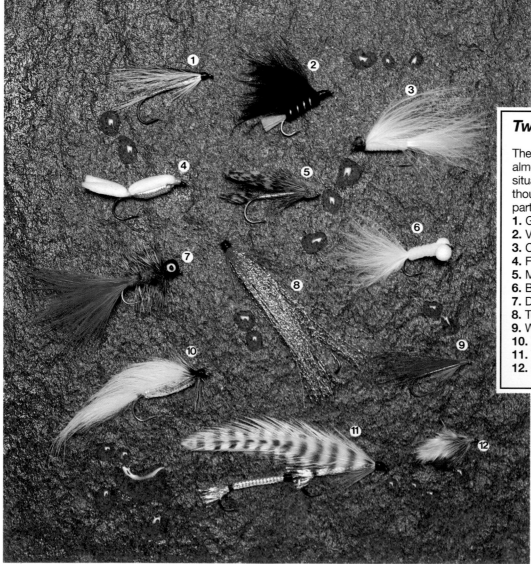

▲ *Tying some lures (such as the Baby Doll or Goldie) isn't as difficult as you may think.*

There's plenty of room to manoeuvre your fingers around large long shank hooks (sizes 6-10).

Twelve modern lures

These twelve trout lures can cover almost any stillwater angling situation that you may encounter, though each was created for a particular purpose.
1. Goldie
2. Viva
3. Cat's Whisker
4. Floating Fry
5. Muddler Minnow
6. Booby
7. Dog Nobbler
8. Tube Fly
9. Whisky Fly
10. Zonker
11. Tandem Lure
12. Mini-lure (Jack Frost)

 **Tip** Level leaders

When distance casting isn't crucial, the most economical way of attaching lures is to use a long level leader – 6lb (2.7kg) for example.

Use a double grinner or a water knot for droppers.

Tip *Lead core fry*

Try using a floating fry pattern with a HI-D line. You can make the pattern dive and then bob up to the surface.

Tying a Baby Doll

The Baby Doll, originally tied by Brian Kench for Ravensthorpe Reservoir in 1971, is illustrated for two reasons. It is one of the easiest lures for a beginner to tie, and it is another very popular reservoir lure, passing for a roach or perch fry.

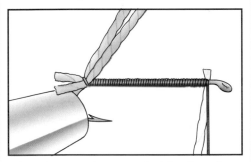

1. Starting near the eye, wind the thread down to the bend of the hook to form a secure bed. At the bend, tie in 2 or 3 lengths of fluorescent green wool, leaving tails 5-7mm long. Bring the thread 2mm from the eye. Catch in a length of fluorescent white wool (or a substitute material).

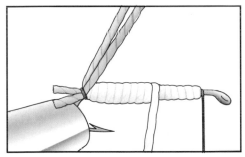

2. Wind the white wool down the hook shank in neat butted turns and then back up towards the eye. Secure the white wool 2mm before the eye with 2 wraps of thread. Cut off the excess wool.

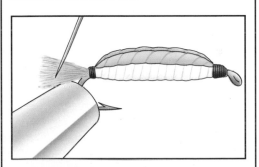

3. Bring the green wool over the back of the lure and secure with 2 turns of thread. Clip off the excess, and build a neat head. 'Pick' out the tail with your needle, forming the single tail.

fish. Today, however, Muddlers come in every colour imaginable.

All have the classic buoyant head of spun deer hair. When retrieved, the fly's bulbous head makes a disturbance in the water which really turns trout on.

Booby This style of lure, originally tied by professional fly dresser Gordon Frazer, has

▼ **With the net nearby, this angler pulls a rainbow trout close to the boat.**

Mini-lures, fished loch-style, can be good substitutes for traditional wets on many southern stillwaters.

proved absolutely deadly. The combination of marabou tail and buoyant eyes (made of Plastazote) produces a ducking, diving action similar to that of the Dog Nobbler.

Because the Booby is buoyant, use a very fast sinking line (Hi-D) and a short leader, so the fly fishes just above the lake bed. The retrieve is a slow figure-of-eight. Takes are so positive that the Booby is often swallowed.

Dog Nobbler This was *the* lure of the 1980s. Invented by Trevor Housby, the Dog Nobbler took the stillwater scene by storm. Since the early 1980s it has accounted for literally thousands of trout, many of them of specimen size.

As you retrieve the Dog Nobbler, its heavily weighted head and long marabou tail

◀ *There are no definitive rules when choosing a lure. Experience coupled with trial and error are often the only ways to find a successful pattern for the time of year and the particular water.*

coarse fish about 7.5-10cm (3-4in) long or as a general attracting pattern.

Whisky Fly This hot orange eyeball-burner was devised by the late Albert Willock to catch cruising summer rainbows. Orange flies, particularly those as bright as the Whisky Fly, prove deadly when the trout are in the upper water layers.

During the warm summer months, especially when the fish are feeding on daphnia, 'orange madness' takes hold of trout. A Whisky Fly fished fast just below the surface can produce spectacular results.

Zonker The Zonker originates from the USA. It has a body of mylar tubing and a wing fashioned from a thin strip of rabbit fur, making it a very mobile and effective pattern. It's tied in a wide range of colour combinations, but grey and silver ones make great fry imitations.

Tandem Lure This is basically two long shank lures tied together 'in tandem' – one after another. Although this style of dressing is often used to imitate small coarse fish, any lure pattern may be dressed in this way. The joint between the two hooks is flexible 20lb (9kg) nylon monofilament.

Mini-lure Although lures are usually large, there are times when trout still want the pulsing movement of marabou – but in a short-shanked version. Here the mini-lure comes into its own. This style has become popular in competition fly fishing on still-waters where there is a limit on the length and size of the flies used.

▼ *Though imitation has gained an important place in lure design, the order of the day is still colour and flash.*
    Lures take more stillwater rainbow or brown trout than any other type of fly.

produce a wiggling motion. This erratic movement is the attraction of the lure. Effective colours include black, white, orange, yellow and olive.

Tube Fly This specialist lure is tied on lengths of fine plastic, aluminium or brass tubing. It has a treble hook at the end instead of a standard long shank hook. The Tube Fly can be tied either to imitate small

Seasonal salmon flies

Stan Headley shortlists his seven favourite salmon flies and offers his experience in selecting the right ones for the right time of year.

▲ *Low-water conditions in mid summer (such as here on the River Spey in Scotland) require small patterns fished near the surface on a floating line.*

Salmon don't feed in fresh water, yet they take lures and flies. This is surely an angling enigma. But even more of a puzzle is that salmon take some flies more readily than others, depending on the time of year and the clarity of the water.

Even though there are no concrete answers as to why salmon take, in Stan's opinion you generally need large, colourful flies fished deep in spring and late autumn when the rivers are high and possibly coloured. Small, dull patterns fished near the surface catch more fish under low-water summer conditions. At this time the salmon can be wary and often uncooperative.

It seems logical, therefore, to classify salmon flies by season rather than by their size or colour.

Spring and autumn flies

On the whole, patterns for the colder months of the year tend to be big, bright and sometimes heavy. They are frequently tied on tubes or wire shanks (often called Waddingtons or waddies) which may be as much as 10cm (4in) long.

1. Willie Gunn (Waddington) This pattern probably catches more salmon in the spring than any other. It's most commonly tied on a Waddington shank. Yellow, orange and black are good colours for early patterns. In heavily peat-stained water reduce the proportion of black hair to produce a brighter fly. In areas of clear water use a fly with more black hair.

2. Fast Eddy (tube) Stan Headley specifically designed this pattern for the River Thurso in Scotland where flies with a touch

Headley's top seven

1. Willie Gunn

2. Fast Eddy

3. Garry Dog

4. Collie Dog

5. Stoat's Tail

6. Munro Killer

7. Ally's Shrimp

Tip *Tubes on the cheap*

Buying plastic tubes in a tackle shop can be expensive. Make your own substitute for plastic tubes with stiff shop-bought carp booms. Use scissors to cut tubes in various sizes and then carefully heat the end of the tube with a match to form a collar.

of green work well. Fish the Fast Eddy from mid-March to mid-May. It's also effective during a clearing spate.

3. Garry Dog (tube) is another popular spring and autumn fly. Because of its bright colours the fly is effective in peat-stained waters and in clearing floodwater. Traditional dressing gives it a mixed wing of yellow and red, but yellow and orange can be even better.

4. Collie Dog (tube) This pattern, easy to tie, has exploded on to the salmon scene in the past few years. Tied on a short tube body with a wing of hair up to 23cm (9in) long, it has revolutionized spring fishing in many areas. Versions with smaller wings work well in the summer.

Salmon may come up from great depths to take the fly, which can be fished on intermediate or floating lines. It's usually tied on an aluminium tube with no body dressing.

Small in summer

With the exception of shrimp imitations, Stan has found that summer salmon usually take dull patterns – not bright ones.

5. Stoat's Tail (double) Simple but deadly, this fly is used on floating or intermediate lines and catches a fair share of salmon. Some anglers give the fly a yellow tail.

6. Munro Killer (double) Originally tied for fishing on the Spey, this fly now catches salmon all over the world. Basically it's a jazzed-up Stoat's Tail – the dashes of colour make it supreme in the peat-stained waters of northern Scotland.

7. Ally's Shrimp (long shank treble) In western Scotland's fast spate rivers shrimp patterns reign supreme – and this is perhaps the best. Though brighter than most summer patterns it is the exception to the sombre/summer rule. Don't be without one when fishing from June to August. Ally's Shrimp is also good in large sizes when salmon become aggressive in late autumn.

▲ *This cracking, fresh-run springer took a big fly fished slowly on a fast-sinking line.*

Dressed to kill?

Overly ornate, fully dressed salmon flies like this Durham Ranger (right) are works of art – they look beautiful and take great skill to tie. But it has to be admitted that their function is rather more suited to luring fly tyers and fishermen than attracting big salmon.

Elaborate patterns such as these are hardly necessary – and can often be detrimental when it come to fishing, says Stan Headley. Far more practical, in his opinion, is a set of bare-boned, proven patterns.

Tip The humble trout fly

"Any fisherman who finds himself on a salmon river with only his trout fly box need not despair," says Stan. "There are many trout flies which tempt salmon, and the standard Muddler can catch more than most.

"Traditional wets such as the Soldier Palmer also work well."

GAME FISHING

TECHNIQUES

Rainbow trout: strategies for success

In 1884 the wild rainbow trout was imported to Europe from the USA. In Britain you can find rainbow trout in most if not all fisheries.

Compared with the native European brown trout, rainbows are easier to rear and are able to stand higher water temperatures and lower water quality. Rainbow trout also rise more readily than browns and, as anyone who has hooked one knows full well, make many fanatical, often unstoppable, bids for freedom.

Fishing for rainbows

There are only a few places in Britain where rainbow trout reproduce naturally, the River Wye in Derbyshire being the most noted example. Almost all small fisheries, however, breed or buy-in rainbows.

You should begin your apprenticeship on small stillwaters, for you stand a far better chance of seeing and catching rainbows than on reservoirs or even large gravel pits.

Nymph fishing – using imitations of immature aquatic insects – is probably the most common method of catching trout on small stillwaters. Attach a Black Buzzer, Hare's Ear (variant), Pheasant Tail Nymph or goldhead nymph and then cast to cruising trout. It's a good idea to experiment with the retrieval speeds to see what's working on the day.

Use the countdown method to explore all depths. Cast out and, before you begin to

▶ *An early winter's day on Leominstead Lake (Hampshire) pays off as a rainbow trout comes to the net. On many small stillwaters you can fish for rainbow trout all year round – there's no close season.*

retrieve, count to ten (for example). Repeat the process adding on ten or so seconds after each cast. If you hook a trout, remember the number at which you stopped counting and began retrieving, and repeat the process.

Lure fishing There are imitative lures which represent coarse fish fry and brightly coloured ones which provoke aggression and curiosity. Some fisheries may ban certain types; check before you go. On the bank use the same procedure as with nymphs, experimenting with retrieval speeds and a

◀ *If you are new to the sport, it's a good idea to let someone experienced net your first trout.*

> **Tip** *Gear up*
>
> Watching the rainbows continually pass up your offering – be it nymphs, lures or dry flies – is frustrating, to say the least. This, however, is part of stillwater angling. What can be done?
>
> Lengthen your leader and reduce the breaking strain of the tippet. Try to cast directly in front of the trout and use the induced-take method.
>
> If that fails, cast out and retrieve your nymph with a very slow figure-of-eight retrieve (1in/2.5cm per second).

variety of different depths.

The dry fly Using an artificial fly that floats on the surface of the water is an underrated method of catching stillwater rainbows. Though simple, it requires a bit of patience.

In most stillwaters trout have specific patrol routes. On some waters you can actually see them cruising along the margins. Attach a dry fly such as a Hare's Ear Emerger or White Wulff and cast about 1m (1yd) in front of the trout – then wait. When casting, make sure you don't slap the water with your line.

You'll be able to see the trout take the fly. A word of warning, however: don't strike immediately. Wait until the fish has taken the fly and turned down into the water. Then lift the rod firmly. As a general guideline, wait about three seconds after the trout surfaces.

Dry fly fishing is effective even if you can't see the trout patrolling the water. Sometimes you may have to wait up to ten minutes without recasting.

If it's windy, cast straight out towards the middle of the water, and allow the wind to sweep the fly in an arc to the margins. Repeat the process. If you get impatient, retrieve the fly very slowly.

Alternatively, give the fly an occasional twitch by quickly lifting your rod. (The trout can sense the surface vibrations very well.) Overall, dry fly fishing on stillwaters is successful if you have the patience to allow it to work.

Once you catch a rainbow you'll soon see why it's a furious fighter. A word of advice – don't attempt to bring the fish in too quickly, or it may break off. Allow the trout to take line, but keep constant tension on the line. You won't lose too many fish if you play them patiently and have suitable monofilament line. Don't attempt to use 2lb (0.9kg) nylon. As a minimum, use 5lb (2.3kg) b.s. line. Enjoy the battle.

▼ *Many anglers reckon that the fighting abilities of stillwater rainbows (such as this specimen) are second only to salmon.*

The overhead cast

You can't get a fly into the water without casting, so you need to learn to cast properly before you start fishing. Peter Cockwill shows you how.

Casting styles

The overhead cast is not the only way to throw a fly line. Later you may wish to use other styles including the roll and side casts for cramped conditions, and the single and double-haul casts for when you need to fish at longer distances.

C asting requires timing and technique, not muscle, so an hour spent with a qualified instructor could save a lot of frustration. Some of the better venues provide tuition and very often let novices fish free of charge until the first fish is landed.

With or without professional instruction, the only way to perfect your casting style in safety is to practise with a leader but without a fly. The best place for this is in your garden or an empty field, not at a water.

Two casts in one

Casting a fly is done in two stages – a back cast and a forward cast. The rod is designed to work best with about 10-12m (11-13yd) of line worked through the rod rings on to the ground in front of you.

In the first stage – the back cast – you lift the line off the ground and swing out through the air, behind your head. In the second stage – the forward cast – you throw the line on to the ground, leaving your fly about 12m (13yd) from where you are standing. Ideally both the fly and fly line should land softly, so that it won't cause much of a splash when you come to cast on to water.

Recasting

After you have slowly retrieved some of the line to give fish the chance to bite, you have to recast. It's a good idea to practise this on dry land. The procedure is similar to before except that now you have 4m (13ft) of fly

Teaching organisations

You can get details of casting instructors from the fly fishing press and from some tackle shops (particularly those that specialise in game fishing tackle). You can also contact the Association of Professional Game Angling Instructors direct.

● The Association of Professional Game Angling Instructors,
c/o Mr D Downs,
The Mead,
Hosey, Westerham, Kent, TN16 1TA.

▶ *Good casting technique is more important than many anglers realize. It allows you to present a fly to wary fish in a natural way.*

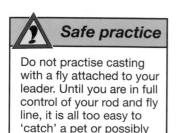

⚠ Safe practice

Do not practise casting with a fly attached to your leader. Until you are in full control of your rod and fly line, it is all too easy to 'catch' a pet or possibly someone's ear.

line in a pile at your feet.

Make the back cast, holding the line below the first rod ring with your free hand to prevent the spare line slipping. As the line is travelling out in front of you in the forward cast, release the spare to slip through the rod rings. In this way you recast the full length. This is known as 'shooting' the line. Also try casting on a windy day at various angles to the wind.

You'll often have to cope with this when fishing and it can make a difference to where the fly ends up. This will stand you in good stead when you get down to the water, as it is rarely completely windless.

Practise these basic techniques until they feel natural. Don't make your first ever cast at the water's edge and expect to catch fish. You'll be too busy untangling your line from nearby trees.

Practising the overhead cast

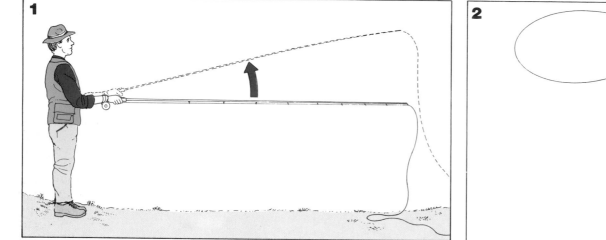

1. Work about 10-12m (11-13yd) of line through the rod rings on to the ground, or water, in front of you. Starting with the rod in the horizontal position, raise your forearm until it reaches the vertical, keeping your wrist stiff and straight. Accelerate smoothly through this movement and the line will lift off the ground to stream out behind you, over your shoulder.

2. Stop the rod in the upright position – don't allow it to drift back past the vertical. Loop an elasticated sweat band round your wrist and rod butt (as shown) to stop you cocking your wrist. This stops the rod going too far back which would throw the line downwards.

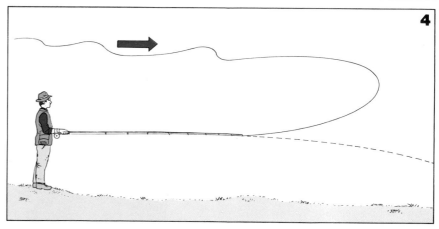

3. Allow a short pause for the line to straighten out behind you. If you don't wait long enough, the line can become tangled and you could end up with the fly line and leader falling about your ears.

4. Lower your arm until the rod is horizontal, keeping your wrist rigid. The rod action flicks the line out in front of you to land gently on the ground or water. If the line lands with a thud (or splash) you have lowered your arm too fast or too far. All your movements should be smooth and use the minimum force required to get the line where you want it. If you are too jerky or violent, you'll get tangles, or cause the fly to 'crack off' (which is exactly what it sounds like). The timing of these steps will come with practice.

Targeting stillwater brown trout

Many reservoirs around Britain contain both rainbow and brown trout, yet browns, very different in character, aren't caught nearly as often as rainbows. Tony Blakeman explains.

Both the native brown trout and the imported rainbow are reared in stew ponds and stocked into Britain's rivers, ponds, lakes and reservoirs from 8oz to 20lb (0.23-9kg) or more. But unlike nomadic rainbows, browns are very territorial, establish particular feeding habits and live in deep water, rarely making their presence known to anglers.

Catching recently stocked browns (or rainbows for that matter) is easy. The fish tend to stay in the area where they were stocked until they adjust to their new surroundings and become familar with the available food. The stocked browns which aren't caught probably move out to deep water, though obviously it is difficult to know that for sure.

▶ *An angler used a Cat's Whisker, fished on a Hi-D, to catch this Grafham brown which was feeding along the bottom on roach.*

▼ *One of the most popular venues for brown trout, Blagdon Water in Avon, has plenty of fly life to produce some excellent grown-on fish.*

Where there is a concentration of fry or even sizeable coarse fish, a large brown will almost certainly be lurking, following the prey and waiting to pounce. A brown of over 5lb (2.3kg) won't hesitate to take a 12oz (0.34kg) roach, for example. One or two of these fish each day may keep the trout content in summer for quite a while, giving it plenty of time to ignore your imitations. A good hatch of fly can also tempt browns to the surface to feed.

▲ *Bank anglers fish the deep water off the dam wall on Grafham Water. Low light levels give the brown trout security to venture towards the bank in search of food – this is especially true when deep water is located close in.*

Fishing from the bank

Before beginning, always have a look at the catch returns and, more importantly, talk to local anglers for up-to-date advice about the best fishing areas.

Some of the most notable general areas are boat jetties, which always attract fry. These in turn draw fry-feeding rainbows and browns. Keep a lookout for seagulls wheeling in the air and plunging into the water for fry. The chances are brown trout are harrying their prey from below just as the gulls are from above.

Sunken islands with deep water nearby and valve towers are other good areas to locate browns.

Methods Your best chance of taking a big brown trout from the bank of a reservoir is early in the season or at the end of the season. Of the two, the early season is better, because the banks have been rested all winter long, and the trout can patrol very close to the bank.

Cover as much water as possible. Start by fishing close in and then and only then should you bang out a long line. A stiff rod with a WF or ST (shooting head) 7-9 is ideal. Floating, intermediate, Wet Cel II (medium-fast sinking) and Hi-D lines are essential.

It's hard to beat a floating line and a team

Imitative flies aren't the only ones which catch browns. Jeremy Herrmann prepares to land a brown caught on a Pink Tadpole from Blagdon Water.

of nymphs or buzzers for brown trout all season round. Because they aren't as aggressive as rainbows, you're far likelier to succeed with the imitative approach. Hare's Ear and Damsel Nymphs in sizes 8-12 as well as Pearly Buzzers and Thorpe Buzzers in sizes 10-14 work well.

With the wind blowing from left to right (assuming that you're right-handed) cast out perpendicular to the waves and allow the wind to swing the line around. When fishing flat water, use a slow strip or figure-of-eight retrieve. The count-down method enables your flies to explore all depths.

If that fails try fishing in deep water with a Wet Cel II and a marabou lure, experimenting with different colours – but especially black and green. Vary the retrieves – slow figure-of-eight, long, slow strips interrupted by the occasional quick jerk or hand-over-hand which is one of the best ways to fish big lures these days.

Using a Booby on a Hi-D is a very effective way of fishing the bottom without constantly getting hung up on weed or debris. Alter the leader length from 15cm (6in) to 3m (10ft). With a short leader, retrieve slowly so that the fly doesn't dive and pick up weed. You can fish the fly much more erratically with a longer leader. Many big browns fall for the Booby each season.

For the boat angler
Boat anglers should also give attention to deep water marks, sunken islands and shallow plains. Where bank fishing is prohibited or inaccessible, boat anglers can target browns undisturbed near the shoreline.

A brown trout from Colliford Reservoir in Cornwall crashes on the surface. Browns are better known for their deep, dogged style of fighting, rather than surface-crashing style.

Anglers fish loch-style on Grafham Water. This method, which catches both browns and rainbows, allows you to cover a lot of fish-holding water.

▲ *Tony Blakeman hoists aboard a good trout from Draycote Water. Some days large lures are most successful; other times you can catch browns on the dry fly, and sometimes you can't catch at all! They follow but won't take.*

▼ *Superb browns such as this 3½ lb (1.6kg) grown-on fish don't come too often. That makes catching them all the more a special occasion.*

sedge imitations work very effectively too.

Floating and Hi-D Along with a floating line and nymphs, anglers often catch browns using a Hi-D line and large marabou lures such as tandems or tube flies. These attractors can be over 15cm (6in) long and tied in bright colours to irritate the fish or in white and grey to imitate coarse fish.

One of the most popular boat methods for covering a large area of water, and certainly one that improves your chances of finding fish, is using the rudder. Check that it's legal before beginning. The rudder allows the boat to move in and out of bays and follow the contours of the bank. Again blast out a lure as far as you can to allow the line to sink and to produce a sufficient arc. Browns usually hit as the fly speeds up when coming around the arc.

The tactics and retrieves when boat fishing aren't a great deal different from bank fishing styles. One advantage of boat fishing is that you can hang the flies at the end of a retrieve – this often results in many last-second takes.

Patchy sport

Brown trout fishing can be very frustrating, to say the least. You may have days when big trout follow but just won't take. The fish just play games with you. Sometimes two fish follow the same fly. A noted area can be fished hard all day and might only result in follows. The same place the next day may well fish its head off.

It's also hard to say that the fish you'll catch will be a brown trout. When fishing big established reservoirs, you never really know what's going to grab your offering – it could be a big pike, a rainbow or a brown. Unless you see your quarry there's no way of telling. This is why big browns always hit the angling headlines.

Loch-style Welsh, Scottish and Irish waters contain wild browns used to eating insects at all levels of the water, but especially just below the surface and in the surface film. Small wets and dries fished on floating or intermediate lines are the order of the day. A 3lb (1.4kg) brown from such waters is an excellent trout.

Useful flies for these regions are mainly palmered. Bibio, Zulu, Soldier Palmer and Bumbles are excellent bob flies. Small wets such as Butcher, Wickham's Fancy, Greenwell's Glory and Black and Peacock Spider all take trout. Dry flies such as Daddy Longlegs and various mayfly and

Fly fishing from reservoir banks

You don't always need to go out in a boat to catch reservoir trout. They often come within casting distance to feast on fry, buzzers and margin-dwelling corixae. Reservoir specialist Tom Saville explains.

To enjoy bank-fishing to the full, you need the appropriate tackle and the correct strategies as the seasons change.

Proper equipment

A 10-10½ft (3-3.2m) carbon fly rod (rated AFTMA 7-8) is powerful enough to cast 25m (27yd) of line and reach trout which are holding well out. Don't attempt to fish a reservoir with a short rod because you won't have the leverage to hook a fish at a distance.

It's easier to cast weight forward lines than straight or double-taper ones because

▲ *Early in the season brown and rainbow trout are reluctant to venture into the cold shallow water (under 3m/10ft deep) along the reservoir margins.*

◄ *This is what bank fishing is all about – reading the water, selecting the right flies, casting effectively and, finally, safely landing big trout.*

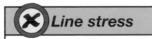 **Line stress**

Try not to aerialize more than the tapered section when false casting with WF lines. The line hinges in mid-air, breaking down the coating at the point where the tapered section joins the level section.

the weight is concentrated in the first 10m (33ft). A 7 or 8 is ideal for bank fishing.

Floating lines are used most of the time – the fast sinker or Hi-D is reserved for fishing deep water. Attach the fly line to 75m (82yd) of backing, and use a needle or nail knot to connect a 30cm (12in) butt section of 25lb (11.3kg) stiff mono to the fly line. Tie a loop in the butt section so that you can change leaders quickly.

For most work on reservoirs, fish with the longest leader you can manage – ideally, twice the length of the rod, with two 10cm (4in) droppers at 1.2m (4ft) intervals from the tip. The overall leader length should not be less than 5m (16ft).

A popular nylon strength for most reservoir work is 6lb (2.7kg). Learn to tie the blood loop or double grinner knot for making droppers. You can help to avoid tangles by attaching the heaviest fly on the point and the bulkiest fly on the top dropper.

In addition to good waterproof clothing, thigh waders and a large landing net, other

This well-marked brown trout, taken from the shore of a Midland reservoir, fell for a size 12 nymph fished on a long leader.

essential equipment includes a fly fisher's waistcoat (with plenty of pockets to hold tackle), scissor-pliers, priest, fly box, polarized sunglasses, an assortment of nymphs and lures and a bag to keep your catch fresh.

Seasonal tactics

It goes without saying that you need to adjust your approach as the seasons change.

In April most reservoirs open for fishing. The water is still cold after months of winter temperatures, and the trout are fairly lethargic. Unless a hatch of flies (midge pupae or buzzers) brings the trout to the surface, they swim near the bottom and can be tempted to take a slow-moving weighted black lure. Lures such as the Viva, Tadpole or Cat's Whisker with their mobile marabou tails or wings are best. With the lure on the point, put a Black Buzzer Nymph on the middle dropper and a Black Zulu on the top dropper. Size 10 hooks for all three are suitable.

Using your floating line, cast out, and then wait until the flies sink well down. Retrieve slowly with the rod tip about 20cm (8in) above the surface to keep in direct contact with the line and flies – this increases

The double haul

1. When you need to punch out a lot of line, use the double haul, a cast which dramatically increases the line speed.

The angler begins by holding the rod level with the water. With his left hand he grasps the line. There's about 10-15m (11-16yd) of line extended in a straight line.

2. With the fly line still held in one hand, the angler lifts up quickly on the rod as if he were making a normal cast. Notice his left hand; it is near the top of his head as he brings the rod up.

3. On the rear power stroke, just **when the butt of the rod is at about a 90° angle** to the water, the angler pulls the fly line down 30cm (1ft). This is the first 'haul'.

Hi-D strategies

When used with a Hi-D line and a short leader, the Booby (far right) dives and bobs, pulsing the mobile marabou.

You can make floating fry (right) dive enticingly and then rise to the surface. All that surface action brings rainbows from afar.

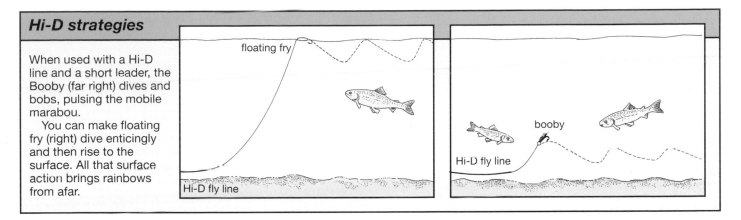

your chances of hooking a trout.

Early in the season the best places to fish are the dam walls and gently shelving banks where the depth is about 3m (10ft) at a comfortable casting distance.

Don't fish with a wind coming directly behind you because the water temperature is then at its coldest. Fish near the downwind shore with the wind blowing from the direction opposite to your casting arm. For example, if you're right-handed, fish with the wind blowing from left to right.

For deep water, use fast sinking line. Loop about 50cm (20in) of 7lb (3.2kg) nylon to your 25lb (11.3kg) butt section, and attach a buoyant Black Booby. Cast as far as you can, and again wait until the line sinks to the bottom.

The Booby is now suspended just above the bottom. Leave it static, keeping a good hold of your fly line, or you can retrieve it slowly.

In May and June prolific hatches of buzzers usually occur. As the year progresses the water gets warmer, and the trout become more active. Try a Pheasant Tail Nymph or a Gold Ribbed Hare's Ear Nymph on the point, with Buzzer Nymphs on the droppers. If you see adult midges on the surface, attach a winged wet fly, similar

Tip Casting well

Though you can learn the casts yourself, personal casting tuition from an expert helps to iron out any problems that you may have and provides you with many helpful insights.

Some waters have resident casting instructors. It is advisable to book well in advance.

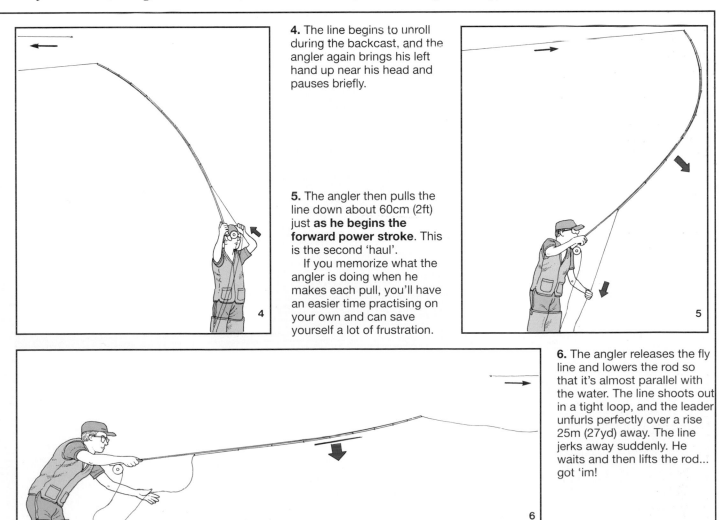

4. The line begins to unroll during the backcast, and the angler again brings his left hand up near his head and pauses briefly.

5. The angler then pulls the line down about 60cm (2ft) just **as he begins the forward power stroke**. This is the second 'haul'.

If you memorize what the angler is doing when he makes each pull, you'll have an easier time practising on your own and can save yourself a lot of frustration.

6. The angler releases the fly line and lowers the rod so that it's almost parallel with the water. The line shoots out in a tight loop, and the leader unfurls perfectly over a rise 25m (27yd) away. The line jerks away suddenly. He waits and then lifts the rod... got 'im!

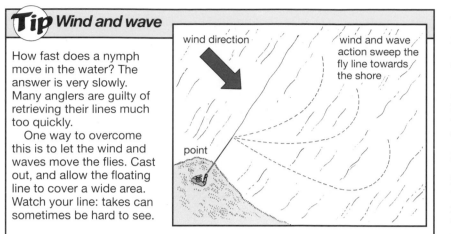

Tip *Wind and wave*

How fast does a nymph move in the water? The answer is very slowly. Many anglers are guilty of retrieving their lines much too quickly.

One way to overcome this is to let the wind and waves move the flies. Cast out, and allow the floating line to cover a wide area. Watch your line: takes can sometimes be hard to see.

wind direction

wind and wave action sweep the fly line towards the shore

point

in colour and size, to the top dropper.

If trout are rising regularly, ensure that your flies hang just below the surface of the water by applying grease to your leader. If there's no surface activity, try a weighted Stickfly or Montana Nymph on the point; let it sink well down, and retrieve slowly.

In late June and early July there are many hatches of sedge flies, especially in the evenings, and the trout feed enthusiastically on them. Popular sedge imitations that you can try are Invicta, Green Peter, Wickham's Fancy and Fiery Brown.

Buzzers are still on the trout's menu, and the fish are now likely to be tempted by imitations of hatching flies emerging at the surface. Offer 'dry fly' patterns such as the Shipman Buzzer or Hopper – both treated with floatant – but again make sure the leader sinks. Allow the flies to drift around without retrieving. When your fly is taken, wait a few seconds before striking.

In August the weather can be very warm – but as you probably know, trout don't like

Back off!

Don't get too close to another angler – even if he's catching fish. It's courteous to stay at least 50m (55yd) away. You can still see what he's doing and learn from him.

warm water. The coolest water is found along the shore from which the wind is blowing (with the wind at your back). So choose your location accordingly.

Trout often feed on coarse fry in mid-season. You usually see big splashes around marginal weedbeds as the trout slash into the shoals. Such is the force of the attack that some fry are stunned and float to the surface. The trout return to pick them off. You can catch these trout by offering them a floating Ethafoam Fry. Just cast it out near the activity: resist any temptation to move it! The trout takes it like a dry fly. It's vital to wait a couple of seconds before striking, or you won't hook the fish very well.

As autumn approaches, wet and humid weather encourages hordes of craneflies to appear in the surrounding grassland. Some of these are blown on to the water and prove an irresistible mouthful for trout.

Experiment how far out to fish the fly. If there's no response close in, use the wind from the windward shore to drift the floating 'Daddy' a long way out. When you get a take, don't strike immediately: let the fish take the fly down first.

◄ *Cracking rainbow trout such as this one are often the target of the bank angler early in May and June – times when distance casting isn't essential.*

▼ *The lure of the bank at dusk: moving to shallow water to hunt for roach and perch fry, brown trout come well within casting range.*

Boat fishing on reservoirs for trout

Early season trout are not always the easiest fish to find – but they're there. Bob Church, Britain's best known reservoir fly fisherman, shows you where they lurk.

▼ *Some reservoirs, like Rutland Water (below), are huge and can be quite daunting to an angler used to smaller waters. Drifting – as these anglers are doing – can often be an excellent way to locate and catch trout. A short cast is often more successful than a long one as you don't scare fish which are close to the boat by casting over them.*

Although there are a number of small reservoirs in Britain of 60-100 acres, most are around 300 acres with some, such as Rutland Water, covering more than ten times this area. On these 'inland seas' a boat can help you get the best of the sport – as long as you know how to handle it and where to position it.

Most reservoirs are not the featureless places that some people imagine them to be. There are bays and headlands, valve pumping towers, submerged islands and many other features. These areas fish well at different times of the day and in different seasons – using various techniques. Taking a boat out means you can fish any of these places – and if the action's slow, it's easy and quick to move to another spot.

Using a boat can be dangerous, so fish with someone else unless you are highly experienced. Before you and your partner set out from the jetty, make sure that your boat has all the essential equipment.

You'll need an anchor – the kedge-type is best because it holds bottom firmly without being very heavy. (It has blades which dig in when you pay out enough line.)

If the boat has an outboard motor, and most do, make sure there are a pair of oars under the seats for emergencies. Nothing is guaranteed to ruin your day more effectively than being adrift in 3000 acres of water waiting for a rescue boat.

Check the rowlocks aren't damaged and that there is a life jacket or a buoyancy aid for you and your fishing partner. There should also be a bailer beneath the seat to get rid of the water you bring into the boat with your wet tackle and, with any luck, your fish.

For control over your drifting speed, a drogue (a small parachute dropped in the water and used to slow the rate of drift) is essential. One of 130cm (50in) square is just right. Obviously this is only useful for fishing on the drift.

⚠ **Water sense**

Bob Church recommends that you wear a buoyancy aid whenever you're afloat, no matter how well you swim. You may never need it, but too often anglers using boats drown unnecessarily.

▲ *The start of the day at Llyn Brenig in North Wales – time to make sure everything you need is there, and stowed away tidily.*

> **Tip** **Using the anchor**
>
> When fishing at anchor, you must avoid any noise which may scare off the fish. Drift or paddle to your intended anchorage from upwind, have the anchor rope untangled and ready to drop, and drop it *quietly*.

▲ *Landing fish in a boat shouldn't be any harder than it is from the bank. Just draw the trout over the net.*

Spring sport

Early in the season, the water is beginning to warm up and weeds are starting to grow in the shallower water. These weeds are a haven for insects and fish fry which attract the bigger fish. Areas of shallow water accessible only by boat are usually great places to find early season trout.

Headlands often continue underwater for

A WINDY SPRING DAY ON A RESERVOIR

Make sure you avoid anchoring too close to anglers wading from the bank.

There is often a hatch of chironomids (bloodworm) in sheltered bays during the afternoon.

rainbow trout

Both rainbows and brownies are attracted to areas of shallow water by the mud and silt stirred up on a windy day.

brown trout

hundreds of yards, providing areas of shallow water. This type of feature produces some prime fishing from April to mid-May. The weedy ridge provides food and shelter for the trout and many can be caught before sport tails off in late summer. Approach the ridge downwind – to avoid scaring the fish you want to catch – and drop anchor about 60-80m (66-87yd) from the shore and 20m (22yd) upwind of the ridge. The fish lie close to the bottom, over and around the ridge.

In a light to medium wind, drop the anchor out from the central stern position – this stops the boat swinging about. In a higher wind with waves of 60cm (2ft) or more, tie up from the bows to reduce risk of capsizing. Some anglers tie up from the central rowlock, leaving the boat broadside to the wind. If you do this, then even if you stay right way up, the extra area presented to the wind can cause the anchor to drag along the bottom over the ridge – spoiling the fishing.

Submerged islands provide very similar opportunities in mid to late spring. The shallow water over these areas also encourages weed growth and provides shelter for trout. Both types of hotspot fish well with a wave of 60cm (2ft). This can stir up the water, colouring it slightly over ridges and

▲ *A good wind producing waves like these often makes for the best trout catching conditions in the early season. These anglers afloat on Berkshire's Queen Mother Reservoir have anchored near the dam wall to fish deep. Fish often wait for food swept in by the waves.*

Boat handling

Fishing from a boat offers you the freedom of the water, but with it goes a certain amount of responsibility – both to other users of the water, and to yourself. Here are some simple rules which you should follow whenever you step into a boat to help you fish safely and with consideration.

● Most waters insist on your wearing a buoyancy aid. Though these tend to be brightly coloured, presumably to aid rescue, they won't put the fish off as long as you don't stand up making yourself visible to trout for miles around.

● Standing up is a bad idea in any case as small boats are not very stable.

In windy conditions, anchor from the bows for greater stability and safety.

Early season fishing is often best when the wind is raising waves of 60cm (2ft) or over.

rainbow trout

rainbow trout

brown trout

Headlands often continue underwater for a long way. They provide shallow water which encourages the growth of weeds early in the season.

Trout tend to feed close to the bottom in the early part of the season.

Weeds attract the trout because of the insects and small fish they shelter.

● Always make sure that the boat is fully equipped before setting off.
● Don't go out alone unless you are very experienced in boat handling.
● Keep bulky or heavy items in the centre of the boat to maintain stability. Lay rods along the gunwales, and make sure you don't have to stumble over your gear to move around the boat.
● Make sure you can easily reach your equipment while in the boat.
● Treat other water users with respect. Don't motor in front of other anglers to try to 'steal' a good fishing position, and always leave at least 50m (55yd) between you and the nearest angler.

Top reservoirs

Reservoir trout are usually stocked at around a pound (0.45kg) in weight, and reach 2lb (0.9kg) in three or four months. This means that a four pounder (1.8kg) has grown on to that weight and has had time to get used to its surroundings – making it a wild fish. This is a different proposition from fish stocked at that weight. Bob recommends the following reservoirs for a good scrap with brown and rainbow trout.

- **Blagdon Lake,** Somerset – 350 acres
- **Carsington Reservoir,** Derbys – 600 acres
- **Chew Valley Lake,** Somerset – 1000 acres
- **Draycote Water,** Warwickshire – 600 acres
- **Eye Brook Reservoir,** Leics – 350 acres
- **Farmoor Reservoir,** Oxfordshire – 400 acres
- **Grafham Water,** Cambs – 1500 acres
- **Hanningfield Reservoir,** Essex – 1000 acres
- **Kielder Water,** Northumberland – 3300 acres
- **Ladybower Reservoir,** Derbs – 500 acres
- **Llyn Brenig,** Clwyd – 1000 acres
- **Pitsford Reservoir,** Northants – 800 acres
- **Ravensthorpe Res.,** Northants – 100 acres
- **Rutland Water,** Leicestershire – 3300 acres

islands and creating a trail of colour downwind. Such a trail acts rather like groundbait and can attract fish from quite some distance.

Other styles

Sometimes the obvious hotspots fail to produce, and that's when you must search for your fish. In a mild spring, you can try drifting. This is most effective in 2.4-4.6m (8-15ft) of water, with the fish tending to lie near the bottom. Always use the drogue except in the lightest of breezes. Without it, you'll find yourself drifting too rapidly towards your flies.

At the end of a drift, pull in the drogue and motor back upwind to start another from a new position to the left or right. That way you cover a large area of water. When you find a fish or two, use the same drift-line until you stop catching. Don't motor over the area down which you're going to drift or

▲ *Late afternoon to dusk is traditionally a good time for hatches of insects that prompt trout to feed.*

you'll scatter the fish. Use the deep water at the middle of the reservoir for this, and make sure you steer well clear of other anglers' lines of drift. Etiquette on the water is more than just politeness – if everyone simply motored wherever they wanted, there would be more accidents and fewer trout caught.

In the sheltered, tree-lined margins of the reservoir there is often a hatch of chironomids in the late afternoon. This is another good place to hunt for trout in late spring. Anchor far enough away from the shore to avoid scaring the fish you want to catch – but not so far that you can't cast to them. If you see trout rising, they are probably taking the emerging pupae trapped in the surface film of the water. Etiquette again demands that you anchor no closer than 50m (55yd) to the nearest boat – and watch out for anglers wading from the bank.

◀ *The frayed tail of the brown trout (top) shows that it has been recently stocked, whereas the rainbow is full-finned and wild.*

Dry fly fishing

Casting a dry fly to a trout and seeing the fish take it or turn away at the last moment makes the heart of even the most seasoned angler beat faster. John Roberts takes a closer look.

Dry versus wet

Dry-fly fishing allows you to see the fly as it drifts downstream: unlike wet-fly fishing, you know if it's working as it should or not. Again, when it comes to bite detection, you can see the fly when the fish takes it and strike accordingly.

▼ *There are few things to match the excitement of watching your dry fly being engulfed by a brown trout on a clear chalk stream.*

Trout often feed at the surface of the water on newly hatched aquatic insects or female flies returning to lay their eggs. Terrestrial (land-based) flies and other insects are also important food items as summer progresses.

Matching the hatch

If you want to catch a feeding trout, your best chance is to offer it an imitation of the natural fly it is taking. By looking at the water or along the river bank you can discover what the trout are feeding on.

Size is an important feature. Few fish are duped by a fly too small or too large. Also take into consideration the shape and colour of the natural insect's body, legs and wings. Is the dry fly designed to copy a sedge fly or a dun (a newly hatched upwing fly), an egg-laying spinner or a terrestrial? Wings don't have to be included – often the blur of the hackle is a sufficient suggestion.

Rise forms

Trout feeding at the surface reveal clues about the insects they are consuming. The simple or plain rise is the commonest form. Trout taking duns, motionless adult sedges and most terrestrial insects produce regular concentric rings on the surface – sometimes with a tell-tale bubble.

When a trout moves quickly to grab a fly off the surface, it causes a splash, displacing a lot of water. This is the slashing rise, a signal which suggests the trout is taking fast-moving, hatching sedge pupae. If sedges aren't around, the trout may be feeding on large terrestrial insects. Fish a sedge pupa imitation in the surface film of the water. If that fails, try a large terrestrial.

The dimple, sip or kiss rise is difficult to detect on rippled or fast water. It's much easier to see on calm stretches. The trout moves unhurriedly to its prey – knowing the food can't escape – and sucks the insect in without breaking the surface of the water, producing very gentle ripples.

Spent spinners, stillborn flies or those trapped in the surface film are the likely

How a river trout takes an insect

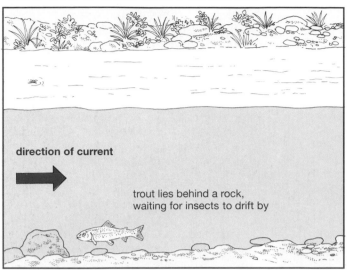

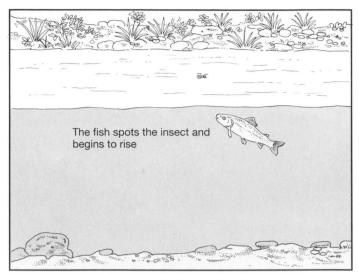

direction of current

trout lies behind a rock,
waiting for insects to drift by

The fish spots the insect and
begins to rise

Seeing a trout rise is a welcome sight. But many anglers don't take into sufficient account *the depth of the water or the speed of the current.*

The depth and speed of the river affect where the trout makes its rise and where the angler sees the rise. In this position the trout is about 90cm (3ft) from its lie.

> ### **Tip** Real illusion
>
> Though dry flies catch trout even when the fish aren't rising, you might create the illusion that a hatch is occurring by casting to a lie several times. This may stimulate the fish to feed.

items the fish is going for here. A trout feeding in this way is usually stationed very close to the surface and feeding frequently. Because there is often plenty of food, trout do not move very far to feed. Present the fly in line with the trout.

▼ *A prime time to fish a dry fly is during an evening insect hatch. Offering an appropriate imitation to a wild brown trout is often successful – and great fun.*

Proper presentation

Selecting the right pattern is half the problem; the other half is presenting the fly correctly. Drag, the main concern for the dry-fly angler, occurs because the speed of the current varies across the surface of the river, and the line pulls or 'drags' the fly at an unusual speed. A fly which doesn't drift exactly where the current takes it looks unnatural, and trout refuse it. There are exceptions to this (mainly egg-laying

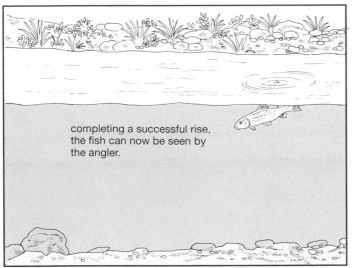

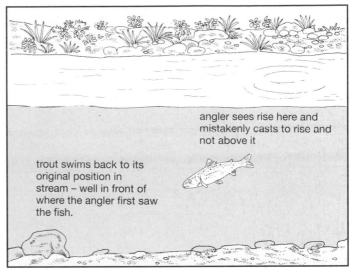

Trout have an angle of view of 97° irrespective of depth. The *size* of a trout's window increases as it swims deeper and decreases as it swims towards the surface.

The trout is usually about 60-120cm (2-4ft) upstream of its rise, but remember you still need to cast about 90cm (3ft) in front of the lie, so the fish can see the fly coming.

sedges), but 95% of your presentations must be drag-free.

You can overcome drag by casting the line leader and fly on to water which has a *minimum* variation in current speed. You can also cast slack or excess line on to the water, so the current has to straighten it before drag can begin.

If you cast across the current, any faster water creates a downstream belly in the line and causes the fly to drag. You can avoid this by mending the line – flicking the line upstream so that the belly moves upstream of the fly (shown on page 186).

On smooth, unrippled surfaces mending line may alarm fish. A reach cast moves the line in the air on the forward cast so that it lands upstream of the fishing zone. The longer a fly is allowed to drift, the more likely it is to drag. Another answer is to fish with short drifts.

Presenting the fly downstream offers some advantages – the fly is the first thing the trout sees, and the leader and line are less visible. Fishing this way can be a very effective way of taking shy fish.

Fishing tips

If rising trout refuse the artificial fly, there are a number of things you can do. In moderate to slow water – where trout can take a long, hard look at the dry fly – use a pattern a size or two smaller than the one you tried first. You can also try a low-riding pattern which rests in the surface film. Copying an emerging or trapped fly in this way is often successful. In fast water where trout might

▶ *When you're fishing in ultra-clear water and trout are refusing to rise to your fly, use a fly a size or two smaller. If that doesn't work, try a bushy sedge pattern.*

Mending the line – across current

This technique is very effective if you're trying to avoid 'drag' – when the current grabs the line and pulls the fly at an unnatural speed.

If the line is straight or if the fly is starting to drag, you can create a belly in the line by flicking the rod upstream (left in this case) to allow the fly to drift freely in the current.

But mending the line on very calm parts of the river may spook the fish.

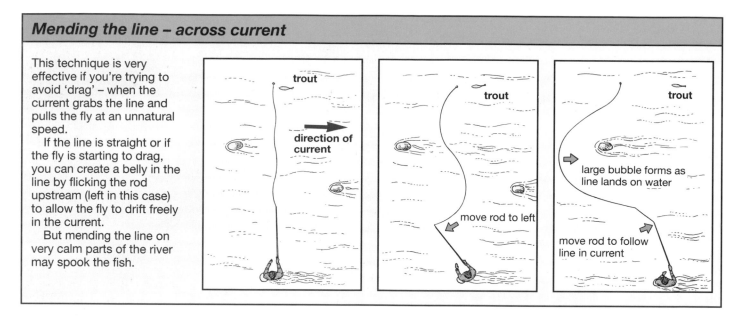

easily miss a fly, move up in size to make sure they see your imitation.

Another possibility is to offer them a food source such as a bushy sedge or a beetle pattern that might be more attractive. If that fails cast upstream and, as the fly drifts 30cm (1ft) or so in front of the trout, twitch it gently. This singles it out from motionless natural flies and gives it some life. Adding a bit of life to the fly is perhaps one of the most difficult characteristics to give to an artificial.

If trout aren't rising or if you can't find them, try searching the faster water with an attractor pattern such as a Wickham's Fancy. Or cast a terrestrial pattern in slow water so that it lands with a 'plop' that attracts the attention of lethargic fish. At dusk use a bushy sedge pattern. Fish it downstream, giving it an occasional twitch. Using a finer leader (which makes the line less visible) or softer nylon (which allows a freer drift) may also help. Fishing the dry fly often means continually changing your approach to tempt shy fish. The problems that the trout presents are part of its charm.

▼ *Probably the worst time to fish is mid-day in summer. Extreme stealth and patience are needed on small, slow-flowing rivers.*

Tip Skating flies

This is an effective technique when trout refuse to rise. Apply a floatant to an Elk Hair Caddis, and grease the leader and 1.2m (4ft) of the fly line.

Cast downstream or across. Lift the rod tip, skipping the fly across the surface to imitate a caddis fly trying to fly.

Fly fishing for salmon

Fly fishing is probably the most challenging way of fishing for Atlantic salmon. Veteran salmon angler Arthur Oglesby recommends equipment and tactics which should increase your chances of catching the fish.

Though Atlantic salmon don't feed when returning from the sea to spawn in fresh water, you can still catch them with lures, plugs, natural baits or flies. No one knows for certain why they take – but take flies they do! Perhaps the salmon have some memory of feeding which triggers a response to strike. They may also hit lures or flies out of sheer aggression or to defend their lies from intruders.

To fly fish effectively for salmon, you need to switch tactics as the seasons change. There are two overall approaches – the big fly fished deep for early and late-season salmon and the small fly presented near the surface for late spring, summer and early autumn fish.

But it's important not to be too dogmatic about your approach. Though anglers fishing during the early season catch mostly on large sunk flies, you might also tempt

▶ An angler fly fishes on the River Helmsdale in northern Scotland during the early season (March).
   At this time of year, use a fast sinking line to present the fly deep. But keep moving from pool to pool to find fresh-run fish.

salmon with a small sparsely dressed fly. Remember, if one particular tactic isn't working, experiment to find one that will.

Early and late season

The water is generally cold and sometimes high during the early and late season. The salmon are reluctant to move too far, so you need to use a heavy brass tube fly and a sinking line to drop the fly to the fish's level.

▼ The reward of finally catching a salmon on a fly far outweighs the price you sometimes have to pay in terms of hard work and long hours.
   Here a delighted angler cradles a cracking 8lb (3.6kg) salmon, caught in late April.

Equipment Anglers plump for a double-handed fly rod between 13-18ft (4-5.5m) long for most of the salmon fly fishing in Britain. You can control the line easier with a double-handed rod than with a shorter rod. And better line control means better presentation.

Also, you can cast farther and more effectively with a double-handed rod – especially if the area behind you is obstructed with foliage – punching out the line quite a way with a Spey or Double Spey cast. But with a short single-handed rod, this is far more difficult – you just don't have the leverage or the power.

Most anglers plump for a 15ft (4.5m) double-handed carbon-fibre fly rod rated for a 10-weight line. Combine this with a weight-forward fast sinking line (such as a Wet Cel II) and a 6ft (1.8m) leader of 15-20lb (7-9kg) breaking strain, and you're nearly ready to begin.

Water craft During the early and late season the salmon hold in sheltered lies where they don't have to expend too much energy contending against the current. The slow, deep pools are prime areas when the water is at its normal level.

Finding salmon when the water is cold and high is fairly straightforward: the fish concentrate near the banks, away from the main channel in the middle of the river.

Fishing in the early and late season To begin fishing for salmon, cast directly

▼ *An angler fly fishes for salmon with a single-handed rod in low-water conditions in early autumn. Notice that he has plenty of room for his backcasts.*

A general guide to salmon lies

1. When the water is high, the salmon may lie close to the bank – sometimes no more than a rod's length away. The current isn't as fast close as it is in the middle of the river.

2. You may need to wade when the river is just above its normal level. The salmon can be spread out, but most lie in the indicated strip.

3. Under normal and low-water conditions (usually in the summer) you can often find the salmon in the deep pools, but it's also worth trying the runs and riffles.

across the river or slightly downstream and across, then let the fly swing around gently in the current. Ideally, you want the fly to drift 1-2ft (45-60cm) above the river bed.

Perhaps the biggest mistake beginners make is to allow the fly to swing around too quickly. Always try to fish the fly as *slowly* as possible. This can't be overstressed, especially when the water temperature is below 10°C (50°F) and fish are reluctant to move around. In fact, a good principle to remember is that the colder the water is, the slower you must present the fly.

It's always better to cover a lot of water quickly in the early season, taking a step or two after each cast, than to plod about the pool or run slowly and aimlessly. This is especially true when there are fresh fish in the pools, and they are still in the process of moving upstream – however slowly.

Fresh-run salmon take flies more readily than resident fish, which have been in the river longer and tend to be more reluctant to strike.

Sometimes casting a long way is helpful,

Down-and-across fly fishing for salmon

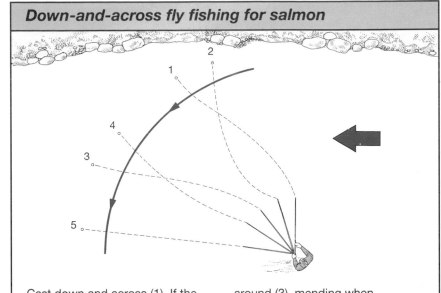

Cast down and across (1). If the water is fast flowing, mend the line immediately (2) to allow the fly to sink and swing attractively in the current. Allow the fly to swing around (3), mending when necessary (4) to fish the fly as slowly as possible (except in low, warm water). Re-cast when the fly is downstream of you (5).

A rough guide to water temperatures and fly sizes

Water temperature	Fly size
0-7°C (32-45°F)	The larger the fly the better. Use tube flies 2-3in long.
7-12°C (45-54°F)	Try using tube flies 1-2in long, or size 4-6 doubles or trebles.
12-15°C (54-59°F)	Small flies work best in warm water. Try fishing with singles or doubles in sizes 6-12. Trout flies may also catch.

but it's much better to know roughly where fish are lying and how best to cover them. It makes sense to hire a ghillie, if you can afford one. He will take you to the most prolific sections of a river. Without local advice, you have to look for deep water and simply learn from experience.

Warm-water fly fishing

Fishing for salmon in late spring and early autumn can be fabulous, depending on the river and the number of fresh-run fish coming through. Your prospects in summer aren't usually that good because most of the fish are residents and the water levels often plummet, but you can get away with using

Five of the best

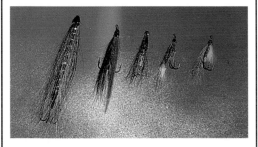

Many beginning salmon anglers carry boxes and boxes of flies to the riverbank. You don't need dozens of patterns – just a range of large and small ones for the different times of the year. Here are some of Arthur Oglesby's favourites (from left to right): Willie Gunn, Oglebug, Stoat's Tail, Munro Killer and Blue Charm.

▶ *An early autumn salmon comes to the net on a Scottish river. The angler used a single-handed rod, floating line and small fly to tempt the fish from the low, clear water.*

lighter gear at this time of year – in some cases your trout rod will do!

Equipment As soon as the water warms above 10°C (50°F) and provided the air is warmer than the water, you can put aside your sunk line tackle and resort to an intermediate or full floating line. The floater is easier to control than a sinking line because you can mend it. Mending prevents the line from dragging in the current and allows the fly to sink to the proper depth.

Sometimes in the very low water of summer you may want to use your trout fly rod (rated for 7-8 weight lines), a floating line and leader of 6-8lb (2.7-3.6kg) breaking strain. Under such conditions it pays to use very small flies (sizes 10-12). Many anglers have taken salmon on trout flies such as Muddlers, Goldhead nymphs and traditional wet flies.

Finding salmon Under low-water conditions throughout the summer, search deep water below stretches of fast water. But you can also find fish in runs and even riffles. Fast water appeals to salmon because its oxygen content is high.

Fishing approaches Though the water may now be lower and warmer than during the early or late season, your tactics for fly presentation are basically the same as before. Obviously, the fly fishes much closer to the surface when you use a floating line, but again swing it over the salmon (or probable lie) as slowly as possible.

Long casts are often necessary on large rivers – where the salmon might be spread out over a large stretch of water. But again line control is more important.

Under low-water conditions you can temporarily abandon fishing your fly slowly. In fact, a fly cast upstream and retrieved sometimes provokes a salmon into taking.

▲ Local knowledge is as precious as gold. Here, a ghillie recommends a fly for normal conditions in the early season.

◄ Salmon freshly run from the sea are silvery white and in top condition. This double-figure beauty was taken on a large fly, fished slow and deep with a fast-sinking line.

Side and reach casts

Even when you have to reach difficult lies, it's important in fly fishing to present the fly as delicately and precisely as possible.

The side and reach casts are just two of the many types of casts developed to overcome very difficult situations in river fly fishing.

The reach cast You see a big brown trout directly across from you in fast water. How are you going to present your dry fly without the line pulling the fly under right away? The solution is to try a reach cast, a slightly modified version of the overhead cast that puts an upstream belly in the line. It's used only when casting across the river.

When you fish with a dry fly, the upstream belly (slack line) allows the fly to drift drag free over the trout. And when you use a nymph or wet fly, the same upstream belly allows the flies to sink, rather than be swept across the current near the surface.

The side cast You're fishing on a small, deep river; its banks are lined with bushes and tall trees. The shade of the trees encourages trout to rise to hatching upwings (iron blues).

You can't use an overhead cast because the water is too deep to wade and the trees are in the way. The side cast allows you to work upstream yet avoid the troublesome tree branches.

Again, in many ways this cast is similar to an overhead cast except that it's done to one side. The important point to remember is that the rod must move smoothly back and forwards at a 90° angle and generally remain parallel to the water.

▲ *This angler uses the side cast from under the bough of a tree to present his fly to a Yorkshire grayling.*

Fly casting

Casting champions spend up to eight hours a day practising. Attach a piece of yarn to your leader and sharpen your skills in your back garden.

▼ *Learning alternative casts may help you catch more fish – such as this handsome brown trout.*

The reach cast (A)... and the side cast (B)

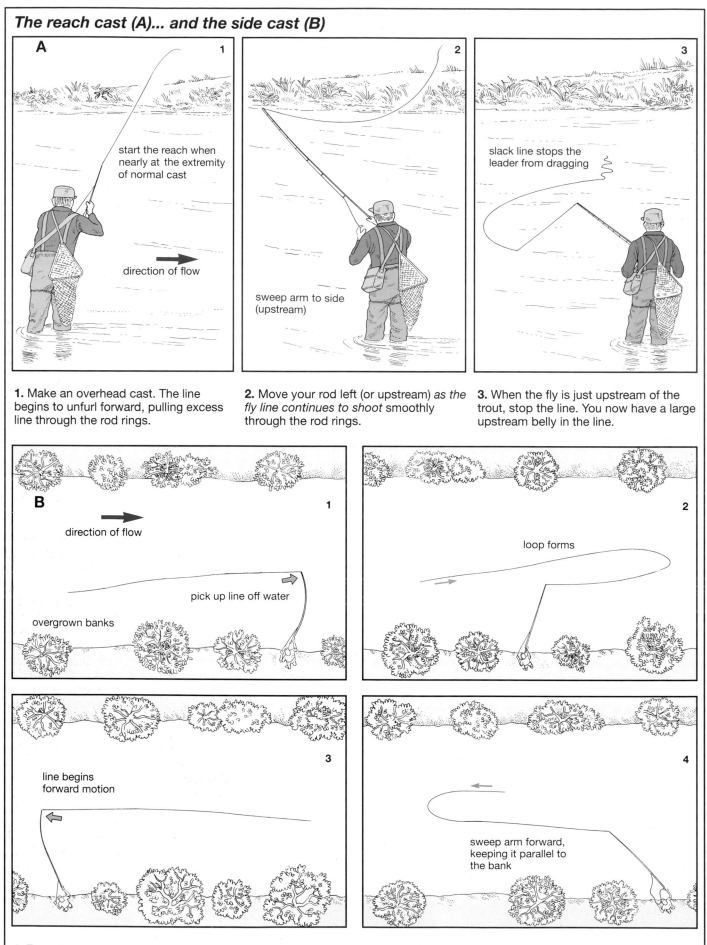

1. Make an overhead cast. The line begins to unfurl forward, pulling excess line through the rod rings.

2. Move your rod left (or upstream) *as the fly line continues to shoot* smoothly through the rod rings.

3. When the fly is just upstream of the trout, stop the line. You now have a large upstream belly in the line.

1. Face the direction in which you want to cast. Bring the rod back to 1pm. *Keep the rod parallel to the water during the cast.*

2 & 3. The line shoots back in a tight loop. When the line is nearly unrolled, bring the rod forward or towards the left.

4. Stop the rod at about 10am. The line shoots forward in a tight loop, and the fly swings around towards the target.

Nymph fishing

Since trout take most of their food below the surface of the water, nymph fishing is perhaps the deadliest type of fly-fishing. Charles Jardine explains both upstream and downstream 'nymphing'.

▲ *Fishing for trout on the Welsh Dee. The gap between two riffles is a perfect place to use a nymph along the bottom.*

Always strike

When upstream nymphing, if you see your line hesitate or twitch at all, strike immediately! Sometimes the nymph gets caught on rocks, debris or weeds, giving the impression that a fish has taken it. There is, in fact, no way of telling until you strike.

A remedy for a rocky, problematic bottom is to put on a lighter pattern which won't snag so easily.

Nymph fishing in its literal sense is angling with the imitations of immature insects such as mayflies, caddis flies, midges and others. But it also applies to other underwater creatures such as shrimps and corixas (lesser water boatmen). Even snails are labelled under the term 'nymph'.

Getting set up

Nymph fishing on rivers requires light fly line – AFTMA 4, 5 or 6 – to present the fly delicately without slapping the water. It doesn't matter what the taper or colour of the line is – as long as it floats. A rod with a fast action (middle-to-tip) and 8½-9½ft (2.6-2.9m) long is ideal.

Leaders should always be somewhat longer than the depth you are fishing. For example, deep runs and holes of 2.7m (9ft) require a 3.7-4.6m (12-15ft) leader. For general fishing conditions, though, a 2.7-3.7m (9-12ft) leader is best. To extend the life of a knotless tapered leader, add a tippet section to the end. You then have to replace only the tippet when it's used up, not the entire leader.

Since river fish usually don't grow as big as their reservoir cousins, consider the pliability of the line and the size of the fly when choosing the proper tippet breaking strain. Soft line allows the nymph to move freely and easily in the water, imitating a natural, free-swimming insect. Stiff or thick line hinders the nymph's movement and puts fish off. As a general guideline, hook sizes 18-20 require 1½-2lb (0.7-0.9kg) line. You may need 3-4lb (1.4-1.8kg) line for hook sizes 12-16. Heavily weighted patterns in sizes 6-10 require line up to 5-6lb (2.3-2.7kg).

The upstream approach

One of the most celebrated and effective methods is the upstream approach. There are two basic variations of this style of fishing, the dead drift and the induced take.

The dead drift is simply casting upstream of a trout (or a likely lie) and allowing the fly to run with the current towards the fish.

The induced take is similar to the dead drift, but just as the fly is about to reach the quarry, move the nymph either sideways or upwards by quickly lifting up the rod tip while pulling the fly line. This imitates a fleeing, panic-stricken insect and stimulates the trout to feed.

Water craft is vital when fishing upstream: you should have a good idea where the trout are, or where they are likely to be, so that you don't waste time fishing in inappropriate stretches of water such as shallow runs only about 15cm (6in) deep.

Another important yet often overlooked consideration is choosing a correctly weighted pattern which fishes at the trout's level. If a trout's lie is just off the bottom in very deep fast water, for example, you need a heavy nymph to get right down to the fish. The alternative is to cast far enough ahead of the lie so that the fly has extra time to sink to the required depth.

Whether you use the dead drift or the induced-take method of upstream nymphing, keep a low profile – kneel on the bank or cast from behind the cover of tall grass.

Another point which may help you catch wary trout in clear rivers is to change the angle of your cast. If you are casting to a trout directly upstream, your line lands above the feeding fish – this could spook the trout. But by casting upstream and across, you place the line and leader at a slight angle to the fish, helping to conceal the fly line.

In clear water – where you can see the

▲ *Though more common on stillwaters, dragonfly nymphs also thrive in the slow-moving rivers of southern England.*

Nymphs scurry along rocks and weeds and are fairly good swimmers.

Perfecting the roll cast

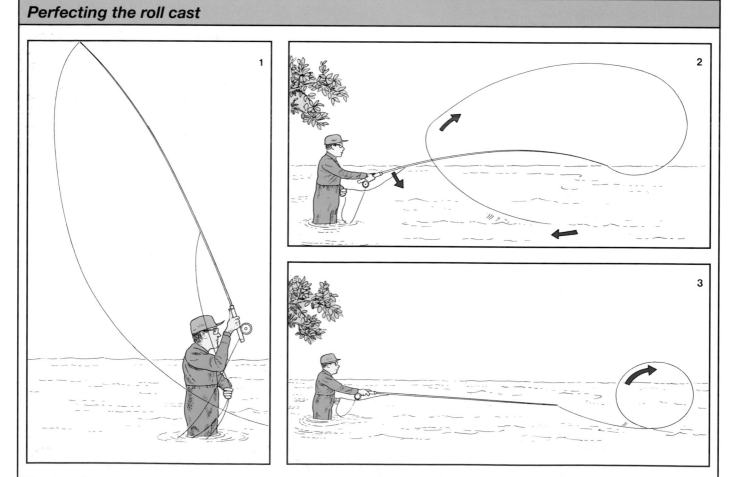

Use the roll cast when trees prevent an overhead cast. Raise the rod up until the line forms a belly behind the rod **(1)**.

Bring the rod down hard and fast – as if you're hitting a nail with a hammer. Your arm completes a 90° angle **(2)**.

As the rod is thrust downward, the line is picked up off the water and hurled towards the target in a circular form **(3)**.

fish – detecting the take isn't difficult. A trout or grayling's sudden movement upwards, downwards or to the side usually indicates that the fish has hit your nymph. A speedy but gentle lift of the rod sets the hook. Whatever the water conditions, if you don't see a fish but your leader stops or twitches in the current, strike! Your attitude should always be to strike first – ask questions later. Trout and grayling can sometimes spit out imitations as quickly as they take them.

When trout are surface-feeding the same principles of upstream nymphing apply – though there are distinct parallels with dry-fly fishing. G.E.M. Skues founded this style of angling in the early 1900s; later it came to be called 'emerger' or 'damp' fly-fishing. Follow the same principles as with the dead-

▲ The upstream approach is an effective method for fly-fishing small rivers such as this West Country water. This angler is using short drifts to work the nymph in front of and behind the boulders.

The outlaws

On some rivers fishing the nymph upstream is banned while on others (chalk streams) fishing it downstream is illegal. Make sure you *check* the rules before you go.

drift method, but use a pattern (such as a sedge pupa emerger) which hangs in the surface film, and cast closer to, but still upstream of, the rising trout or grayling. Takes are again visual. They look like an ordinary rise – if you see one anywhere near your fly, set the hook immediately.

The basic upstream nymph tactic is applicable throughout the season, and by varying the weight and style of your artificial you can accommodate everything from the surface-feeding brownie to the bottom-grubbing grayling.

Downstream nymphing

Another method of nymph fishing is the traditional 'down and across' technique. Drag on the nymph isn't too much of a disadvantage when fishing downstream. Cast across the stream and let the current sweep the nymph down. This is one of the easiest methods of fly-fishing because there isn't much casting involved.

By controlling the line flow, you're not limited to imitation solely by appearance – you can make a heavily weighted nymph, for example, 'swim' in a deep pool by gently twitching the fly upstream and then letting it move down again. This adds life to the nymph.

Water craft isn't as important when fishing downstream. An intimate knowledge of the river's deep pools and seething eddies isn't necessary because your nymph covers a wide fish-holding area, and you take a few steps downstream after working a stretch.

Unlike fishing upstream – when the current has control of the fly – 'nymphing' downstream allows you to dangle a tantalizing fly just above a sunken log, a boulder

Pattern points

Too many anglers take far too many nymphs with them. All you really need are a Stickfly, Pheasant Tail Nymph, Gold Ribbed Hare's Ear, Montana, Damsel and Dragonfly Nymphs, GE Nymph and various shrimp patterns.

When fishing with nymphs (upstream dead-drifting especially), ensure that the tippet section and fly descend rapidly through the surface film. Leader-sink agent should be applied after every 10 or so casts.

If the leader has any grease on it, it is more visible to the trout. Degreasing is crucial when fishing emergers in the surface film.

Some river and stillwater specials

▶*From left to right: the Stickfly (1) imitates a caddis fly nymph; the Montana (2) suggests a stonefly nymph; and the Dragonfly Nymph (3). Most imitations are tied on long shank hooks, sizes 6 to 16.*

or a snag-strewn heap of branches: you can explore the river without worrying too much about losing your favourite fly.

There are certain disadvantages when fishing downstream, though. First of all, you can sometimes be visible to the trout. The importance of stealth cannot be overstressed. Walk quietly to the bank; fish from the cover of vegetation; and wear drab clothing. This is especially important on calm stretches of shallow water. Fish with a lot of line out in such places.

A second disadvantage comes when you try to read takes. Generally, you can feel them more than you can see them. If you're not careful and controlled when setting the hook, you could easily pull the nymph *away* from the trout's mouth (since the fish usually points or faces towards you).

Hooking isn't usually a problem when you're fishing upstream because the trout is in front of you or at your side – striking pulls the hook *into* the fish's mouth.

Some say fishing the nymph is much more problematic than using the dry fly (especially when detecting takes). But this deadly style of fly-fishing isn't beyond the reach of anyone. Proficiency and confidence come with practice and patience.

◄ *Nymphs trundled slowly along the bottom often attract the attention of big grayling, such as this 2½lb (1.1kg) River Test resident.*

▼ *Major insect hatches occur at dawn and dusk. An 'emerger' (one fished in the surface film) is your best choice at this time.*

Chalk streams for trout

The vast weed growth on England's startlingly clear chalk streams creates perfect resting and feeding places for trout, says river fly fishing expert Charles Jardine.

Fishing for trout in summer on one of the rare, idyllic chalk streams of Southern England is something all too few anglers experience these days – the expense and difficulty of booking puts it out of the reach of most. But should the chance come your way, you'll find it pays to understand what makes chalk streams special.

▼ *A beautiful rainbow comes to the net from this clear, reed-fringed stream on a fine day in late summer – tempted by a dry fly.*

Streams to try

The problem with chalk streams is that there are not very many of them. Since they offer such magnificent fishing, owners charge heavily for fishing rights. They are also booked up months in advance. The fisheries listed here offer some day ticket fishing at a reasonable price.
● **Dever Springs Trout Fishery,** near Andover, Hants. (Tel 01264 72592.)
● **Rockbourne Trout Fishery,** Rockbourne, Fordingbridge, Hampshire SP6 1QG. (Tel 017253 603 or 01425 52479.)
● **Rooksbury Mill Trout Fishery,** Rooksbury Road, Andover, Hampshire. (Tel 01264 52921.)
● **Powder Mills Fishery** (part of Albury Estate Fisheries), Chilworth, near Guildford, Surrey. (Tel 01483 570419.)

Since all rivers and streams owe their existence to rain, you might expect them all to have a similar flow and appearance – but this is far from the case.

The streams that thread their way down mountains and hillsides and tumble through valleys – although fed to a certain extent from springs – rely almost entirely for their water on rainfall and snowfall. They trickle down or run in spate according to how little or how much water has fallen to swell the flow. Chalk streams are quite different. Their water comes mainly from springs fed by deep underground resources (aquafers) which collect and hold huge amounts of rainwater.

As a direct result the true chalk stream offers fish one of the richest, most stable of all freshwater habitats. The chalk stream is 'born' on the downlands of eastern and southern England. Rain works its way through the porous chalk, gathering calcium, phosphates and other nutrients, and comes to rest in aquafers deep below the surface. Eventually the water appears in springs at ground level, creating the infant chalk stream. It can take four months – or even longer – for the water to surface in a spring after falling as rain.

Chalk streams are fed by underground springs which maintain a high water level and keep the temperature fairly constant in summer.

water crowfoot

Undercut banks provide sheltered lies for trout and grayling.

Unique features

This process of delay creates a variety of special features. The temperature of the water is remarkably stable. Even in the warmest weather it is rare for a chalk stream to rise above 12°C (54°F) – or to fall lower than 9°C (48°F) in cold weather.

The ever-present system of springs, often along the river's entire length, provides a con-

▲ *Chalk streams are famous for their lush growth of weed which provides trout with excellent cover and also harbours a host of insects for food. Hollows in undercut banks are favourite lies for the fish.*

▶ *The extreme clarity of most chalk streams means it's essential to approach the water with extreme stealth and caution – this dry fly angler on the River Itchen has found a handy patch of tall plants to disguise his presence.*

SUMMER ON A SOUTHERN CHALK STREAM

Dense bankside vegetation and overhanging trees also supply shade and security to fish – especially in the summer months.

Mayfly nymphs, and freshwater shrimp hide in the weeds.

brown trout

Chalk streams are rich in aquatic insects and plant life. The ample food and shelter often support large numbers of big river trout.

The stream bed is usually gravel, silt or a mixture of the two.

The speed of the current is much slower near the bottom of the river. Trout often lie in deep holes in very slow water, waiting for nymphs or freshwater shrimps to drift past.

Tip *What to wear*

Sombre, unobtrusive clothing is a must when you are fishing ultra-clear chalk streams.

If the water is not too deep, wading can make casting easier. Wear thigh waders with cleated rubber soles that give a good grip on gravel, but bear in mind that wading isn't allowed everywhere.

sistent level of water and also a permanent saturation of vital calcium, nitrates and carbon dioxides. These, in turn, give rise to the startling clarity and purity of chalk streams.

Speed of flow is also fairly constant. A chalk stream is far less likely to flood or suffer the huge variation in flow of other rivers. Flow in a chalk stream is balanced, though swift – it runs at about 4mph (fast walking pace) along its length from source to mouth. Flow of water at the surface is much faster than it is deeper down.

Finding trout lies
These rich, stable conditions mean plant and animal life prospers. Anglers often think chalk streams are for game fish only – even now most of the larger rivers have salmon and sea trout runs, though they are more familiar as trout rivers. But the richness of chalk streams in fact encourages most running water fish – roach, dace, barbel, chub, pike and grayling can all reach specimen weights here.

Weed growth in chalk streams is heavy, rooted in the gravelly or pebbly bed. Look for trout sheltering among the thick swathes of

water crowfoot and banks of starwort that create excellent lies in the channels – perfect resting and feeding places for the fish.

Man-made hatch pools and weir pools, with their reverse flows and overhanging trees, are all-important fish-attracting features. The hatch pool pushes water through a small controlled opening, creating a mini weir pool. This makes for a fast central cur-

▼ *All's serene on the Itchen at Abbots Worthy near Winchester. Where weed growth is not too dense, spend some time studying the water for signs of fish.*

rent which divides and reverses to either side. Trout lie in this highly oxygenated area, waiting for food to come their way.

Overhanging trees on any water offer fish abundant security and shade. They are not so important in chalk streams, but they are still places the canny fly fisherman finds well worth investigating – lots of flies and grubs fall on the water from them and the fish appreciate the shade when the rest of the stream is in bright sunshine.

Undercut banks Trout favour holes and lies tucked under the banks and hollowed by erosion and water movement. The fish are often shielded by reeds, grasses and other plants that also harbour a variety of insects on which the fish feed. These are places you should explore, though because they are so close to the bank, you'll need to exercise extreme caution and stealth.

Follow the feeding The lush weed growth, which has to be cut at regular intervals on most streams to regulate flow and avoid localized flooding, harbours a vast array of aquatic insects. Most chalk streams have a healthy population of ephemerals (upwinged mayflies) and caddis (sedges), as well as small two-winged flies (diptera) such as midges and smuts. Every time you go down to the water to fish, check to see if the trout are feeding on one insect to the exclusion of others. When they are – imitation is the order of the day. Most fly fishing on chalk streams is concerned with the use of an imitation of an upwinged nymph (wet) or a dun (adult, dry), though a dry sedge, especially near nightfall in the

summer, can be deadly. You'll find that fishing upstream with a dry fly is the only permitted method on most chalk streams until August, when a nymph may be used.

Check the flow Although the variation of flow in a chalk stream is not as dramatic as it is in other types of river, different depths do affect the speed of the water. Some sections offer elongated shallows which the fish seem to favour during the evening. Slower, deeper sections often hold larger trout, but don't be deceived into choosing larger flies. Colonies of small diptera and other insects mean it's essential to use tiny flies (size 18-20) on fine tippets of 1½-2lb/0.7-0.9kg b.s.

Overall, however, a chalk stream averages a depth of 1.2-1.8m (4-6ft) and is fairly uniform along its length – making trout location fairly constant.

▲ *Retrieving line on the River Wylye in Wiltshire. The white flowers are water crowfoot. The weed growth on streams like this is often so dense that it has to be cut and cleared several times a year.*

◄ *A healthy brownie is returned to its home in the River Test. The gravelly river bottom here is typical of chalk streams.*
This angler is wearing polarizing glasses – vital for spotting fish.

Chalk streams

These are some of the chalk streams of E. and S. England. The lower reaches of some do not have all the chalk stream features.
● **Berkshire** R. Lambourn; R. Kennet.
● **Buckinghamshire** R. Chess.
● **Dorset** R. Frome; R. Piddle; R. Stour.
● **Hampshire** R. Avon; R. Itchen; R. Test.
● **Hertfordshire** R. Lea (above Chingford).
● **Humberside** Foston Beck and Driffield Beck (tributaries of R. Hull).
● **Wiltshire** R. Wylye.

Fishing for grayling

Understanding the grayling's feeding habits is essential.

T he grayling is a beautiful fish, so sensitive to pollution that you'll find it only in clean, clear rivers. The season is the same as that for coarse fish, but fly fishing for them is best from late July or August – when the fish have recovered from spawning – through to early spring.

Basic equipment

You need the same equipment, and similar artificial flies, as for river trout fishing. An 8½-9ft (2.6-2.8m) rod, with a 4-5 weight floating double taper line, is suitable in most situations – Yorkshire Dales rivers, Welsh Dee or chalk streams.

The leader, whether for a single dry fly or for nymphs or wet flies, should end in nothing heavier than 3lb (1.3kg) b.s.

Top and bottom feeding

Grayling fishing techniques are much the same as those used for brown trout in rivers – and the fish live in the same habitat and eat the same food. Grayling are both bottom feeders and surface feeders, rising to the surface to take gnats and other insects.

Grayling waters

A few waters are open to the general angler: parts of the **River Ribble**; the **Avon** near Salisbury; the **Welsh Dee** at Bala and Corwen; the **Derbyshire Wye** from the Peacock Hotel at Rowsley; and parts of the **Yorkshire** and the **Derbyshire Derwent**.

But because of damage from pollution and water abstraction, many waters are highly preserved and can be fished only with special permission.

▶ *Four dry flies to try for grayling. From left to right: Terry's Terror, Treacle Parkin, Grayling Witch and Red Tag. Many anglers find that grayling are particularly attracted to the colour red.*

▼ *In warm weather grayling are found close to the banks of fast streams, and in glides of good depth. In the winter they move into deeper, warmer water.*

The Red Tag

Perhaps one of the best known grayling patterns, the Red Tag is at least 140 years old. It can be fished wet or dry. Terry's Terror and Treacle Parkin are variations.
Hooks: Sizes 14-18
Thread: Brown
Tag (tail): Scarlet or bright red wool
Body: Peacock herl
Hackle: Natural red cock or hen

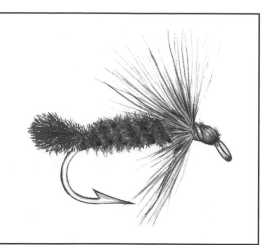

Tip   Other baits

Flies are not the only food grayling go for. Bait fishing with maggots, small red worms or brandlings is effective in autumn and early spring. They also take bread and natural baits such as caddis larvae and grasshoppers.

▼ *A lovely autumn-caught grayling. This fish often uses its long sail-like dorsal fin to create resistance against the current as the angler plays it in.*

Unlike trout, they don't adopt a position in mid water. After a rise the grayling returns at once to the bottom.

Grayling are shoaling fish and all go on the feed simultaneously – when you've found one, you are likely to find more. Shoaling persists throughout the year, the fish gathering in more compact groups the colder it is. All this means your approach to grayling fishing should be different from that for the territorial brown trout.

Choose your flies

In most cases, your aim should be to match the hatch, just as in trout fishing, using artificials to imitate olives, pale wateries and gnats. Fish for grayling at the depth at which they are feeding. If you see a shoal steadily picking off small dark olives at the surface, for instance, try a size 14 dry Blue Dun – it's an old pattern, but the fish go for it. In general grayling prefer flies in sizes 16 to 20 or even 22.

Surface fishing Often the rise of a grayling occurs in the form of tiny sipping rings. The mistake is to think that they are taking a fly from the surface. Countless anglers have suffered frustration as their dry flies have been ignored. The fact is that the fish are taking pupae trapped just under the surface film.

This is where tiny size 18 (or smaller) dark artificial flies are necessary, fished just under the surface, and where the Red Tag – another very old pattern – comes into its own. The nearer the surface it is used, the smaller it must be.

In the north, the spider type of wet fly is much used for sub-surface fishing. Patterns such as Snipe and Purple, Water Hen Bloa and Partridge and Orange are all effective on size 14 hooks.

River bed fishing For grayling feeding on the river bed, a size 14 or 12 leaded shrimp may be necessary. A whole series of flies, such as Sawyer's Grayling Bug and William Rufus, are weighted with copper wire for quick and deep penetration of the stream. In winter, when the shoals may be tightly packed in a deep pool, a heavy nymph or bug – such as the Killer Bug – which sinks right down to the level of the fish may be your best bet.

Sea trout in fast-flowing freestone rivers

In the middle of a hot summer, when ordinary trout fishing during the day is next to impossible, try fishing for sea trout at night. Bill Pennington explains what types of river features you should be aware of.

Attempting to describe one particular river as being a typical sea trout water is virtually impossible. The fish run any river system with clean water and enough gravelly headwaters for spawning.

At one time sea trout ran most of the rivers in the British Isles. Now, however, the runs are more often associated with west coast rivers, although some on the east coast – such as the Scottish Dee, Spey and Tweed – have prodigious numbers.

The River Lyn in Devon, the Glaslyn in Wales, the Kent in Cumbria and the Echaig in Scotland are sea trout rivers which could serve as suitable models. There are many more, but in character they are all very similar: boulder-strewn rivers that die away to near trickles in summer but, following substantial rains, become transformed into raging torrents.

When and where?

The peak runs of sea trout occur in June, July and August, so if you are planning a week's fishing holiday, mid July is your best

▼*Though sea trout fishing is usually done at night, you can still tempt them from the deep pools during the late afternoon and evening. Here an angler plays a medium-sized sea trout from a deep pool on the River Spey near Grantown, Scotland.*

Sea trout rivers

Bill Pennington recommends the following rivers for sea trout.
- **River Coquet, Northumberland** Ticket information from tackle shops in Warkworth, Northumberland.
- **River Dart, Devon** Tickets and information from Wheeler Sports, 44 Fore Street, Totnes, Devon.
- **River Glaslyn, Gwynedd, Wales** Tickets and information from the Angling and Gun Centre, Madon Street, Porthmadog, Gwynedd (tel 0766 512464).
- **River Kent, Cumbria** Information available from Kendal tackle shops.
- **River Lyn, Devon** Ask at tackle shops in Lynmouth, Barnstaple or Minehead.
- **River Nith, Scotland** Tickets available from W. & W. Forsyth, Solicitors, 100 High Street, Sanquhar, Dumfries and Galloway.
- **River Spey, Scotland** Contact Strathspey A.A., 61 High Street, Grantown, Scotland.

Up the rivers

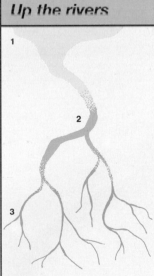

1. Sea trout enter the lower stretches of river any time between late April and June.
2. In July and August they move to the middle parts.
3. In September and October they are in the upper reaches and headwaters – ready for spawning.

▶ *Generally speaking, most of the sea trout move to the shallow stretches after dusk has fallen and can be taken on flies fished fast and close to the surface.*

Tip *The gear*

A 10-11ft (3-3.4m) rod which is rated for AFTM 6/7 line is the best choice. Take a floating and sinking fly line and plenty of nylon (6-10lb/2.7-4.5 kg) for making tippets.

Sea trout flies are legion. Limit yourself to Butcher, Dunkeld, Mallard and Claret and Invicta in sizes 6 to 10. Also take along a few tandem lures.

If you're going spinning, take some spinners and spoons in various colours.

choice, but other months are worth trying.

Water height is of paramount importance to the upstream movement of fish on most rivers. Until the first significant floods of late May and early June, there is no considerable influx of sea trout into the river systems.

Sea trout don't spread themselves evenly throughout rivers from the onset of these spates. Drought years concentrate fish in the lower beats and estuary until late in the season. Some river systems – in particular the big rivers – have genuine early and late runs of sea trout. The River Tweed system is a good example.

Once in the rivers, sea trout show a marked preference for pools with sluggish, deep water. They stay here during the day, especially if this section is blessed with a tree canopy. The fish love shaded pools where they can lie with some security from prying eyes.

A typical pool has a fast-water run at the throat, leading into a deep, tree-covered central part which in turn runs off into a

riffles

medium-paced glide

At dusk sea trout begin to be more active. Tell-tale signs are splashing and leaping.

deep pool

A SEA TROUT RIVER AT TWILIGHT

Deep, sluggish pools, shaded by trees and bushes, are prime lies for sea trout during the day.

long shallow tail.

During the daylight hours most fish are concentrated in deep water. But as night approaches they tend to move up into faster water at the throat of the pool and also drop back into the pool's tail.

The trout won't move all together: the deep water always holds fish. The best lies in the pool are usually tenanted by the better-quality specimens which may not actually leave the pool at all during the night.

As the night progresses, sea trout again swim to deep water and then have a tendency to stay put until first light when, once again for a short period, they move into the fast water at the throat and tail of the pool.

For anyone new to a section of river, there is no substitute for daylight reconnaissance to locate fish – provided the water clarity allows for it. Take careful note of the positions of sea trout, so you know where to fish your fly or spinner during the night.

Some truly wild rivers have deep, slightly coloured water and steep, tree-lined banks which don't make reconnaissance easy. But

The faster, shallower stretches of river contain many sea trout at night. Darkness gives the fish confidence to venture out from the safety of the pools - though some fish remain in the pools all night.

there is no need to despair: sea trout are very obliging in betraying their presence. As darkness falls, you can often hear them jumping and splashing repeatedly in the gathering gloom. Again, mark well the position of the leaping sounds, and concentrate your angling efforts there.

▲ *Incredibly powerful, a fresh-run sea trout surges downstream on the River Lune in Cumbria.*
Usually, the longer a sea trout is in fresh water, the harder it is to catch.

riffles

fast water

Gravelly headwaters and clean water are needed for sea trout to spawn.

◀ *Fishing in complete darkness offers you the best chance of success, for sea trout are very wary and easily spooked.*

Tip **The approach: a brief**

1. It's dangerous wading in fast rivers at night.
2. Wait until it's dark before you begin fishing a pool. Leave the tail of the pool for a further hour before fishing there.
3. Always be conscious of your flies and the water speed. Keep the flies moving through the water during the first few hours of night fishing.
4. When sunk-line fishing in deep pools, work your flies as slowly as possible, and be alert for gentle takes.

is clearly defined by the fish themselves. Suddenly, as if a switch were thrown, the pools become lifeless – though the occasional fish may splash in the darkness.

Sea trout are loath to respond to a surface fly, and the angler must now revert to a deeply sunk lure up to 7.5cm (3in) long. fish it very slowly on a sunk line, and stick to the deep-water sections of the pool or to specific lies that you have noted previously.

The third phase doesn't last long – from the first signs of dawn into proper daylight. Sea trout activity during this period is generally confined to the faster water at the throat of a pool when the fish once again respond to the same tactics as in phase one.

Whenever you fish, be careful when wading into a fast-flowing river at night. Always carry a reliable torch and a sturdy wading stick with a rope handle.

▼ *A fresh-run sea trout from the River Conway in North Wales.*
One of the best times to fish for sea trout is just after a summer spate when the water has dropped and cleared, and a new stock has moved up the river.

Why fish at night?

Before deciding on a strategy to catch sea trout, you must accept one strange fact: the fish don't feed while in fresh water. So how do you go about catching a non-feeding fish, you may well ask? If it is not feeding why does it take any form of lure? This is a puzzling question. But as the sea trout can't tell us themselves, we'll have to accept that they do and be thankful.

Sea trout are very shy, flighty and wary creatures. Although they can be caught during daylight, they are much more responsive to lures at night. They feed heavily at sea at dawn and dusk and continue to be active at these times. But this memory dims with time in freshwater. They become progressively more and more difficult to catch the longer they're in the river.

Your best time to take fish, therefore, is directly after a summer spate when the water has dropped and cleared and when the stocks have been replenished from fresh-run fish. At this time they can be very obliging and easily caught. But three weeks later they can be totally different propositions and very difficult indeed.

Times for fishing

There are three distinct phases to sea trout behaviour from dusk to early morning.
The first phase is from dusk to three hours later when sea trout are very active. They rove, splash about in the pools and are responsive to a fly fished quite fast and close to the surface.
The second phase runs from three or so hours after dusk until the first signs of dawn appear in the eastern sky. This period

SEA
FISHING

TACKLE AND
TECHNIQUES

Hooks

The best rod, reel, line and bait in the world are wasted with the wrong hook, advises top Southern sea match angler Tony Kirrage.

The golden rule is always to match the size and type of hook to the size and type of fish you are seeking and the size and type of bait you are using.

It's largely a matter of common sense – a small, fine wire hook suitable for dabs is clearly not up to the job of landing a shark, while even the greediest dab would be hard pressed to get a huge, forged hook designed for shark fishing into its mouth.

Equally, a small, fine wire hook cannot be expected to hold a whole mackerel bait, nor a large, forged hook a tiny harbour ragworm.

Yet many anglers – some of them quite experienced – too often choose the wrong hook for the job. They still catch fish, of course, but they would catch many more if they gave a little more thought to their choice of hooks.

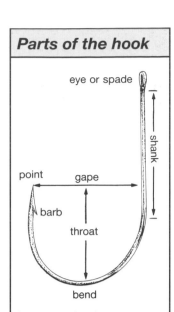

Parts of the hook

eye or spade

shank

point

gape

barb

throat

bend

Large sea hooks are usually eyed, while small ones sometimes have spade-ends.

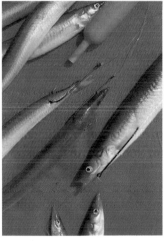

▲ *Aberdeen hooks are best for delicate baits such as these sandeels as they do little damage to the bait.*

◀ *Long shank, fine wire Aberdeen hooks and fresh lug are the perfect combination for small-mouthed flatfish such as this plump 3lb (1.4kg) summertime plaice.*

Basic hook types

Aberdeen

Needle-sharp, this fine wire hook has a long shank and a round bend. It is ideal for delicate baits, such as worms, sandeels and prawns, as it does little damage to the bait.

Limerick

This is a medium wire hook with a short shank and a wide gape. It is excellent for bulky baits such as peeler crab, as the wide gape prevents the bait from masking the point.

Uptide

Also with a short shank and a wide gape, this hook is forged for greater strength. It is excellent for fishing large, bulky baits such as peeler crab for cod and bass.

O'Shaughnessy

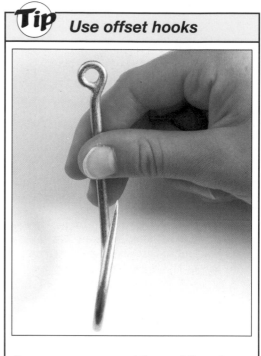

Made of thick, stainless steel, this medium shank and medium gape hook is ideal for strong fish such as conger. It is also used when you have to heave out smaller but still hard-fighting fish like wrasse.

Hook types

Five main types of hook cover the sea angler's needs, not counting freshwater hooks for mullet fishing or treble hooks attached to pirks, spinners and trolling lures. The five are: Aberdeen, Limerick, Uptide, O'Shaughnessy and Seamaster.

The hook for the job

Below are the recommended hook sizes and types for most of the popular fish sought in the seas around Britain.

Mullet are wary, small-mouthed and hard-fighting fish. Use short shank, forged, size 8 and 6 freshwater hooks when fishing with small, delicate baits such as bread and harbour ragworm.

Dabs, plaice and flounders For these small-mouthed fish, choose size 4 and 2 Aberdeens when fishing with worm baits in calm seas. These hooks can also land bonus codling and bass. In choppy seas use a larger and stronger size 1/0 Aberdeen. When fishing for flounders with peeler crab, use a size 4 or 2 Limerick.

Sole Small hooks are essential as sole have very small mouths. Size 6 and 4 Aberdeens are best for worm baits.

Tip   Use offset hooks

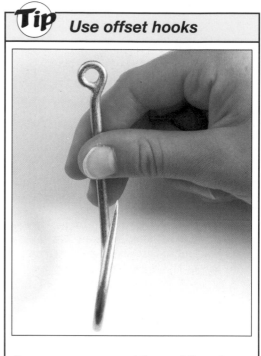

For some reason, you hit more bites when using hooks with offset points. Some hooks come with their points already offset. If not, you can offset the points with pliers.

▶ *The strikingly coloured wrasse is not a big fish but it fights well, has a bony mouth and lives among rocky and often kelp-infested shores – all of which means you must use a strong hook such as an O'Shaughnessy.*

Eels Use size 4 and 2 Limericks for shore fishing with peeler crab as bait.

Whiting A bold biter that rattles and thumps your rod tip, this is nevertheless one of the hardest fish to hook. Use an extra sharp size 1 Aberdeen.

Bass When fishing over rocks, large hooks are essential to land hard-fighting bass. A size 6/0 Uptide is favourite for crab baits, a size 6/0 Kamasan B940 Aberdeen – a stronger, thicker wire Aberdeen – for worm and sandeel baits. When fishing over sand, a size 2/0 is big enough.

Wrasse A strong, sharp hook is needed when fishing off rocks for these hard-fighting, bony-mouthed fish. A size 1 O'Shaughnessy is ideal.

Cod Use size 1/0 and 2/0 Uptides for shore fishing. In these sizes Uptides are also small enough to hook any smaller fish

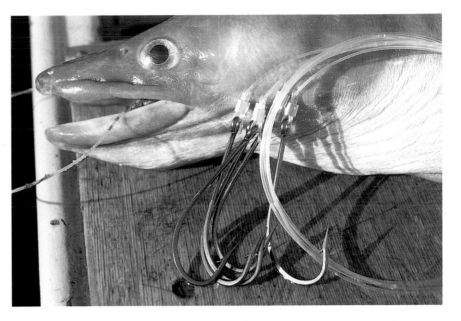

▼ *A wide range of hook sizes is used in sea fishing around Britain, reflecting the different fish you can catch and the variety of baits you can use. The basic range, in ascending order of size, is: 8, 6, 4, 2, 1, 1/0, 2/0, 3/0, 4/0, 5/0, 6/0, 7/0, 8/0, 9/0, 10/0, 12/0 and 14/0.*

about, such as whiting, dabs and flounders. When boat fishing for cod you need a larger, stronger hook – a size 5/0 or 6/0 Uptide or O'Shaughnessy.

Pollack and coalfish Use size 3/0 and 4/0 O'Shaughnessy hooks with artificial eels and fish baits. For delicate baits such as

▲ *Congers are all muscle. To have any chance of hauling one from its lair you need a strong rod, strong line, a large, strong O'Shaughnessy hook – and last but not least, a strong back.*

Hook sizes (reproduced actual size)

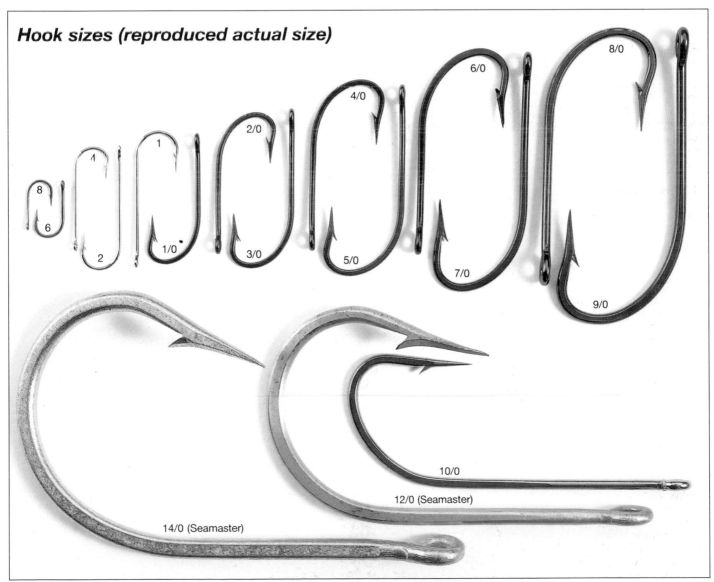

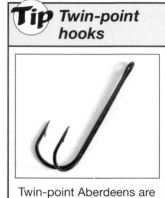

◀ *A dogfish from the deep is brought alongside the boat. Size 2/0 or 3/0 Kamasan B940 Aberdeens are ideal for this hard-mouthed fish. They are made from thicker and stronger wire than normal Aberdeens.*

Tip Twin-point hooks

Twin-point Aberdeens are a recent and very effective innovation for shore fishing with worm baits, because the bait stays on the hook so well. Squeeze the two points together and push a baiting needle on to the single point formed. Thread the worm up the needle on to the shank and line. Remove the needle and the two points spring apart, stopping the worm sliding off the hook.

king ragworm and live sandeels, choose Kamasan B940 Aberdeens in the same sizes as the O'Shaughnessy hooks.

Dogfish and smooth hounds Extra sharp size 2/0 and 3/0 Kamasan B940 Aberdeens are ideal for these hard mouthed fish.

Conger, ling and tope You need a big, strong hook when fishing with large baits such as whole mackerel for these large, hard-fighting fish. Use size 7/0, 8/0, 9/0 and 10/0 O'Shaughnessy hooks.

Sharks The recommended hooks for boat fishing with very big baits for these very large and powerful fish are size 10/0, 12/0 and 14/0 Seamaster hooks. A Seamaster is a short shank, medium gape hook made of even thicker and stronger wire than the O'Shaughnessy.

Care of your hooks

Keep your hooks sharp or you will miss bites and lose fish. One retrieve over rough ground is enough to blunt any hook. For small hooks, buy a sharpening stone and touch up the point every cast. For large O'Shaughnessy and Seamaster hooks, use a metal file to sharpen the point and the edge from the point to the barb.

When you pack up, never put used hooks back in with unused ones – the salt water will rust them all in days. If you decide to throw your used hooks away, wait until you get home before doing so. If you decide to keep and re-use them, rinse in fresh water, dry thoroughly, wipe with an oily rag and store in a dry place.

✖ Bait-holder hooks

The popular bait-holder hook has barbs cut into the outside of the shank. The idea is that these barbs stop the bait sliding down on to the bend. In fact, all they do is weaken the hook. Bait-holders also tend to be made from brittle metal, so avoid using them.

Six essential knots

Many knots used in sea angling have only very specialized uses. For general shore and boat fishing the beginner need actually know very few, says Mike Thrussell.

Learn to tie the following half dozen knots – they are essential components of safe, secure and trouble-free tackle set-ups.

Tucked half blood knot The standard half blood knot can come undone under pressure. By tucking the tag end through the knot a second time before drawing it tight you greatly increase the knot's reliability.

This is a simple and effective knot for tying hooks, swivels, lead links and so on to your main line or traces.

Uni knot This is an alternative to the tucked half blood knot. It is more complicated but is good for tying on hooks when threading worms up the shank and on to the line; the tag end lies flush against the line and does not burst the worm.

Use the same knot to tie an effective stop knot/slider knot on your main line with a separate length of lighter line.

Spool knot Tying line to the spool of a multiplier reel with a bulky knot can make the spool empty unevenly when you cast, cut-

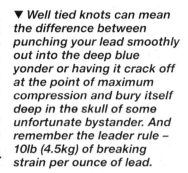

▶ A conger eel takes the mackerel bait and battle is joined. The strain imposed on your tackle when heaving a big fish away from a wreck and up through the water is immense. Therefore you cannot afford the slightest weakness in your tackle. Not in your hooks, not in your line – and certainly not in your knots.

ting distance and increasing the risk of a bird's nest. With a badly tied spool knot there is also always the possibility, however remote, of a fish stripping all the line from the reel. A well tied, reliable spool knot gives you added confidence when a big fish takes a lot of line.

Provided it is tied correctly, the spool knot illustrated overleaf never comes undone and, more importantly, sits flat on the spool, allowing the line to wind on and come off

▼ Well tied knots can mean the difference between punching your lead smoothly out into the deep blue yonder or having it crack off at the point of maximum compression and bury itself deep in the skull of some unfortunate bystander. And remember the leader rule – 10lb (4.5kg) of breaking strain per ounce of lead.

Mike Thrussell's six essential sea knots

1. Tucked half blood
Use instead of the standard half blood knot for tying on hooks and swivels.

2. Uni knot A harder knot to tie than the tucked half blood but a better choice when using worms, as the tag lies flush with the line and doesn't damage the bait.

Knots **1** and **2** are both more secure if you double the line through the eye of the hook or swivel.

3. Spool knot A simple but secure knot for tying line to the spool of a multiplier reel – the spool of a fixed-spool reel too, for that matter.

4. Blood loop A very useful knot to know, especially for boat fishing over rough ground. It creates mounting points for traces without the need for swivels, beads and booms and the like, so if you snag up and have to pull for a break, the cost of your losses is kept to a minimum.

5. Tournament leader The smallest, neatest and, most important of all, the strongest knot for joining two pieces of line of unequal diameters.

6. Blood knot This is a good knot to use when tying together two lines of roughly the same diameter.

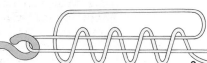
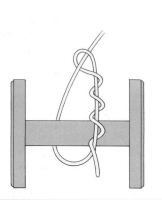

evenly for trouble-free casting.

Blood loop When fishing over rough ground, where tackle losses can be high, this knot is an effective way of creating mounting points for hook traces and does away with the need for expensive swivels and booms.

If you tie the loops in very long they are ideal for presenting muppets and artificial eels above a pirk when wrecking; simply thread the loop through the eye of the hook, pass it over the point, then draw tight. You can stiffen the loops beforehand with short lengths of thin plastic tubing so the hooks hang clear of the main line.

Tournament leader knot A shock leader knot needs to be small and neat so that it passes smoothly through the rod rings when you cast. Also, the smaller the knot, the less weed it collects.

The tournament leader knot is the smallest, strongest knot there is for joining two pieces of line of uneven diameter. It is so-called because it is used by many top tournament casters.

If you use a multiplier reel, always lay the knot to one side of the spool before casting, otherwise it can cut your thumb badly as it leaves the spool.

Blood knot This is a good knot for joining two lines of roughly equal diameter and is very strong under a direct pull. It is a little bulky, but not so much that it doesn't pass smoothly enough through the rod rings when you cast. Maximum strength is achieved by making sure that each length of line is wound at least eight times around the other.

Tip Use clippers, not teeth

Use nail clippers not teeth to trim knots unless you enjoy regular visits to the dentist! You don't need to leave a long tag. If you have tied the knot correctly, next to no further tightening occurs. About 2mm of tag proud of the knot is plenty.

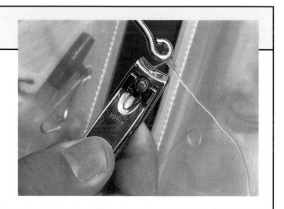

◀ *A fine double-figure cod to put a broad grin on any angler's face. Such fish are strong and heavy enough to expose any weakness in your tackle, yet every year many big fish are lost because of inadequately tied knots.*

Tip Tight lines

All knots should be drawn tight slowly after being lubricated with saliva to eliminate friction burns, which weaken line. Don't tug sharply on the line to tighten a knot – it stretches and weakens it. A knot that won't tighten easily is badly tied and should be scrapped.

Leads and booms

Lead weights and booms are the basis of most saltwater terminal rigs. John Holden explains the when, why and how of using the huge variety available.

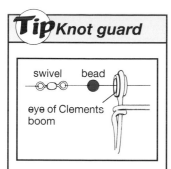
Saltwater tackle relies heavily on weights and booms to get the bait to where the fish are feeding in a way they find attractive. There is a large and often confusing variety of both kinds of terminal tackle – much of it designed to do a fairly specialized job. Knowing when to use each item of tackle can save you time and hassle and make your fishing more satisfying.

Weights for saltwater

Choosing the right lead weight is important in both beach and boat fishing. Many beginners make the mistake of thinking that size is all that matters – the deeper the water and the bigger the waves, the heavier the lead should be.

Simply increasing weight to overcome tide, waves and so on seems a logical plan and, for lowering baits straight down into deep water, it works. That is why an egg or cone-shaped lead, weighing between 6oz-2lb (170-900g), has become the usual choice for general boat angling.

For bottom fishing over very deep marks swept by powerful currents, experienced anglers use wire line instead of Dacron or monofilament. Wire line is much thinner than nylon of the same breaking strain and so presents much less resistance to the current. This means that less lead is needed to hold bottom.

Wire line has the added advantage that it does not stretch like nylon, so bites are much more positive in deep water. To be effective, line and weight must be chosen as a team. Always ask the skipper's advice, otherwise your baits may never reach the bottom.

Wired leads

For surfcasting and uptide boat fishing, there are other considerations besides

▶ In a boat you can reach marks well offshore, but away from the shelter of the coast, tides can be very strong. This requires the use of heavy weights to reach the sea bed. If the tide is not too strong, light tackle such as this pirking gear is much more sporting and more fun.

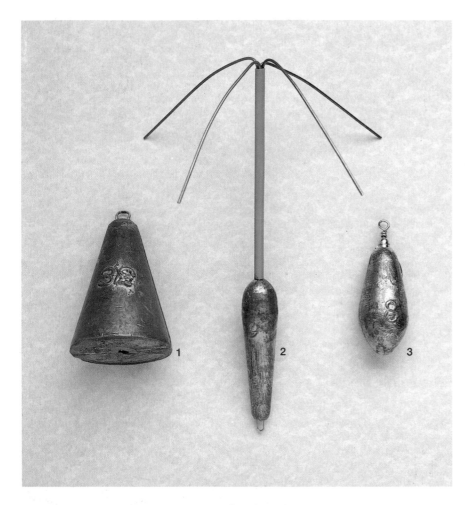

▲ *A selection of boat leads for a variety of situations: A 2lb (900g) conical lead for general boat use (1), a 6oz (170g) wired uptide lead for boat casting (2) and an 8oz (227g) bomb (3) for fishing in light tides.*

weight. Long casting – essential in many cases – requires the use of bomb or torpedo-shaped leads. Also, few fishermen, or their rods, can handle more than 6oz (170g). Besides, even a massive chunk of lead alone cannot possibly anchor tackle against strong lateral tides. If you were to use a plain lead on most cod or bass beaches, the tackle would be swept back ashore within a few minutes. The answer is to use a wired lead. These are available in weights of between 3-8oz (85-227g) and in fixed or breakaway forms.

A fixed-wire lead has wires sprouting from the nose which act as mini grapnels, anchoring the tackle to the sea bed almost regardless of wind and tide. An 8oz (227g) wired lead sits tight where a 24oz (680g) plain weight rolls uncontrollably. The only drawback is that the wires sometimes get caught up on the retrieve. They are supposed to bend out of the way of snags but, as every angler knows, rocks and weeds can be remarkably clever when it comes to stealing tackle.

The breakaway lead is designed to overcome problems with the retrieve. The wires are fixed during the cast and while the bait lies on the sea bed, but they swivel free to trail behind when you recover your tackle. This combination of high grip and easy handling has made the breakaway the standard choice for beachcasting and uptiding. The best weight for long distance casting is 5¼oz (150g) and it copes well with most conditions and bait sizes.

Other weights

Heavyweight eggs and wired bombs are the main weapons against water depth and tide. Often the angler has no choice but to use them even though they require heavier tackle than the fish themselves deserve. Sometimes though, the sea lies calm with little or no tide. This is the time to let your tackle roll slowly along the sea bed. For this you'll need a 2-6oz (57-170g) plain torpedo or bomb for beach and uptide fishing, and 4-10oz (113-284g) for boat fishing in deeper water.

For spinning the weights must lie close to the line to minimize water resistance during the retrieve. The best weights for this are Jardine spirals which you can change without cutting the line, or Wye leads which help to reduce line twist. Pierced barrels are also used for spinning, though as they slide freely on the line they need to be held in place with beads and stop knots. This freedom of movement makes them a good weight for float fishing as you can easily change their position.

Sea booms

The boom has been the foundation of successful terminal tackle in sea fishing for

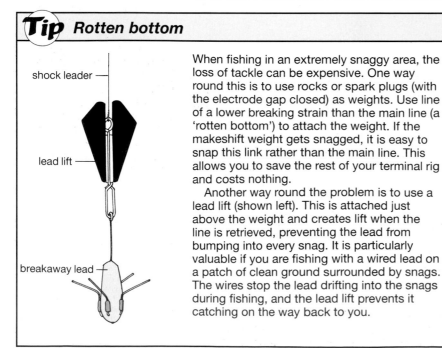

Tip **Rotten bottom**

shock leader

lead lift

breakaway lead

When fishing in an extremely snaggy area, the loss of tackle can be expensive. One way round this is to use rocks or spark plugs (with the electrode gap closed) as weights. Use line of a lower breaking strain than the main line (a 'rotten bottom') to attach the weight. If the makeshift weight gets snagged, it is easy to snap this link rather than the main line. This allows you to save the rest of your terminal rig and costs nothing.

Another way round the problem is to use a lead lift (shown left). This is attached just above the weight and creates lift when the line is retrieved, preventing the lead from bumping into every snag. It is particularly valuable if you are fishing with a wired lead on a patch of clean ground surrounded by snags. The wires stop the lead drifting into the snags during fishing, and the lead lift prevents it catching on the way back to you.

▼ *You've often got to cast a long way to reach the fish from the beach, which means streamlined leads and rigs. A bait clip can be useful to hold the snoods in flight.*

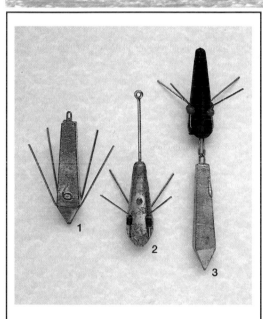

For beachcasting in strong surf, you need a wired lead. A wired torpedo (**1**) has soft brass wires which can be bent with a tug. A breakaway lead (**2**) has rigid wires which swivel when retrieved. A plain torpedo and clip-on plastic breakaway (**3**) – used with another breakaway, they increase grip more.

many years. There are two separate types of boom – one to carry weights and one to carry hook snoods. Nowadays most are made of tough plastic, though you can certainly still get metal ones as well.

Snood booms are stiff extenders which link the hooklength to the main line while preventing tangles by holding the two lines apart. French booms are based on the traditional wire paternoster, but more modern plastic booms and 'bait arms' do the same job. Thread them on to the line

and hold them in place with stop knots.

Fold-flat booms work on the same principle but have the advantage of lying alongside the leader for casting. Casting distances improve and baits are less liable to damage as they aren't left to flap during the cast. Once underwater, the boom swings out at right angles to the leader once more. You need a bait clip to hold the baited hook in position and it is important that you assemble the whole rig accurately to ensure clean disengagement.

Weight-carrying booms are key components of sliding rigs for boat and heavy beach fishing. One of the best sliding booms for light tackle is a link swivel with a short length of rigid plastic tube pushed tightly into the eye. This tube carries the reel line. Booms like this can be bought, or made at home from plain swivels and a short length of plastic sleeve – the tube from a ballpoint-pen for example.

These DIY booms are excellent for light boat work of all kinds, but they should not be used for long range casting unless the line running through the tube is at least 50lb

Breakaways

The breakaway lead ready for casting (**1**). The rollers sit in grooves on the lead, holding the wires rigid for grip. When retrieved, the wires swivel out of the way (**2**). In really rough conditions some anglers increase the tension needed to break the grip by looping an elastic band around the wires before casting.

(22.7kg) breaking strain. You would perhaps be wiser to avoid the sliding boom arrangement altogether for long range work.

Short range congering and tope fishing from the shore, deep water fishing and heavy uptiding call for a weight boom that is tough and which protects the line running through it. The traditional Clements and Kilmore booms are of brass or stainless steel wire with one or two ceramic-lined eyes for the line. They work well, but are quite expensive and have now been largely superseded by nylon bodied booms with stainless steel weight clips.

Booms with two eyes should always be attached with the 'tail' (the eye which is not directly above the weight) pointing towards the hook. This helps ensure greater running smoothness and prevents tangles, which is after all, the purpose of the rig.

The variety of booms and leads available is supposed to make fishing easier and more effective, not to make things difficult, so select your terminal tackle with an eye to the fish you are after and where you are fishing. But remember, simplicity is the key – if something is not doing a useful job in your rig, get rid of it.

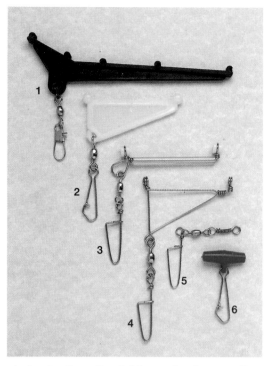

▲ *A selection of weight carrying booms: the Eddystone boom (1), Clements booms (2-4), a Kilmore boom (5), and a more modern type of plastic boom (6).*

▲ *A circular watch grip (left) and a pierced coffin (right) are useful over soft muddy ground as they are flat and do not sink into mud very easily. However, they are no good for long casting and the watch grip is prone to twisting over and over in a strong tide.*

▲ *The banana shaped Wye lead (1) is ideal for spinning, as is the Jardine spiral (2), which can be moved easily. The pierced barrel (3) can also be used for spinning, or for float fishing and the pierced bullet (4) is perfect for fishing with a heavy float.*

Fold-flat boom and bait clip

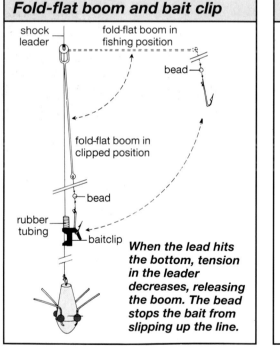

When the lead hits the bottom, tension in the leader decreases, releasing the boom. The bead stops the bait from slipping up the line.

A sliding boom rig

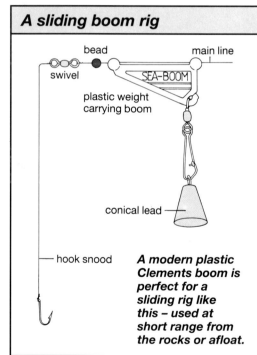

A modern plastic Clements boom is perfect for a sliding rig like this – used at short range from the rocks or afloat.

▶ *Sliding bait booms (1-3) are easily repositioned. Plastic booms (4-5) are held in position with beads and stop knots. A metal version of the plastic boom (6). A three way swivel with beads (7) is an inexpensive way of attaching a snood. The French boom (8) is held in place by twisting the line around the central projecting loop, making it very easy to reposition.*

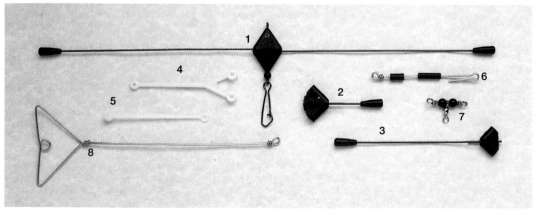

Fixed-spool reels

According to sea angling journalist Bob Gledhill, the idea that fixed-spool reels are somehow second-rate is wrong. Here he explains why these reels should have a place in any sea angler's kit.

The fixed-spool reel still suffers from an image problem in sea angling. It is regarded as somehow being the trademark of a below-average angler. Remarks like these have not been so common in recent years but the idea still exists that real sea anglers don't use 'em.

Pointless comparisons

Fixed-spool reels are easy to use and – ironically enough – it is this that has led to their poor image. It is true that, compared with multipliers, they are very easy to cast with and are usually chosen by beginners for this reason. But an unfair association seems to have grown up between the fixed-spool and the novice.

The issue is further muddied when a multiplier and fixed-spool reel are placed side by side and the advantages and disadvantages of each traded off in a 'which-is-best' competition. This is nonsense. Both are important tools.

A positive picture

Fixed-spool reels differ fundamentally from multipliers. With a multiplier the spool's axis is perpendicular to the rod and line is given out or taken in as the spool rotates. With a fixed-spool reel the spool's axis is parallel to the rod and, unless the drag is slackened – which it rarely is – does not rotate. Instead, line is wound on to the spool over a lip at the front, by means of a bale arm.

The fixed-spool reel's design has several benefits for shore and boat anglers.

Over-runs can be an exasperating problem for the shore angler. (This is where the spool continues to rotate after casting, releasing line and causing horrendous tangles.) With a fixed-spool reel this can't happen. The spool is stationary, so no matter how mistimed the cast or bulky the bait, the line behaves.

▼ *The fixed-spool reel is one of the sea angler's most versatile tools and should have a place in even the most experienced fisherman's tackle box.*

Afraid of the dark? One difficulty when casting from the shore at night is gauging just when the lead is going to land. With a multiplier this means that slowing the spool as the lead approaches the end of its trajectory becomes pure guesswork. Since most anglers are anxious that the reel should not over-run, they tend to err on the early side and shorten their cast quite considerably. With a fixed-spool reel you don't have to worry about over-runs so there is no need to shorten the cast.

The high retrieval rate means that tackle can be dragged up to the surface very quickly. For shore fishing the reel is usually loaded with 15lb (6.8kg) line, but when fishing in weed you can use heavier lines with the fast retrieve to winch the tackle clear.

Light weights cannot be cast with a multiplier because of the spool's inertia – it takes a fair bit of weight to get it rotating in the first place. So for spinning from the shore with light lures for fish such as pollack, bass and mackerel, or for float-fishing, fixed-spool reels are the obvious choice.

Boat casting when the target is moderate-sized cod, ray or smaller fish is a task to which the fixed-spool reel is particularly well suited. Oddly enough, although this technique is popular in Holland, Belgium and Scandinavia it is seldom used in the British Isles.

▼ *Some fixed-spool reels designed for shore fishing have a short stubby pick-up instead of a self-engaging bale arm. (With this type of bale the line has to be engaged by hand after casting.) This is to avoid the problem of the bale arm accidentally snapping shut during the cast. Since this rarely happens – except in the fiercest casting tournaments – it is a feature that the majority of sea anglers needn't bother with.*

Filling the spool

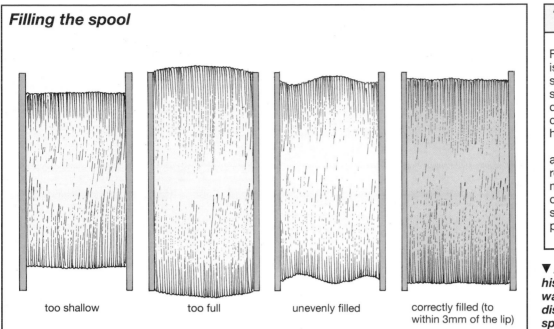

too shallow

too full

unevenly filled

correctly filled (to within 3mm of the lip)

Tip **Even line lay**

For trouble-free casting it is important that the line should lie evenly on the spool. If your reel doesn't do this automatically you can solve the problem by hand.

Note where the humps and troughs are when the reel is full. Then remove most of the line and wind on compensating humps so that as the reel fills the profile becomes level.

▼ *A hopeful angler punches his bait out into the open waters. Casting moderate distances with a fixed-spool is a relatively simple matter even for the novice.*

A limitation

Although fixed-spool reels are versatile they have a drawback. They are unsuitable for boat fishing with heavy sinkers in deep water. The high retrieve rate, combined with the right angle through which the line is pulled as it comes on to the spool, makes it difficult to pull up heavy weights without a pumping action. Fixed-spool reels are not as strong as heavy duty multipliers and break down under severe stress.

Buying a reel

Of the scores of fixed-spool reels available only a few are suitable for sea fishing. Most are not robust enough to cope with casting heavy weights (and this is true of many freshwater reels which look as though they might do the job). Rather than rushing out

Tip **Finger protection**

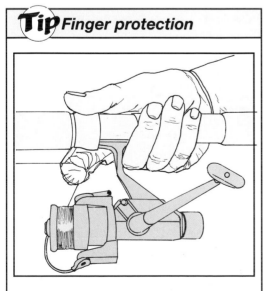

When casting, the finger that traps the line can be cut by the line slipping over it at extreme pressure. You can prevent this by wearing a finger stall.

and buying one on appearances, it is better to read carefully through some manufacturers' catalogues. Robustness and ability to withstand the corrosive action of salt water are the main requirements.

Prices vary widely and in general price is a good indicator of quality – the higher the price the better the reel. Most tackle dealers can be relied on to give a fair assessment of what a particular reel can do without giving you the hard-sell. Top models in the expensive ranges are superior – containing more ball races, machined to closer tolerances and made from better materials than cheaper models. This means that most are stronger and last longer. But some of the budget-priced reels can still cast long distances.

Service and spares Make sure that you can get spare spools for your reel so you can store different breaking strains for all the types of fishing you intend to do.

The largest recognized manufacturers tend to offer the best after-sales service but

▶ *This angler looks suitably pleased with the garfish he caught on a spinner. Fixed-spool reels are the obvious choice for light lure and float fishing simply because multipliers are not capable of casting light weights.*

▼ *Debates over whether fixed-spools or multipliers are better for long distance casting are only relevant to tournament casters. The average angler should concentrate on technique rather than tackle here – since it is largely the angler's skill and not the reel which is responsible for long casts.*

recently there has been an irritating trend among manufacturers towards bringing out new models every couple of years or so and deleting the old models – making it difficult to get spares.

Loading your reel

You need to take care over just how much line you put on the reel and how it is loaded. Incorrect loading is one of the few ways in which the fixed-spool reel can cause problems for the sea angler.

The rule is that the profile of the line on the spool must be level and should come to within about 3mm from the lip of the spool. (If you are a smooth caster then the gap can be reduced to 2mm or even 1mm.) Fill the spool to the brim and the line will simply spring off the front when it is not supposed to, causing tangles. Put too little line on and the friction – caused by the line having to drag over the lip at right angles from deep inside the spool – will seriously shorten your cast.

As well as being about 3mm from the lip, the line should be laid level over the spool. Cheaper reels form humps and troughs in the level while the expensive ones don't or shouldn't. To correct the humping tendency of the reel, hand wind compensating humps and troughs into the level of the spool.

Cleaning and maintenance

Compared with multipliers, the construction of fixed-spool reels is quite simple, making cleaning and maintenance much easier.

Apart from rinsing in fresh water, drying and spraying with water repelling spray such as WD-40, the only regular maintenance required is to run a finger carefully round the lip of the spool to check that no nicks have appeared which might damage the line.

Beachcasting

Casting champion, record holder and instructor Paul Kerry discusses the off-the-ground cast. The most easily learned beachcasting technique, with practice it can hurl a bait out over 175yd (160m) or a plain lead over 200yd (180m).

What it's all about

The aim of any cast is to propel a sinker and bait as far as is possible. You do this by giving the weight as much speed as you can. A flexible rod absorbs some of the power of the cast, so a stiff pole is best, and the longer the better for off-the-ground casting. A long rod produces a longer sinker arc.

However, fishing with, say, a 30ft (9.1m) rod would be nigh-on impossible. Also fishing with a totally rigid broom pole makes bite detection difficult, provides no sort of shock absorber for playing fish and would not cushion any jolts within the cast.

What you need therefore is a rod of 12-13ft (3.65-3.95m), with a soft tip for bite detection and shock absorption and stiff lower sections to transmit the power of the cast directly to the sinker.

Early in the cast, much of the power you exert goes into bending the rod. Any good casting style compresses the rod early and fast – locking up the blank. All the power you apply afterwards goes into speeding up the sinker.

Casting techniques have come a long way in the last 20 years. The refinements involved allow serious shore anglers to put a bait an extremely long way out if the need arises. The improvements in technique have been accompanied by significant developments in tackle design so that average anglers with less refined methods can also achieve good distances.

The ultimate

The pendulum cast is probably the ultimate technique for tournament and beachcasting. However, it can be a little too much to go straight on to this from an overhead thump. It's best to work on your casting in three separate stages.

Start with the off-the-ground or South African cast, progress to a simple side-to-side type pendulum and finally, when you are ready, move on to the full-blooded pendulum cast. To get you started, this feature covers only the off-the-ground cast. The more advanced techniques are explained in most books on beachcasting.

The three-stage approach has two main advantages. Firstly, casting off-the-gound teaches important lessons about body rotation and punching the bait out, while the side-to-side pendulum gets you used to the idea of a moving lead before you try to master the intricacies of the pendulum proper.

The second advantage is that each of the stages is itself a good practical casting style. You may find the off-the-ground cast suits you perfectly, letting you blast your baits over the horizon. In that case there's no need to look any further.

Off-the-ground

The off-the-ground cast starts with a static sinker, so you can check that everything is set up correctly before you even move. With a pendulum cast, once the sinker starts to move towards the set up position, it's too late to check.

Also, the final punch and release is very similar for all three casts. For these reasons, off-the-ground is the place to start.

With the rod fully compressed, Ian Golds begins the power stroke, punching his baited rig well over 150yd (137m) to find feeding plaice at Hayling Island.

The set-up – the angles

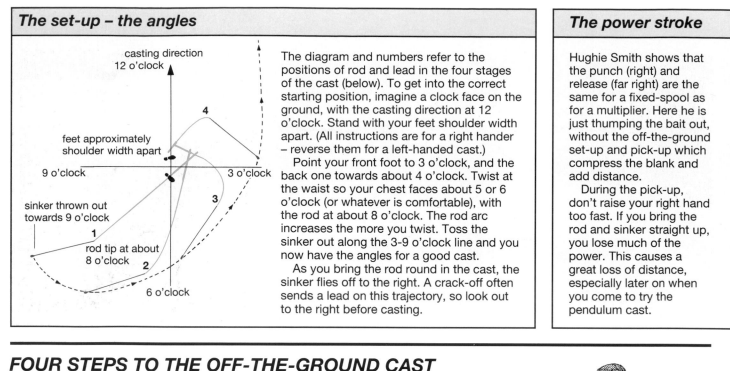

The diagram and numbers refer to the positions of rod and lead in the four stages of the cast (below). To get into the correct starting position, imagine a clock face on the ground, with the casting direction at 12 o'clock. Stand with your feet shoulder width apart. (All instructions are for a right hander – reverse them for a left-handed cast.)

Point your front foot to 3 o'clock, and the back one towards about 4 o'clock. Twist at the waist so your chest faces about 5 or 6 o'clock (or whatever is comfortable), with the rod at about 8 o'clock. The rod arc increases the more you twist. Toss the sinker out along the 3-9 o'clock line and you now have the angles for a good cast.

As you bring the rod round in the cast, the sinker flies off to the right. A crack-off often sends a lead on this trajectory, so look out to the right before casting.

The power stroke

Hughie Smith shows that the punch (right) and release (far right) are the same for a fixed-spool as for a multiplier. Here he is just thumping the bait out, without the off-the-ground set-up and pick-up which compress the blank and add distance.

During the pick-up, don't raise your right hand too fast. If you bring the rod and sinker straight up, you lose much of the power. This causes a great loss of distance, especially later on when you come to try the pendulum cast.

FOUR STEPS TO THE OFF-THE-GROUND CAST

Step one – the set-up

Step three – the punch

Step one With your feet set and torso twisted (see above), get the rod ready to pick up the lead. Hold the left arm out straight – hand on rod butt, at about eye level. Bend your right arm with the hand at shoulder height. The rod points down with the tip about 30cm (12in) off the ground. Make minor adjustments until comfortable.

To start with your weight is on your back foot, with the toes of your front foot just touching the ground for stability. In a good cast your weight transfers on to the front foot, putting your body weight behind the cast, as in any throwing action, such as shot putting or hitting a golf ball.

Step three Now that the rod is well compressed and the sinker is moving in an arc, you must punch it into the sky. The left hand pulls the butt end back and across into the chest, while the right hand punches upwards and forwards. Put your full weight behind your right hand. It helps the arms complete the punch and accelerates the sinker even more. At this stage the rod should be at about 45° to the horizontal.

The punch

The release

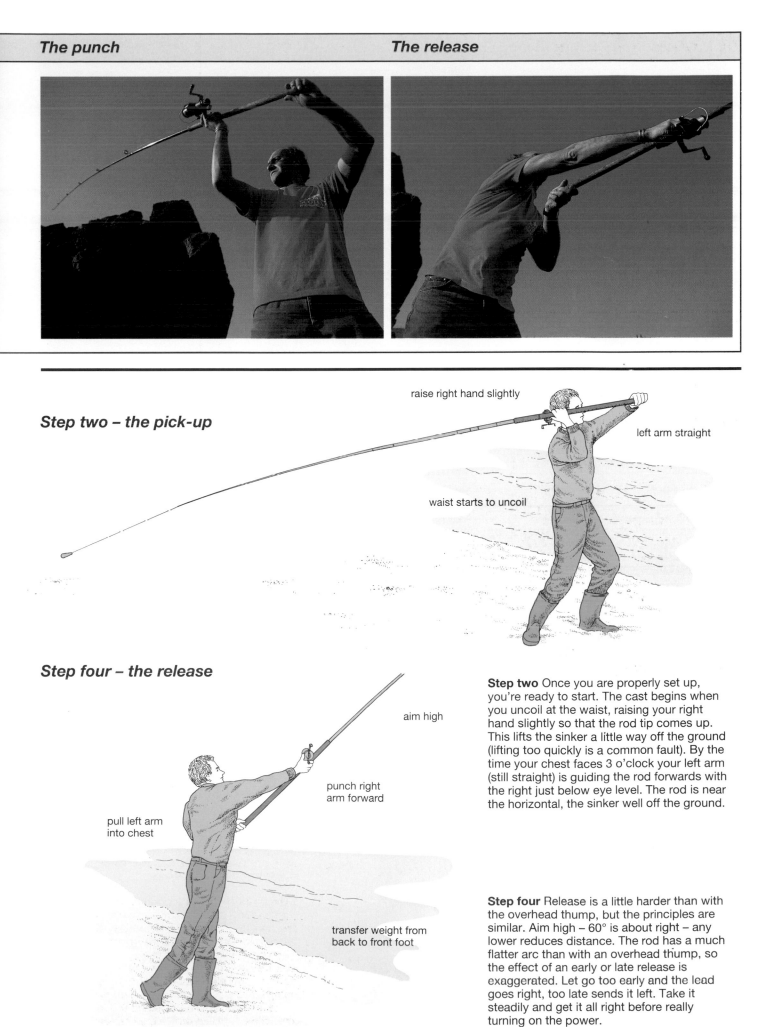

Step two – the pick-up

raise right hand slightly

left arm straight

waist starts to uncoil

Step four – the release

aim high

punch right arm forward

pull left arm into chest

transfer weight from back to front foot

Step two Once you are properly set up, you're ready to start. The cast begins when you uncoil at the waist, raising your right hand slightly so that the rod tip comes up. This lifts the sinker a little way off the ground (lifting too quickly is a common fault). By the time your chest faces 3 o'clock your left arm (still straight) is guiding the rod forwards with the right just below eye level. The rod is near the horizontal, the sinker well off the ground.

Step four Release is a little harder than with the overhead thump, but the principles are similar. Aim high – 60° is about right – any lower reduces distance. The rod has a much flatter arc than with an overhead thump, so the effect of an early or late release is exaggerated. Let go too early and the lead goes right, too late sends it left. Take it steadily and get it all right before really turning on the power.

Tip *Experiment with position*

The length of drop, degree to which you twist and angle at which you throw out the lead all depend on you. The longer the drop, and the greater the angles, the greater the potential distance – and problems. Get comfortable when you set up, and don't try too much too soon. You can always increase the angles later.

Steady as a rock

The off-the-ground cast teaches you all you need to know about the power stroke and release. It is also a highly useful cast in its own right. With a long rod, it can cast well over 200yd (180m) on a field.

When you've got everything right you can feel it, and distance comes without effort. Once the cast is flowing sweetly, you can really turn on the power. You might find you're happy with this cast and have no need to try a pendulum, but if you do mean to learn the pendulum, the off-the-ground cast is the best way to start.

▶ *For decent cod like this from the beach, distance casting can be a real advantage. They are one species for which a good style gives you a definite edge – so get practising in time for the winter!*

▼ *Chris Clark in perfect release position. The rod is aimed high, and all his weight is now on the front foot. The rod tip is flexed slightly to the right, indicating that this is the way the sinker swings round – as it does with all powerful casts.*

Multiplier reels

Whether you're a confirmed fixed-spool caster who's wary of multipliers, or a regular multiplier user who wants to know how to get the most out of your reel, casting champion Paul Kerry has the answers.

Multiplier reels are very popular among sea anglers. Indeed, they are the only realistic choice for most heavy boat fishing. On the beach too, many anglers see them as indispensable, but there are still plenty who regard them with suspicion.

This comes mostly from the dreaded backlash or overrun, which is all too possible with a multiplier but which cannot happen with a fixed-spool reel. However, it is easy to avoid once you know what causes it and what steps to take to set up your reel properly.

Tip *Less line*

Setting up the braking on a multiplier is vital to avoid backlashes but there are other factors. Too much line adds weight and forces the brakes to work harder. A smooth casting action and evenly laid line are also essential.

On open beaches, light line of 15-18lb (6.8-8.2kg) b.s. and a well set up narrow-spooled reel can help you cast a long way – putting you among the fish instead of catching nothing.

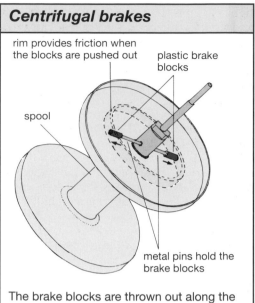

Overruns and backlashes

Because the multiplier is a development of
the original revolving spool centrepin, the
spool must revolve to pay out or recover
line. When you cast with one, the weight
and speed of the sinker as it flies out to sea
pulls line off the spool, making it rotate.

At first the speed of the lead determines
how fast the spool rotates. However, wind
resistance slows the lead, so if the spool
doesn't slow down as much, more line comes
off the spool than the lead needs.

This extra line forms loose coils which
can then catch on the spool as it rotates.
Before you know it the line is winding back
on to the spool but this time it's going on
backwards! Instead of the line coming off
the spool, the excess line is now being
wound back the other way.

With your lead flying in one direction,

With or without?

Baitcasting reels come
with or without a level
wind. The ABU 6500C
(right) has one, the Daiwa
7HT (left) does not. The
level wind mechanism
uses some of the spool's
rotation to drive a line
guide across the face of
the reel. Some casters
reckon to lose 10-15m
(11-16yd) with the extra
friction of a level wind.

For less experienced
casters, the extra braking
effect of a level wind on a
multiplier, coupled with the
evenness of line lay (vital
for smooth casting), may
actually help you get good
distance without endless
overruns.

and the line being wound back in the other,
the least you can expect is an almighty jerk
and a huge tangle. Often your terminal
tackle cracks off as well, which can get
expensive if you make a habit of it.

This can happen with just the plain lead
used in tournament casting. Add to that the
air resistance of a three hook paternoster
and a headwind and you can see how a session of overruns and crack-offs has produced many a committed fixed-spool user.

Braking reels

The solution is to slow the rotation of the
spool in time with the lead – to brake the
spool. That way there's no excess line. With
primitive multipliers, using your thumb to
slow the spool's rotation during the cast was
a good way to do this.

There's no need to thumb the spool of a
modern multiplier if you set it up properly –
the braking is built-in. Overruns are then
more easily avoidable, being due to uneven
line lay or a jerky cast.

Ideally, the spool supplies the sinker with
just enough line so that resistance is almost
zero. This is hard enough to achieve even
under tournament conditions, where your
sinker isn't slowed by bait and traces.

When fishing, you can't expect perfection.
The best you can hope for is that while the
sinker has to pull line from the reel, it
doesn't have to pull too hard, causing you to
lose distance.

The simplest form of braking is using
the end cap or caps. These are the caps on
the side plates of your reel which take up
the side-to-side play of the spool as you

◄ *It doesn't matter how you cast – with a
simple thump to a full blooded pendulum –
if you're not smooth you'll get overruns.*

tighten them. If you take up all this play and then tighten up a touch more, the extra tension acts to slow down the spool. If you rely too heavily on this kind of braking, you can wear holes in your end caps.

Another way to vary the braking of your spool is to lubricate the bearings with oils of different thicknesses. You might be surprised at the difference between reels lubricated with 3 in 1 cycle oil and with SAE 90 gear oil. The thin 3 in 1 is fine for tournament casting, whereas the thicker gear oil provides plenty of braking for a beginner.

This works for all reels, though ball bearings hold the oil longer than plain bush bearings. Indeed, you may find you have to remove the end caps about every ten casts to re-lubricate bush bearings.

The best is built-in

The above two methods work well, but for efficient braking and control they are best used on a reel that features built-in brakes. The most common types are centrifugal and magnetic brakes.

▲ *All distance casting calls for a shock leader. If you use a brightly coloured one, as here, it's easier to see in dim light.*

> **Tip** *Watch the wind*
>
> The better you cast, the less braking you need, but conditions also have an effect. A tailwind produces less resistance to your bait and lead than a headwind, and so calls for less braking. Magnetic brakes can be a boon here. With them you can easily adjust the braking as conditions change.

◀▼ *Alan Yates uses a pendulum cast to help his rod to lock-up early in the cast. Note that he mounts his reel at the butt end of the handle (below). He says it tends to smooth out the cast and give him greater leverage.*

Centrifugal brakes are very popular and work on a simple principle. Two brake blocks are mounted on a pin which is fixed to the spindle next to the spool. As the spool rotates, the brake blocks are thrown out along the pin and rub against a special drum around the pin – a bit like drum brakes on a car. The friction this causes slows the spool.

Removing one of the blocks reduces the braking, as does decreasing the size of the blocks. However, to change the braking you do need to take the spool out.

Magnetic brakes are a fairly recent idea, but they don't seem to have caught the imagination of many shore anglers. Some systems involve a single magnet which attracts the spool and is moved closer to it for more braking. Others involve banks of magnets which attract each other.

They have a dial which allows you to

change the braking externally. It can be a great help if you want the reel to react to changing conditions such as a headwind getting up, or a change of bait size.

The reel for the job

The heavier the spool, the more momentum it has when it starts rotating, and so the harder it is to slow it. This is why multipliers designed for distance casting have light graphite or alloy spools. Similarly, narrow spools are better than wide ones and since line itself has weight, a fuller spool means more overruns.

Small multipliers with light spools are the easiest to control and give the best distances. For general open beach work with lines of 0.35-0.40mm diameter (15-18lb/6.8-8.2kg b.s.), small baitcasting reels such as the ABU 6500 series or the Daiwa 6HM and 7HT are ideal.

Some situations call for ruggedness and winching power instead of very long casts. For mixed ground fishing, where you're using lines of 0.40-0.45mm (18-25lb/8.2-11.3kg b.s.), the ABU 7000, Daiwa SL20

▲ *The classic birdsnest. Avoid it with a smooth cast, even line lay and a well set up reel. You can also get one if you're late thumbing the spool to a stop when the lead hits the water.*

and the Shimano Speedmaster IICFS are powerful but are still capable casting reels.

For really rough ground fishing where casting potential is unimportant but where robustness is vital, powerful reels like the ABU 9000 and 10000, the Daiwa Sealine and the Shimano Speedmaster III are the best choices. They have the strength to allow you to wind heavy lines on to the spool under enormous pressure without breaking.

Whatever multiplier you use, set the braking to suit your abilities. It's no fun constantly losing terminal tackle and line. A tournament caster may be prepared to risk the odd crack-off for an extra yard or two. But if you always worry about cracking-off, you won't be able to concentrate on improving your technique.

Reel set-up by reel type and casting ability

Reel type	Line level	Lubricant setting	Brake	Casting ability and conditions
No built-in braking system eg: Daiwa Sealine, Penn 160, Shimano Speedmaster III	spool ¾ full	SAE 90	–	beginner
		SAE 30	–	average caster most conditions
		SAE 20/50	–	good caster max. range
Medium capacity centrifugal brakes eg: ABU 7000, Daiwa SL20 Shimano Speedmaster IICFS	spool ¾-⅞ full	SAE 20/50	large blocks	beginner
			2 small blocks	average caster most conditions
			1 small block	good caster good conditions
Small capacity centrifugal brakes eg: ABU 6500, Daiwa 6HM or 7HT	spool ⅞ full	SAE 20/50	large blocks	beginner
			2 small blocks	average caster av. conditions
			1 small block	good caster good conditions
		3 in 1	1 small block	tournament
Small capacity magnetic brakes eg: ABU Mag or Ultra Mag, Daiwa PMF55	spool ⅞ full	SAE 20/50	dial setting ¾-max	beginner
			¼-¾	average caster av. conditions
				good caster good conditions/ tournament

▲ *Cod fishing from steep shingle beaches often calls for big casts – which means a good casting style and a well set up reel.*

Rigs for shore fishing

England International Alan Yates provides a comprehensive range of simple yet effective sea rigs to meet most shore fishing situations.

▼ *At rocky venues such as this in Devon, the weak-link rig (or rotten bottom) in a single paternoster is your all-round best choice, but keep the hooklength short to try and minimize tangles.*

S implicity is the key to successful terminal rigs for shore fishing. It's easy for novices to become bogged down in the technical aspects of rigs, and terminal tackle is one area where the armchair experts excel.

Complicated combination rigs may look fine on paper or hanging from a rod tip, but they often turn into a tangle of monofilament when they hit the sea bed. That is not to say that they can't catch any fish – they can. However, a more balanced and efficient rig may help you to catch more.

With the exception of a float-fishing rig, terminal tackle should put the bait directly on the sea bed – where most sea fish feed. It should also be streamlined to aid casting, and strong enough to withstand all the rigours of casting and the rough, snaggy underwater features of some venues.

The line of the rig is put under tremendous strain when you cast, so it must be the same breaking strain as the shock leader. An excellent rule of thumb is 10lb (4.5kg) of line for every ounce (28g) of lead. Go under this guide and you risk the line snapping and causing injury – possibly death – to other anglers.

Attach the leads with a link swivel or a clip. Tied directly to a lead's eye, the line can be damaged when the lead is dragged up the beach. Check rigs regularly for damage from sand, rocks and shellfish. For the most part, hook snoods need be no lighter than 20lb (9kg) b.s., with 25lb (11kg) the most suitable. If you are using light lines for flatfish, for example, use booms. The danger of using very light hook snoods is that strong tides can twist and damage them.

The following 10 rigs offer a comprehensive combination to cover most sea angling situations for most species. By placing them in a custom-made rig wallet and labelling them accordingly, you can store them efficiently – and also keep them relatively tangle-free.

swivel trapped between micro beads and Impact Power Gum stop knots

micro beads

Power Gum stop knot

Power Gum stop knot

◄ ▼ *When attaching your snoods, never make knots in the trace, for this weakens the line.*

Telephone wire (below) and mono or Power Gum stop knots (left) allow you to move the snoods along the trace.

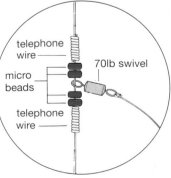

telephone wire

micro beads

telephone wire

70lb swivel

crimp

micro beads

Berkley 40lb swivel

crimp

◄ *To fix the snoods on permanently, you can use crimps (left). Be aware that crimping the line too tightly weakens it, which means that break-offs during casting can be the result.*

1. Basic paternoster This terminal rig provides the overall design and construction for several other rigs. It can be used in one, two or three-hook variations, with a single hook most suitable when you're fishing among snag-strewn ground. It's the most popular shore rig because it is streamlined for casting, and the addition of bait clips aids this even more. Clip the snoods up or down towards the lead.

Hook snoods are positioned along the trace by small swivels which are trapped by micro beads and mono or Impact Power Gum stop knots. Alternatively, you can secure the swivels and beads with wire line crimps or stops made from telephone wire. A proviso is that the hooks mustn't reach the swivel and beads above or below; or they tend to get tangled.

The bait clips hold the hooks and bait close to the main line, making the rig more streamlined. The rig's dimensions, including snood lengths, can be altered to suit the conditions. For example, anglers fishing for dogfish prefer short snoods rather than long ones simply because they reveal bites sooner. But cod anglers prefer long snoods to allow the fish to take the baited hook deeply into their mouths before they move off. Increase the length of snoods to ensure the baited hooks reach the sea bed – this is especially important when you are fishing close in from high pier walls or cliffs.

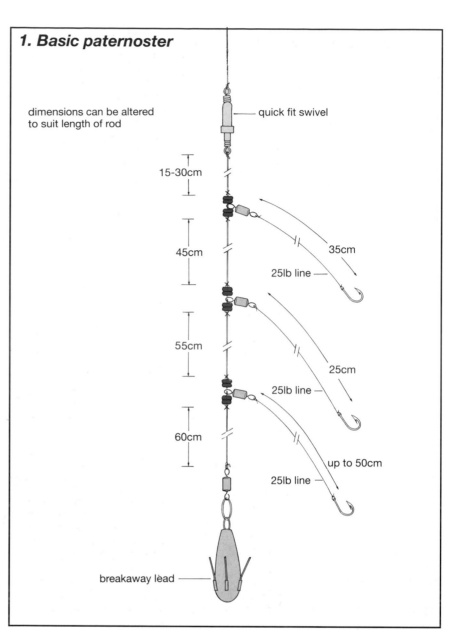

1. Basic paternoster

dimensions can be altered to suit length of rod

quick fit swivel

15-30cm

45cm

35cm

25lb line

55cm

25cm

25lb line

60cm

up to 50cm

25lb line

breakaway lead

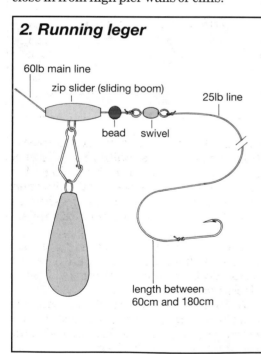

2. Running leger

60lb main line

zip slider (sliding boom)

25lb line

bead   swivel

length between 60cm and 180cm

2. Running leger Used by generation after generation of anglers, this rig is popular among novices when using a single hook. The fact that it allows a biting fish to pull the line through the lead, negating the lead's weight, appears attractive to many anglers. But this offers little real advantage. In fact, a fixed lead is more effective because it helps to drive the hook into a feeding fish.

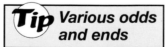

▶ *A single hook paternoster with bait clip (rig shown) or a wishbone rig cuts through strong wind, getting your bait to the target area and holding it along the bottom – where most of the fish are.*

Tip **Various odds and ends**

● Impact Power Gum is available from most coarse angling tackle dealers. Freshwater anglers use it when they are feeder fishing.
● There are special soft crimps which are more suitable for monofilament line. Look for soft crimps which are slightly larger in diameter than the line you are using. Close the crimp with specially designed crimp pliers.

3. Two-up one-down rig

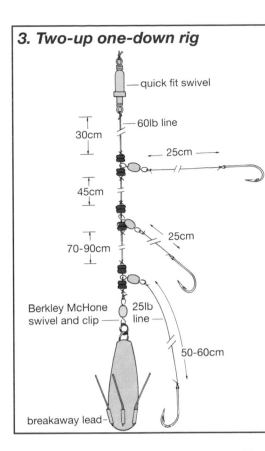

- quick fit swivel
- 60lb line
- 30cm
- 25cm
- 45cm
- 25cm
- 70-90cm
- Berkley McHone swivel and clip
- 25lb line
- 50-60cm
- breakaway lead

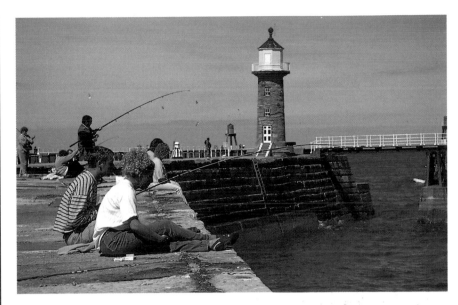

▲ *Mackerel and garfish come inshore in the summer and attract young and old anglers alike.*

Tackle mackerel with a sliding float-fishing rig, and add an extra snood for garfish above the float.

3. Two-up one-down paternoster Two hooks fish above the lead, and another hook, attached to a long trace, fishes below the lead. This rig is popular with anglers fishing from piers or steep shingle beaches.

It is suitable for all bottom-feeding species, and it is ideal in very strong tides. To keep the baits hard along the bottom when the tide is very strong, use short snoods. If you're using a fixed-grip lead, a short twisted-wire boom holds the trace clear of the lead.

Tip **Bait clips**

If you are going to make your own bait clips from wire, remember that the tubing and wire used must fit tightly on the rig's line. Domestic lighting cable, size 1mm, is compatible with 50lb (23kg) plus breaking strain leader.

4. Swivelling wishbone rig

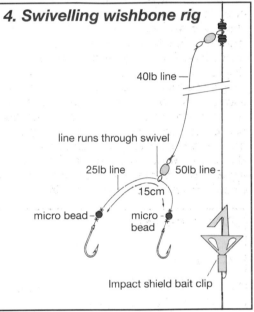

- 40lb line
- line runs through swivel
- 25lb line
- 50lb line
- 15cm
- micro bead
- micro bead
- Impact shield bait clip

5. Pennell rig on single-hook paternoster

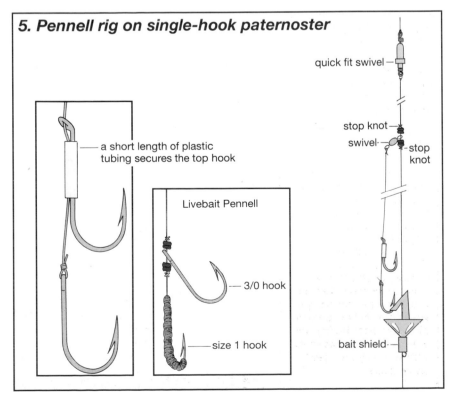

- a short length of plastic tubing secures the top hook
- Livebait Pennell
- 3/0 hook
- size 1 hook
- quick fit swivel
- stop knot
- swivel
- stop knot
- bait shield

4. Wishbone rig The wishbone evolved from the need to cast baits a long distance. It is a streamlined rig using a single bait clip to present either two small baits or one large one. As with most of the rigs shown, it is suitable for all bottom-feeding species – from dabs to cod.

There are two basic designs of the wishbone – the fixed-snood and the swivel versions. Both are prone to tangle if used in slack tidal conditions.

A Breakaway Impact shield bait clip, positioned slightly above the lead, is ideal for clipping down the hooks. The swivelling snood can be 60cm (2ft) long.

5. Pennell rig The name Pennell refers to the inventor and only involves the layout of the hooks on the snood. Popular among bass, conger and cod anglers, the Pennell has two hooks instead of one – this provides an efficient way of hooking fish when large baits such as a whole calamari squid or many lugworms are used. On a simple paternoster the Pennell's snood length can be up to 60cm (2ft).

You can use it either on a paternoster or

running leger. Clipping the baits down at the bottom of the paternoster rig aids casting distance – but this is especially important if you have a large bait.

A type of Pennell rig is excellent when live-baiting for cod. Thread the hooklength through two beads, the eye of a large hook and two more beads. Attach a small hook. Put bait on the small hook, and cast out. You'll soon pick up a small pouting or poor cod which is then left for a big fish to take, the big hook being free to hook the cod.

6. Float rig The sliding-float rig is suitable for float fishing for garfish, mackerel and mullet – and in most situations. By adjusting the stop knot you can fish a variety of depths as long as you add weight to the rig a little way below the float. When fishing in shallow water for surface-swimming garfish, add a fixed hook above the float.

Tip Clip the bait up or down?

Casting with a hook clipped down helps to hold it on the bait clip, but if the bait moves far up the snood, away from it, then you are unlikely to hook a fish. To avoid this, place a small bead or stop knot on the snood above the hook to hold the bait firmly.

If you're casting with baits clipped up, the air pressure may force the bait to move around the hook bend; this seems more efficient, but the choice is yours.

9. The slider rig

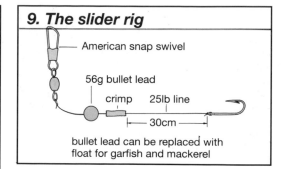

bullet lead can be replaced with float for garfish and mackerel

9. The slider rig As its name suggests, this rig slides down the main line to provide a hookbait on the surface or in mid water for species such as pollack, garfish or mackerel. By adding lead to the snood you can fish it on the sea bed away from the main terminal rig for all bottom-feeding species. It's ideal for fishing close-in for flounders or at long range for most other species.

Include a float or a weighted hook on a snood that slides down the main line as far as the leader knot or the rig's top clip. If using the rig in leger form, you need at least a 2oz (60g) lead to ensure that the bait reaches the sea bed. This rig isn't suitable when you're fishing in a strong tide or among weeds.

6. Basic float-fishing rig

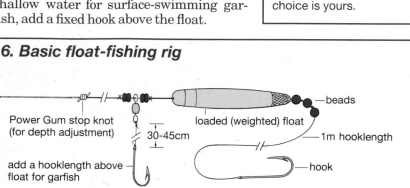

7. Plastic and wire booms

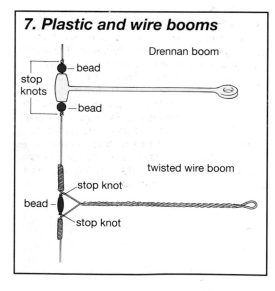

▲ **This excellent shore-caught thornback ray was taken from Co. Clare, Republic of Ireland on a two-up one-down rig.**

10. Conger eel rig

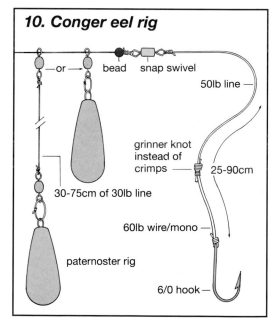

7. Booms The main advantages in using booms are that they distance the snood from the main line and that they enable you to use very light snoods which won't wrap around the body of the rig and break off. There are various types of booms; those made of twisted metal and plastic are the ones used most.

8. Weak-link rig (rotten bottom) This rig is good for single hook fishing over very rough ground such as heavy kelp beds or shallow rocky reefs. The lead is attached to a small open wire clip. After the rig hits the water, the lead falls off the clip. If the weight gets snagged on rocks, the light line breaks easily, freeing the rest of the rig.

10. Conger rig For conger fishing use a large hook (6/0 minimum). A wire or heavy mono length (100lb/45kg) stops the conger's small but sharp teeth from biting through the hook snood. This is when the single hook sliding trace is suitable, although the sliding paternoster is more popular.

8. The weak-link or rotten bottom rig

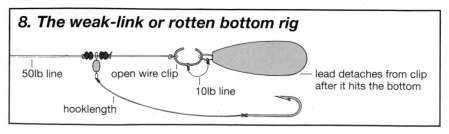

Treyarnon is typical of north Cornwall's beaches. Day is less fruitful than night but you can catch if there's a good tumble. The best state of the tide is about 2-2½ hours before low water – when the gullies become accessible.

Bass on the rocks

According to professional angling guide and tackle dealer Ed Schliffke the secret of successful bass fishing is being in the right place at the right time.

Bass are warm water fish. The time of their inshore arrival and their departure to deeper, warmer waters varies for different parts of the country. On the north coast of Cornwall they usually arrive around the end of March and leave around October. Farther down the west coast – round Land's End, for example – they stay all year round. Although you can sometimes catch them farther north, East Anglia round to North Wales is about as far as they go in any numbers. Often the specimen-sized fish arrive separately from the other fish. In the Treyarnon area this tends to be the last two weeks in July.

So the first thing you need to do is find out when the bass are in. Ask local anglers, fishing guides and tackle dealers and keep an eye on the angling press. It might sound obvious but you won't catch bass if they aren't there!

The right ground

The type of ground is important for bass. Look for an area of rock stretching maybe 50m (55yd) or more from the high to the low water mark and finally giving way to sand. (Steep rocky headlands dropping severely into very deep water are not suitable.)

The main attraction for bass is food. If the rocks are weed-free and polished smooth there won't be much of that. What you are after is weedy, ideally mussel-covered rock, traversed by crab-infested gullies, and riddled with fissures, nooks and crannies stuffed with natural yum! If the gullies

have sandy bottoms then so much the better. The gullies are really the key elements because bass swim up and down them rather like the way we walk up and down a pavement – except they eat their dinners out of them! The angler aims to 'trap' or ambush the bass in these gullies.

Time and tide

Under the right conditions you can catch during the day, but late evening and night are without doubt best. Fishing the tide down to low water is nearly always more

▼ *To catch a fish like this, you have to go out at the right time of the year and under perfect conditions. Bass never make it into some of our northerly waters and even in the south the season varies. So you must find out when the bass are in – if at all. When it comes to bait, peelers are perhaps the greatest bass all-rounder but lug, rag and sandeel can score.*

successful than fishing up to high tide. (In most places, you can work out when low tide is by looking up the time of the high tide prior to a session and adding about six hours and ten minutes.)

For example, let's say that on a particular day low water is at midnight and that sunset's at around 9:00pm. The theory is that during the day big fish (5lb/2.3kg or more) are out in open water chasing shoals of mackerel and pilchards. Twilight offers them security to swim confidently into gullies and search for crabs, prawns, sandeels and other delicacies.

Often they come in for only an hour – just cruising around. In our example this would be around 9:30-10:30pm. The hour either side of low water can be very poor. The reason is that as the gullies empty the bass feeding area widens out once more, making the bass less likely to come across your bait.

Sometimes as the tide begins to flood back into the gullies they concentrate again. You should know straight away if they've returned. If you don't get an indication pretty soon, don't waste time – move on to another mark or knock it on the head altogether. In any case you never seem to get as many fish as on the backtide.

The right conditions

Unfortunately for the holidaymaker – who often hasn't a choice – fishing in the right conditions is essential. If the weather is wrong there's no point bothering.

Daytime bassing is best during a reasonable tumble – when there's a lively wave action. This helps to churn up the bottom, putting plenty of colour in the water and releasing food. For this reason a storm beach with a prevailing wind blowing on to the rocks is best. A bright, sunny day can be okay if there's a lively sea but an overcast day is generally better.

Night fishing isn't easy. Remember that you are casting into tight spaces and you want the bait to stay there. This is difficult enough without the added aggravation of darkness, strong currents, wind and loose weed washing about.

A still evening with very little wave movement – no more than 60cm (2ft) – is essential. (And don't forget, even on a still evening, an area of low pressure right out to sea can bring up a heavy swell, making it unsuitable for fishing.) If you do want to fish a windy night, a lee beach where the wind is blowing over the top is best. Bright moonlight is convenient.

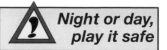

Night or day, play it safe

Some gullies in the Treyarnon area can be 3m (10ft) deep or more and falling into one, irrespective of whether it is full, can be lethal.

● When fishing at night never go alone. At least one of you must know the area intimately.

● Stay close together at all times.

● Unless the moonlight is extremely bright, wear a headlamp. But be careful – outside the beam it is completely dark which can be very disorientating for the wearer.

● If you are fishing when the tide is flooding, beware of getting cut off. Some of the gullies may be 30m (33yd) or more behind you, but they fill eventually!

A typical bass beach – what to look for

Rocky headlands on each side of a surf beach are common features (right). It is around these low-lying rocks that you find bass. Look for fingers of rock jutting out from the main body. Bass must pass these to enter and leave their feeding ground and they make ideal ambush points **(1)**. Gullies into which bass swim in search of food are ideal because you can 'trap' them on the backtide.

Sheltered (lee) beaches are best at night while rougher (storm) beaches are best in the day **(2)**.

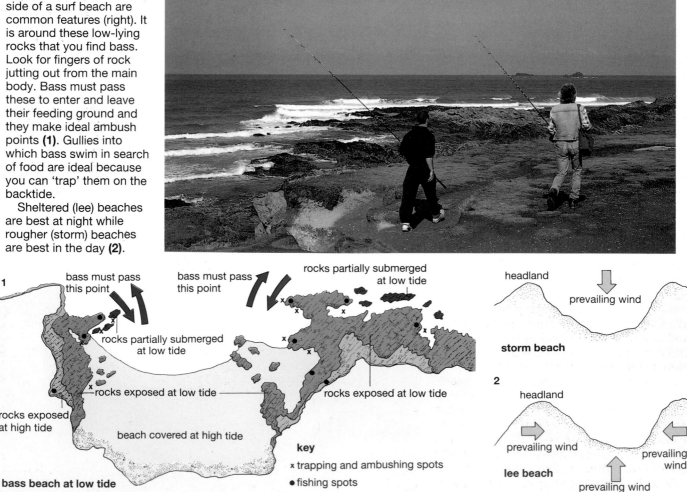

1

bass must pass this point

bass must pass this point

rocks partially submerged at low tide

rocks partially submerged at low tide

rocks exposed at low tide

rocks exposed at low tide

rocks exposed at high tide

beach covered at high tide

bass beach at low tide

key
× trapping and ambushing spots
● fishing spots

headland

prevailing wind

storm beach

2

headland

prevailing wind

prevailing wind

prevailing wind

lee beach

A simple rig and bait for bass

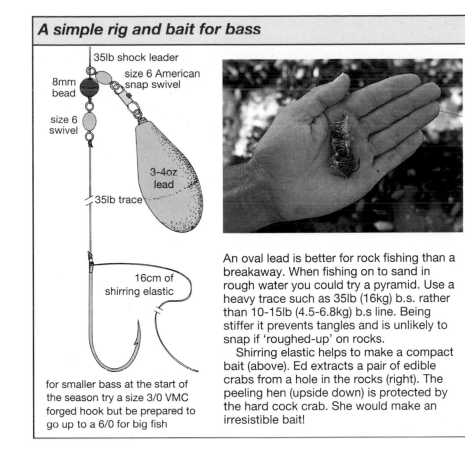

35lb shock leader
size 6 American snap swivel
8mm bead
size 6 swivel
3-4oz lead
35lb trace
16cm of shirring elastic

for smaller bass at the start of the season try a size 3/0 VMC forged hook but be prepared to go up to a 6/0 for big fish

An oval lead is better for rock fishing than a breakaway. When fishing on to sand in rough water you could try a pyramid. Use a heavy trace such as 35lb (16kg) b.s. rather than 10-15lb (4.5-6.8kg) b.s line. Being stiffer it prevents tangles and is unlikely to snap if 'roughed-up' on rocks.

Shirring elastic helps to make a compact bait (above). Ed extracts a pair of edible crabs from a hole in the rocks (right). The peeling hen (upside down) is protected by the hard cock crab. She would make an irresistible bait!

Bass tackle
You rarely need to cast beyond 100m (110yd) and, compared with mullet or mackerel, bass aren't the hardest fighters. A light 12ft (3.6m) carbon beach caster capable of casting 2-4oz (56-113g) or a heavy spinning rod (or even a coarse carp rod) is adequate. A bit of softness in the top is essential in helping you to feel for bites and useful for fighting fish at close quarters, but the rod should not be sloppy. Some reserve power lower down is necessary for casting and helpful if you snag up.

The right technique
You've put together a balanced rig and chosen a likely looking area. The next considerations are: bait, precisely where to cast and what type of bites to expect.

Bait As an all-rounder you can't beat a fresh peeler cut in half with a pair of scissors. On the first cast use two new halves but after that, on each new cast, remove one old half and replace it with a fresh one. This conserves bait while keeping the hookbait attractive. Shirring elastic keeps it compact and holds it on the hook. Fresh ragworm and lugworm are also good – particularly at night when bass hunt by sense of smell.

Casting area The traditional rule of casting just beyond the third breaker may apply to some beaches but often it's not vital. Indeed, sometimes this might involve a cast of over 400m (440yd)! More often than not you can catch bass closer than 50m (55yd) – sometimes right under your feet.

Start by dropping your bait into a likely looking spot – between two rocks at the mouth of a gulley perhaps – and then gradually work towards yourself with each cast, searching the gulley as you go. Especially at night, there's no substitute for having a feel for the tackle and knowing the spot you're fishing like the back of your hand. (Even on a still night you can't tell where a lead has landed by listening for the splash.) Keep a tight line to the bait all the time. If the line is blowing in a great bow around the rocks and the lead is dragging along the bottom, you're fishing in the wrong conditions. Keep the bait still and leave it where it is. Bass fishing is about patience and confidence.

If you are fishing straight out in front you may be fishing into 1.8-2.4m (6-8ft) of water, but don't be put off by much shallower water. In a gulley at night, on a back-

⊗ Missed bites
You do miss some bites. When this happens, don't wind in – leave the bait. Fish often return to it – be patient and confident!

▼ *Ed prefers a good fixed-spool reel, such as this one, to a multiplier. A special switch enables him to engage a preset drag when playing a fish, which means it only gives line when he wants it to.*

Tip *A snag in your favour*

If you are fishing in a sandy gulley and your rig becomes lodged in rock or weed, leave it. If it isn't badly snagged and there's a fish about, then the fish should hit your bait and dislodge it.

ing tide, there may be no more than 60cm (2ft) – just be prepared for the fish to surface as soon as you hit it!

A funny feeling Don't expect bass to pull the rod in – they rarely do. You have to learn to read the bites. Hold the rod all the time and use your fingers to feel the line. It's hard to explain but you have to be really 'switched on' for this type of fishing. Bites on crab can be very gentle, perhaps because the bass are wary of them – they expect a crab to fight back. Often all you feel is a gentle bump – almost as if the lead had dropped into a slight indentation in the rock or between the ripples on the sand. Often this can be a big fish.

Really it's only experience that tells you when to strike. When you feel something suspicious, try tightening up to the lead very gently – so as not to disturb it or the bait – feeling all the while for signs of life. If you do feel a knock, rattle or bump worthy of striking, wind down to the fish as you strike to take up any slack or stretch in the line, and to keep the fish out of the rocks.

▲ *It's easy to see why bass are so attractive to anglers. This one exceeded the MAFF minimum landing size of 36cm (14in). Anything smaller must be returned.*

▼ ◄ *According to Ed you have to be totally 'switched on' while bass fishing. You must hold the rod (below) and feel for bites with your fingers (left) rather than watch the rod top. Often a bite is no more than a very gentle thud. Ed likens it to the feel of the lead drooping into a slight indentation in the rocks.*

Winter shore fishing for cod

Cod are one of the biggest, most widespread species you can catch from the shore in winter, says Alan Yates. So get your kit together, wrap up warm and hit those beaches!

Top cod venues

These marks fish very well but there are many more.
- **Balcarry Point,** Dumfries and Galloway.
- **Chesil Beach,** Dorset.
- **Cullernose Point,** Amble, Northumberland.
- **Dover Breakwater,** Kent.
- **Dungeness Beach,** Kent.
- **Flamborough Head,** Humberside.
- **Hinkley Point,** Somerset.
- **Marine Drive,** Scarboro'.
- **Milford Shingle,** Hants.
- **North Foreland,** Kent.
- **Orford Island,** Essex.

Cod are probably the most popular autumn and winter target for the sea fisherman. Thousands of shore anglers dedicate many hours to them. They grow very big indeed and taste delicious. What more could you ask for in a sea fish?

The British shore-caught record is 44lb 8oz (20.2kg) but any fish over 10lb (4.5kg) is considered a shore specimen. Most shore-caught cod are under 5lb (2.3kg) and are known as codling.

Shoals of cod come within range of the shore fishermen in autumn and stay until spring. The exact timing of this depends on water temperatures. In a mild winter they move in later and move offshore more quickly. In the north of Britain there are inshore cod all year round.

Where and when

Cod are not as common as they used to be due to commercial overfishing. With this in mind, the first task for a novice is finding the fish. Ask about hotspots that are fishing well at your local tackle shop, or join a sea angling club.

No matter where you start, access to deep water close to the shore is of prime importance. Piers, breakwaters, steep storm beaches and rock marks are all popular places to hunt this shovel-mouthed species.

The best times to fish for cod are at night or when the sea is rough and coloured. Cod move close in with greater confidence under cover of darkness or when the sea is stirred up, and plenty of prey animals have been dislodged. Spring tide periods bring the best out of many marks, with the peak time close to high tide.

Baits, big and small

Cod eat almost anything, but while mussels, peeler crabs and ragworm are good baits for codling, lugworm and squid are usually best for bigger specimens.

Small calamari squid fished whole are particularly attractive to big cod. All cod

▼ *Rough weather which stirs up the bottom really seems to suit cod and provides the best chance of a specimen during daylight.*

▲ *If you find a venue that offers easy access to deep water close in, you don't need to be able to cast a long way to reach big specimens like this beauty from Dover Breakwater. Wherever you are fishing, though, fresh bait is essential as cod hunt by smell. A stale bait just won't attract them.*

have big mouths, so a big bait can be the best way to fish selectively for this species and avoid others, such as whiting.

Gear and skills

A 12ft (3.65m) beachcasting rod capable of casting a 6-8oz (170-225g) wired lead over 90m (100yd) is ideal. A sturdy fixed-spool reel filled with 15lb (6.8kg) line is suitable for venues with a snag-free, sandy seabed. For rocky marks and rough ground, you

need the power and ruggedness of a multiplier and 30lb (13.6kg) line.

You can cast a long way with this gear, which is important for cod fishing. If you can't cast very far, stick to venues where casting is not essential – piers and some rock marks. Remember that a headwind makes casting more difficult, as does a large bait, so choose your tactics accordingly.

Fishing night sessions in winter calls for thermal clothes – an umbrella or windbreak is very handy too. But whatever you do, don't forget a gaff or landing net. It's sheer folly to find you can't land the cod you've tried so hard to hook. Get it right and it won't be long before your first cod comes rolling in on the waves.

The Pennell rig

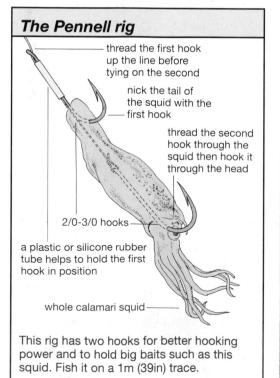

thread the first hook up the line before tying on the second

nick the tail of the squid with the first hook

thread the second hook through the squid then hook it through the head

2/0-3/0 hooks

a plastic or silicone rubber tube helps to hold the first hook in position

whole calamari squid

This rig has two hooks for better hooking power and to hold big baits such as this squid. Fish it on a 1m (39in) trace.

▼ *Cod fishing can be a social activity, and it's safest to fish from rocks in winter in company – they can be extremely slippery.*

Boat fishing for conger

Conger eels often wait inside their lairs for prey to swim nearby, but they may also prowl the ocean depths. Mike Thrussell explains the art of congering.

▲ *Small conger, such as this one, are often taken off reefs and rough ground. Weak tides in summer are your best bet to connect with the snakes of the sea.*

esidents of holes and fissures on rocky reefs, conger eels are the legendary snakes of the sea. Immense, muscular fish of littered wrecks, they are at home hundreds of fathoms down. Wreck conger can reach incredible weights – rod-caught fish in Britain up to 110lb (50kg) with 70lb (32kg) conger common. Specimens caught by commercial trawlers are reported to have exceeded 240lb (109kg).

Despite what many anglers think, conger are not scavengers, eating whatever drifts their way. They are adept killers, well practised in the art of ambushing prey as it passes by their lairs.

War-time wrecks

The best conger fishing is over war-time wrecks in the English Channel. It's here that the 100lb (45kg) fish live, taking up residence inside holes and cracks in the wrecks' hulls. Occasionally you find conger under the debris that often lies alongside these metal monuments.

Away from the wrecks, rough ground,

 **New traces**

If you're not experienced at unhooking fish, never try to take a hook from the jaws of a conger – even a small one. If the conger is large, the skipper leaves the hook inside its mouth, clips the line and re-tackles.

▶ *The skipper marks the wreck with buoys. Get your mackerel flapper or livebait as close to the wreck as possible – even though you may lose a few traces.*

Conger kit

1. 50lb (23kg) class rod (two-piece)
2. Adjustable butt pad
3. Heavy duty multiplier (needs to have a deep, metal spool)
4. Spool of 50lb (23kg) monofilament line

5. Various leads up to 3lb (1.4kg) in weight
6. Packaged conger trace with 250lb (113kg) crimped monofilament with hook sizes from 6/0 to 10/0
7. Barrel swivels (200lb/90kg)

common along the west coast of Britain, also holds conger eels. Commercially caught reef eels off Falmouth have reached 145lb (66kg). When targeting conger you never quite know just how big the next eel may be.

The wrecks hidden in deep water produce eels right through the year. But fishing trips need to be organized around the smaller neap tides – to allow the boat to stay at anchor over the wreck and the bait to remain near the wreck when the tide is running. In deep water conger feed best in small tides and in warm conditions, and in shallow water when light levels are low.

Lines and equipment

Many anglers now resort to wire line because its diameter is finer compared with mono of the same b.s. and, to a lesser extent, it is heavier in weight which allows you to use a much lighter lead. Wire has another advantage – bite detection is better.

Mono suffers from tremendous stretch, so much so that it is often impossible to feel bites in very deep water. The unforgiving nature of wire, though, makes the angler

▲ *A fine conger eel, pulled up from a wartime wreck, comes to the surface, displaying its brilliant white underside.*

Mackerel baits

With its oily flesh, mackerel is perhaps the most readily available and popular bait for conger fishing. The size of these baits indicates that large conger are the quarry.

constantly aware of what's happening to his bait. You need a 4.5m (15ft) length of heavy mono at the end of the wire line just to help absorb any sudden stress on the hookhold when striking and playing fish.

Class tackle To begin conger fishing on the wrecks, whether you choose wire line or monofilament, you would be well advised to select a 50lb (23kg) class outfit. If you use wire, you must use a rod equipped with roller rings.

Your tackle comes under heavy stress and needs to be strong to cope with the power of even an average sized conger. A quality multiplier with a strong spool is essential. Also buy a butt pad to protect yourself from the end of the rod digging into you.

Rigs All conger fishing from a boat is best done with a simple running-leger rig. This means that the lead is static on the sea bed.

▲ *The skipper prepares to unhook the conger at the side of the boat with the trace wrapped around his protected hand.*

The feeding eel can pull line from the reel through the eye of the sinker without feeling undue tension.

Keep the rig set-up as simple as possible. Some anglers recommend wire traces, but commercial monofilament of 250lb (113kg) b.s. is better because it is more supple and less detectable to the feeding eel. The hook trace should be short – no more than 60cm (2ft) to minimize snagging on the wreck. Heavy mono such as this won't knot well; it needs to be crimped to the swivel and the hook.

Hooks shouldn't be too big. Sizes 6/0-8/0 are standard choices, but you may need 10/0s for the very big wreck fish. Carry a sharpening stone and keep the hookpoint ultra sharp at all times.

Bait It's important to realize how conger locate their food – by smell, vibration (through the lateral line) and partially by sight (in the final stages when the eel closes in on its prey). One of the best ways to attract conger is to use a livebait – ideally a pouting or small mackerel. Hook the fish once through its upper lip and lower it gently to the bottom. The conger will sense the

A simple rig

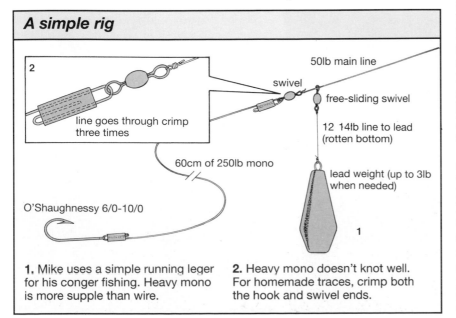

50lb main line

swivel

free-sliding swivel

line goes through crimp three times

12 14lb line to lead (rotten bottom)

60cm of 250lb mono

lead weight (up to 3lb when needed)

O'Shaughnessy 6/0-10/0

1. Mike uses a simple running leger for his conger fishing. Heavy mono is more supple than wire.

2. Heavy mono doesn't knot well. For homemade traces, crimp both the hook and swivel ends.

▶ *An angler watches as the captain reaches for a small, reef-caught conger. At this point the angler should reduce his clutch, in case the fish decides to make a last-minute bid for freedom.*

 **Tip** *Clutch pressure*

Set the drag of your reel at 75% of the main line's breaking strain. This may seem a lot, but if you hook a large specimen, you need to use constant, firm pressure to tire and subdue it.

The amount of line surrendered to a wreck conger must be kept to an absolute minimum in order to keep the fish away from its dark, sharp-edged, rusting lair.

▼ *This is the extraordinary British boat-caught record conger; it weighed in at 110lb 11¹/₂oz (50.22kg).*

livebait's erratic movements and home in for the kill.

Alternatively, you can use deadbaits. Cut a whole mackerel or pouting through the backbone and tail to leave the flanks of the fish still attached to the head. This is called a flapper bait. It provides movement when the bait is on the sea bed, and smell too.

Hook it through the upper lip, or pass the hook through the mouth, out through the gill and then into the flank with the point left clear to penetrate the conger easily.

The take

Conger feed gently – even the colossal ones. You'll feel a series of light taps on the rod tip. Set your reel with the ratchet on and the spool disengaged.

When an eel demands those initial few metres of line, wind the reel back into gear and strike hard to set the hook. Lift the rod, pulling the fish, and as you bring the rod down, wind in line. Repeat the process, pumping the fish up.

It's important to get the conger into open water quickly, for it often makes a dramatic dive straight back to its lair. If the eel's long tail does find the wreck, your chance of successfully freeing it is very slim. Only constant pressure over several minutes may force it to release its grip. Relieving all pressure often results in the conger finding even safer sanctuary inside the wreck.

Allow the skipper to gaff the fish and haul it aboard. As the eel is brought to the side of the boat and the gaff is readied, reduce the reel's clutch so that, if things go wrong, the eel can take line freely and won't be lost if it dives.

Once aboard, the skipper secures the eel in a purpose-built fish holder or in some other escape-proof container. Small eels under 35lb (16kg) are usually unhooked and released straight away so they can prowl the ocean depths once more.

Rough ground boat fishing

Rough ground will test you and your tackle to the limit – but if it's sport you're after, take Trevor Housby's advice and your aching arms may never forgive you!

▲ Rough ground fishing gives you the chance to get to grips with a wide variety of fish and some hefty specimens – as this angler is finding out. The most important thing to remember is to stop a diving fish before it reaches sanctuary.

Fishing from a boat over rough (rocky) ground offers superb opportunities for catching a wide variety of fish. Conger, tope, bull huss, spurdog, ling, pollack, coalfish, whiting, cod, haddock and sea bream all inhabit rocky areas.

These fish tend to gather in the particularly rich feeding areas associated with steep rock ledges and pinnacles. Fish such as conger and huss usually lurk in holes and crevices while other species are more common in the slacker water downtide of a rock formation.

Tough tackle talk
To succeed at this style of angling, you've got to fish into the really rugged areas of rock. Tackle losses are inevitably high, but that has to be expected and accepted.

For all but the smallest species you need fairly heavy gear. You can't afford to hang around when you hook a big fish over rock you've got to hold it hard and hustle it into open water as fast as you can.

For most fish a 30lb (13.6kg) class boat rod is ideal but where there are conger of

▲ A sleek pollack in the peak of condition like this one gives a great account of itself on 20lb (9.1kg) class gear.

Tip Holy buckets!

Take plenty of spare leads and made-up traces for a rough ground trip. Store weights in the bottom of a metal-handled pail and drill holes just below the lip (see below) to hang spare traces.

hang traces from holes – lip of bucket guards the hook points

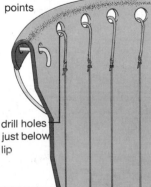

drill holes just below lip

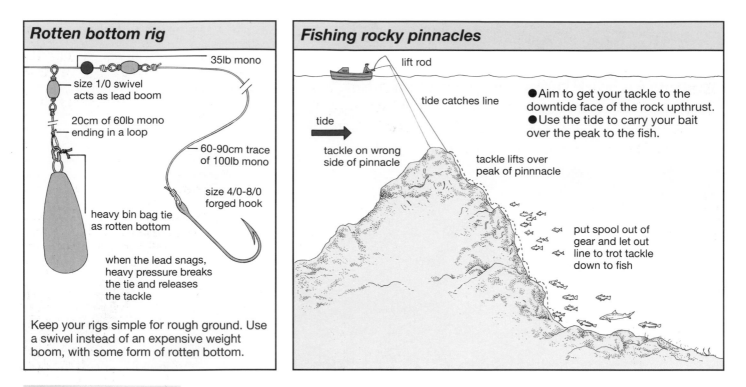

Rotten bottom rig

35lb mono

size 1/0 swivel
acts as lead boom

20cm of 60lb mono
ending in a loop

60-90cm trace
of 100lb mono

size 4/0-8/0
forged hook

heavy bin bag tie
as rotten bottom

when the lead snags,
heavy pressure breaks
the tie and releases
the tackle

Keep your rigs simple for rough ground. Use
a swivel instead of an expensive weight
boom, with some form of rotten bottom.

Fishing rocky pinnacles

lift rod

tide catches line

tide

tackle on wrong
side of pinnacle

tackle lifts over
peak of pinnacle

● Aim to get your tackle to the
downtide face of the rock upthrust.
● Use the tide to carry your bait
over the peak to the fish.

put spool out of
gear and let out
line to trot tackle
down to fish

▲ **Tope are one of the
hardest fighting species
commonly taken over
rough ground. They grow
big too – well over 50lb
(22.7kg)!**

around 40-50lb (18.1-22.7kg), a 50lb
(22.7kg) rod may be necessary. Buy the
best, most rugged reel you can – fishing
over rough ground is a great tackle tester.

For smaller fish a 12-20lb (5.4-9.1kg)
class rod is fine matched with a smaller (but
still rugged) reel.

Pay strict attention to the quality of all
the fittings and furnishings. They are a
helpful guide to the overall quality of the
item of tackle.

Lines and choices

Of the different types of line you can use
from a boat, nylon monofilament is usually
the best choice for rough ground. Dacron is
softer with less stretch and so is nicer to use,
but it parts easily when stretched over rock.
Heavy mono has a hard surface which
resists abrasion.

Wire line is rarely necessary or desirable
for this style of fishing: you don't need a full
set of roller rings on your rod – a tip roller
with ordinary rings lower down is fine.

Match line to rod, but use a breaking
strain slightly over that of the class of the
rod – 5lb (2.3kg) b.s. over is about right
(35lb/15.9kg line with a 30 class rod).
Stepping up the line strength like this
allows you to apply a little extra pressure
when a bigger fish picks up the bait.

Terminal tackle

Keep your rigs as simple as possible.
There's no need to get any more complicated than a running leger with a swivel
replacing the more normal weight boom.

Most of the bigger species want the baits
on or just above the rocks. A rotten bottom
enables you to land fish and recover your rig
even if the lead snags. In areas with little
tide you can use old spark plugs to reduce
costs, attached with a thick rubber band. In
strong flows, however, you need the greater
density of a lead weight to reach bottom.

For whiting, haddock and bream a
simple two-hook paternoster or baited
feathers work well. They present the baits
where these fish want them – slightly off
the bottom.

There is a huge choice of baits but for rock
fishing fresh mackerel and pouting are
hard to beat. For heavyweights a flapper or
head-and-guts are ideal while for the
smaller species a strip works better.

Finally, if you haven't got your own gear,
make sure the skipper has some for hire
when you book. However, the quality of hire
tackle can vary widely, so unless you know
the skipper, try to take your own.

◀ **Big fat cod like this 22½-pounder (10.2kg)
are one of the main attractions of rocky
areas during the winter months, drawing
anglers from all over the country.**

Boatcasting tactics

Boatcasting is a fairly new method, but one that has had an enormous impact on shallow water boat fishing since its development in the 1970s. Mick Toomer explains its uses.

As its name suggests, boatcasting (also called uptiding) involves casting the baits away from the boat. It is most effective in less than 30m (100ft) of water, though it does still have its uses in deeper water.

The best time to boatcast is in a tide run when you're after bigger species. Smaller fish such as pouting can usually be taken more efficiently on conventional downtide tackle.

The advantages
In shallow water, the disturbance caused by the boat's hull and anchor rope tends to scare cautious fish away from the boat. The size of the scare area depends on both the depth of water and the size and type of boat. For an average size charter boat in 12m (40ft) of water, the scare area seems to stretch to some 15m (50ft) on either side of the boat.

As fish move out of the scare area, they tend to concentrate around the edges of the zone. Anglers who find this concentration of fish catch more.

Conventional downtide tactics usually leave the baits in a line downtide of the boat. Fish passing 20m (65ft) or so on either side of the boat may therefore miss the scent trail put out by the baits. Casting the baits away from the boat ensures they are fanned out, so creating a wider scent trail.

Casting into the tide usually requires the use of a wired lead to hold bottom. This means that you can keep your bait on the sea bed with a 5-6oz (140-170g) wired lead where you might need more than 1½lb (0.7kg) of plain lead fishing downtide. A lighter weight is more sporting – allowing both the fish and the angler more freedom – which would make it an attractive technique even if catches were no better than with conventional tactics.

Bait presentation is also different with a wired lead – the bait remains stationary rather than bumping around in the tide as it does when fishing downtide. This point is not yet fully understood, but it is one of the reasons why this technique is successful.

Tackling up
Tackle is perhaps more like beachcasting or pier fishing equipment than conventional boat tackle.

The ideal rod is about 10ft (4.5m) long with a flexible tip and moderately powerful middle and lower sections. Early boatcast-

ers had to use cut-down beachcasting rods but these days there are plenty of purpose-built boatcasting rods on the market. One designed to cast 5-8oz (140-225g) is the best all-round choice.

A multiplier is best for boatcasting but it needn't be hugely powerful. However, it must have a good rate of retrieve and a capacity of around 300yd (275m) of 15-20lb (6.8kg-9.1kg) line. Make sure it has a light alloy spool as heavier metal spools make casting difficult and plastic spools can break under extreme pressure.

With 15-20lb (6.8-9.1kg) line you should use a shock leader of at least 30lb (13.6kg). It makes casting safer and, with a heavy hooklength, gives you a bit of confidence

▼ *The author, Mick Toomer, with a couple of purpose-made boatcasting rods. The reels are powerful without being cumbersome and are capable of smooth casting.*

Boatcasting gear

A purpose-built rod with a flexible tip and a quality reel are required.

Boatcasting terminal tackle

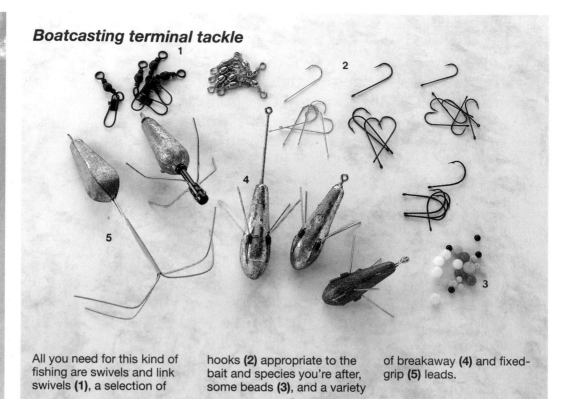

All you need for this kind of fishing are swivels and link swivels **(1)**, a selection of hooks **(2)** appropriate to the bait and species you're after, some beads **(3)**, and a variety of breakaway **(4)** and fixed-grip **(5)** leads.

when a big fish is close to the boat – you don't have to worry so much about losing it. **End gear** usually consists of a single hook rig, with either a fixed or a running trace of 1.2-1.8m (4-6ft). You need a selection of both breakaway and fixed-grip leads of 5-8oz (140-225g) to cope with variations in the tidal flow.

Uptide tactics

The direction you should cast out from the boat depends on the strength of the tide. As the tide increases you need to cast farther uptide and closer to the line of the anchor rope.

To start with, cast about 50m (55yd) uptide at an angle of 45° to the anchor rope.

Fishing outside the scare area

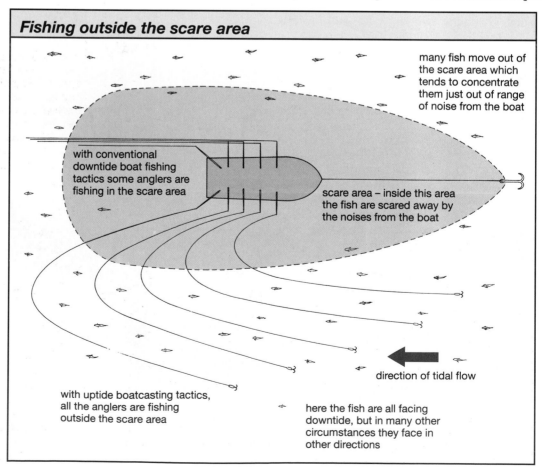

many fish move out of the scare area which tends to concentrate them just out of range of noise from the boat

with conventional downtide boat fishing tactics some anglers are fishing in the scare area

scare area – inside this area the fish are scared away by the noises from the boat

direction of tidal flow

with uptide boatcasting tactics, all the anglers are fishing outside the scare area

here the fish are all facing downtide, but in many other circumstances they face in other directions

Boatcasting end-gear

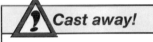

18-20lb main line

swivel

link swivel

— the trace is usually between 1.2m-1.8m long

Pennell rig for cod

wired lead – with either fixed or breakaway wires, depending on the strength of the tide

Find the fish

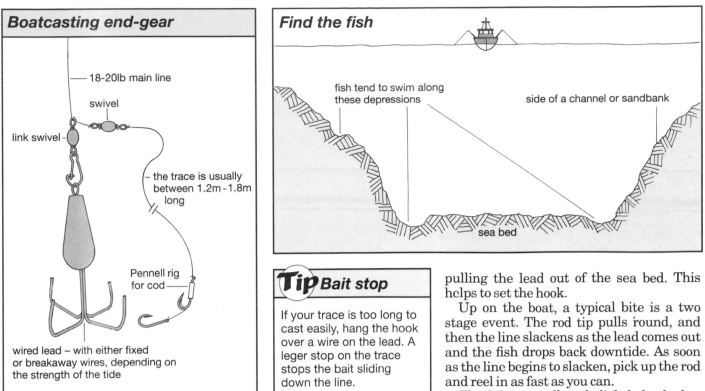

fish tend to swim along these depressions

side of a channel or sandbank

sea bed

Tip Bait stop

If your trace is too long to cast easily, hang the hook over a wire on the lead. A leger stop on the trace stops the bait sliding down the line.

⚠ Cast away!

A boat is quite a cramped casting platform, and safety must always be your first consideration. Make sure you tell the other anglers on board every time you're about to cast away from the boat.

The best way to avoid injuring a fellow angler is to start with your end gear outside the boat and avoid casting over other anglers' heads. This may mean walking to the back of the boat before you cast, but that's vastly preferable to an accident.

Let the line run off the spool even after the lead has hit the bottom. In this way the line forms a bow which tightens in the tide, pulling the grip wires of the lead firmly into the sea bed. The boat's anchor chain and rope works on a similar principle.

The amount of line you need to let out depends on the strength of the tide. Initially you should let the line out until it enters the water downtide at about 15° to the side of the boat. If the lead doesn't hold, use a heavier grip lead, or cast farther uptide and let out a little more line.

Once the lead is fixed in the bottom and the tide has pulled the line taut, put the rod down. The semi-flexible rod tip absorbs the movement of the boat without pulling the wires out of the sea bed. When a fish picks up the bait and moves away, it pricks itself with the hookpoint. The fish then bolts

pulling the lead out of the sea bed. This helps to set the hook.

Up on the boat, a typical bite is a two stage event. The rod tip pulls round, and then the line slackens as the lead comes out and the fish drops back downtide. As soon as the line begins to slacken, pick up the rod and reel in as fast as you can.

The fish is usually only lightly hooked at this stage, and is shaking its head in an effort to dislodge the hook. The sooner you tighten the line, the less time it has to get free. Rays are an exception to this – give them plenty of time to get the bait in their mouth – they rarely drop a bait once they are interested.

Do not stop reeling once you have started. It may be tempting to strike when you start

Tip Concentration

It pays to find any concentrations of fish on the sea bed. These may be due to a feature such as a patch of rough ground or a depression at the base of a sandbank, or to the fish leaving the scare area. Vary your casting distance until you catch a fish and then keep casting to the same area until you stop getting bites.

Smooth casting from a boat

1. Make sure you start with the lead outside the boat and that no-one is in your line of fire.

2. Power the rod smoothly around in a standard overhead thump – just as you might do from a beach.

3. After casting, don't put the reel in gear straight away – leave time for the line to form a bow.

to feel the weight of the fish, but resist the temptation! An early strike allows the bow of line to slacken, giving the fish another chance to shed the hook. Keep winding into the fish until you can feel its full weight downtide of you. Only then should you lean into the fish.

It is very important that you remember to wind the hook home and don't try to strike it there. Set the clutch fairly tight so that you can really wind down into a fish without giving it any line. Once the hook is properly set, you can slacken off the drag a little if the fish is very heavy and likely to take a lot of line.

▶ *Mick Toomer returns a small thornback taken on peeler crab while boatcasting. Many sea species can be taken with this method as long as conditions are right.*

▼ *This fine 64lb (29kg) tope was taken off the coast of Essex. The water is quite shallow in that area, and so it is an ideal place for boatcasting tactics.*

BAITS AND LURES

Ragworm

Second in popularity only to lugworm as a sea bait, the four main types of ragworm between them appeal to a wide range of fish.

Unlike the lugworm, which filter-feeds peacefully in the shelter of its burrow, the ragworm is a voracious carnivore and scavenger that forages relentlessly through sand and mud. Looking somewhat like a cross between an earthworm and a giant centipede, it propels itself along on a mass of bristly 'legs' and seizes its food – small invertebrates, alive or dead – with a pair of extendible, claw-like pincers.

Red rag are the most common type. They grow to about 20cm (8in) long and are usually found in gritty mud. Red rag catch most

▲ *King rag can grow up to 50cm (20in) or more in length and be as thick as your finger. Use them whole for big bass and cod.*

◄ *Red rag in shallow aerated trays of fresh seawater. Kept cool – preferably in a fridge – they will stay alive for a few weeks.*

species but are particularly good in summer for flatfish and bass.

King rag are like red rag but grow to 50cm (20in) or more and prefer sand to mud. They are excellent for big bass, cod, smoothhounds, pollack, coalfish and rays.

White rag are nearly as big as red rag but are much less common. They are found in clean sand and are one of the shore matchman's favourite baits, being deadly for small fish, especially flatties.

Harbour rag, or maddies, are red in colour and grow to only 10cm (4in) at most. They live in soft estuarine mud and are a superb bait for flounders and mullet.

◄ *Harbour rag, or maddies, are as soft as the mud in which they live. Fished on a small hook they are excellent for mullet.*

▼ *White rag are relatively scarce, but no self-respecting shore matchman would dream of turning up for a major contest without them.*

How to hook a ragworm

1 Insert the point of the hook into the head of the worm and thread the whole of the worm lengthways up the shank.

2 Leave the point of the hook inside the worm just before the end of the tail, so that the whole hook is hidden (right).

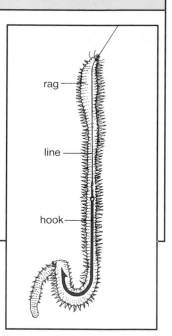

▼ *Flounders are the shore angler's bread and butter fish in many areas. Ragworm is one of the deadliest baits for these popular fish – especially harbour rag.*

Digging rag

To dig rag you need a flat-pronged potato fork, gum boots or waders and a pair of old gloves. Always wear gloves because mud and sand beds often contain hidden pieces of broken glass, rusty tin cans and the like.

To find red, king or white rag, walk slowly across the mud or sand looking down at your feet for tiny spurts of water from small holes in the sand. Trench-dig a patch where the spurts and holes are densest. Break open the clods of sand or mud carefully because rag are soft and damage easily.

To help future stocks, take only large, mature worms and only as many as you really need. And always backfill trenches so there are no nasty potholes for unsuspecting swimmers when the tide comes in.

Maddies are much easier to find and dig. Patches of soft mud pitted with tiny holes yield dozens in a matter of a few forkfuls.

Storing rag

Rag require careful handling and storing to keep them in tip-top condition. Unlike lug, they are only useable live. Frozen, they become too mushy.

Ideally you should use rag within a day of digging them, but it is possible to keep them alive and well for a few weeks. Take only whole, undamaged worms. Any broken ones soon die and contaminate the rest.

Red, king and white rag can be kept in shallow tanks or trays of clean, aerated seawater. Store in a cool, dark place – a fridge, ideally – and check twice a day for dead or dying worms.

The day before fishing, spread the rag out on a tray lined with newspaper or moisture-absorbing particle chips, and put them back in the fridge. If you can get some fresh seaweed to cover them with, all the better. In hot weather or when faced with a long drive, it is best to transport them in a cool box.

Maddies are even more delicate, so need even more careful handling. Rinse them clean of mud in fresh seawater then lay them in a tray lined with newspaper. Maddies keep for up to a week in a fridge.

Hooking rag

Always match size of bait and hook. For flatfish and other small species, thread a single red or white rag on a small, fine-wire Aberdeen. For bigger fish, thread two or three on and above a larger Kamasan B940 (a thicker-wire Aberdeen).

King rag can be used in sections for small fish, or whole for big fish.

Maddies need a very small, fine-wire hook and can be fished singly or in bunches, threaded on or hooked through the middle.

Common and yellowtail lugs

**Each worm is a mini reservoir of potent blood and juices – a bait which sea fish find irresistible.
Successful shore angler Alan Yates tells how you find, keep and present them.**

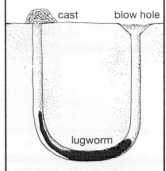

Commons live fairly high up the inter tidal-range in tunnels up to 45cm (18in) deep. At one end of the tunnel is an irregular sand cast created by the worm as it expels inedible particles. At the other end is a depression with a small blowhole.

◀ *Where casts are close to one another digging a trench allows you to gather worms with less effort and back-fill more easily.*

The lug is a natural marine bait but its habitat is so secure that fish rarely encounter it. Sometimes, though, a heavy storm knocks out a sandbank and washes the worms into the surf: then, the fish go on a feeding frenzy.

Lugs take all types of sea fish except for mullet, shark and conger. Digging your own lugs can be a back-breaking business but the rewards of catching plenty of fish using an excellent free and natural bait are certainly worth all the effort.

Worm types

There are two distinct types of lugworm that you can find. They are the common lug and the yellowtail lug.

Common lugworm Commons (other names include blowlug, softlug and redlug) are found in sand and mud fairly high up the inter-tidal range. They have a soft skin and are usually less than 15cm (6in) long but they can grow up to 25cm (10in).

Large commons tend to consist mostly of sand, so the smaller worms are preferable. These have a high water content which causes a fresh worm to explode on the hook,

▼ *A fork is better than a garden spade, there's less chance of breaking the worms. Take a pair of wellies too – bait digging can be a messy business.*

releasing an irresistible scent trail to a hungry predatory fish.

Yellowtail lugworm The yellowtail varies in appearance from one coastal area to another and is known by different names including: gullie, black, runnydown and sewie. It grows to between 10cm (4in) and 30cm (12in) in length but a worm of about 20cm (8in) is a good sized bait.

The yellowtail's tunnel is vertical and goes down as far as 60cm (24in). Because the tunnel goes into mud, its cast is blacker than the common's – the blacker the cast, the deeper the tunnel. The shape of the cast is also distinctive – unlike the common's untidy heap, the yellowtail's cast is almost always a perfect conical heap of spiral coils.

Digging

Dig for lugs when the tide is right out. For best results choose the longest spring tides rather than neap tides which expose the least low tide sand.

Digging commons You can either dig worms individually by following the line of the tunnel from the cast towards the blow hole or, where casts are plentiful, by digging trench-fashion.

If the worm's habitat is fairly dry, use a flat-pronged potato fork. A fork lessens the chance of the worm getting damaged and the flat prongs support the sand so that it doesn't break up, making the sand easier to remove. (If the sand is wetter dig with a lug spade.)

When you've dug down to the worm, don't

⚠ Tide watch

A word of warning: when digging, always keep an eye on an incoming tide. Some beaches (Weston-super-Mare, for example) have a shallow slope and the tide can come rushing in and catch you unawares.

▲ *Handling yellowtails leaves the fingers covered in a bright yellow iodine stain – but this is a small price to pay for such an effective bait.*

▶ *Worms stored in a tray of sea water in the fridge can be kept for up to 2 or 3 months but remove any dead ones straight away.*

Tip **Keep cool**

In hot weather, put a chemical ice pack of the kind used for picnics in the worm bucket to keep them cool, otherwise they will die and go off.

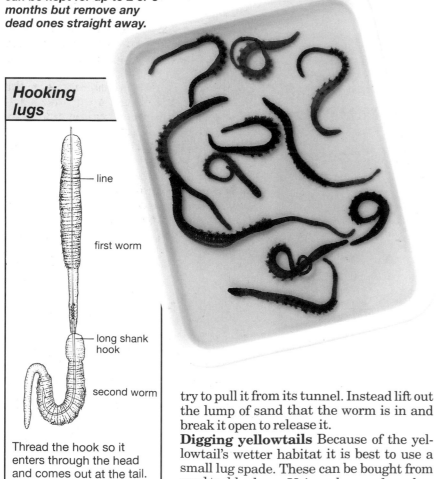

Hooking lugs

line

first worm

long shank hook

second worm

Thread the hook so it enters through the head and comes out at the tail. This lets juices escape, makes the bait look natural and keeps it in one piece when casting.

✖ *Backfilling*

You can often tell where anglers have been digging for bait: the beach looks like a lunar landscape. Apart from looking ugly, holes are a danger to other beach users. Don't be thoughtless, make sure you backfill – fill in the holes – as you go along.

Storage and preparation

In general, fresh, live lugworm is superior to frozen bait but frozen yellowtails can be an effective alternative when fresh bait is not available. Avoid preserved lugworm sold in tackle shops; as a bait it's next to useless.

Commons Because of their high water content, commons are unsuitable for freezing. However, they can be kept alive for up to a week if stored in dry newspaper in the fridge.

It is also possible to keep worms for 2 or 3 months or more by 'tanking' them. Some anglers do this by keeping the worms as they would fish: in an aquarium, with an aeration pump and filter system.

A simpler method of tanking is to put the worms in a shallow bait tray, cover with about 4cm (1½in) of sea water, and keep them at the bottom of the fridge. It is not necessary to use a pump. The important thing is not to put too many worms into one container.

Check the worms daily and remove any dead ones. If you keep a bottle of sea water in the fridge it will be at the right temperature to add to your worms when they need it, but once the tray is set up disturb it as little as possible.

Yellowtails Fresh yellowtails can be stored in the same way as commons. They make an excellent fresh bait because, like the common, they explode on the hook but the tough leathery skin makes them more resistant to attack from crabs and also makes them suitable for freezing.

To freeze, first gut the worm by squeezing out its innards. Next, blanch it by pouring boiling water over it. Then wrap each worm in newspaper and freeze.

Gutted yellowtails stored in the fridge in newspaper are also a useful bait. Check them every so often to see if they've gone off or they'll stink the fridge out.

Presenting the bait

Lugs need a long shank hook so that they stay on the hook. An Aberdeen pattern from size 4 up to 2/0 or 3/0 is ideal.

Worms can be threaded on to the hookshank and snood in twos, threes or fours, depending on the fish you're after. Use fresh worms each cast as the natural juices are quickly sucked out in the sea, making the worms much less attractive to the fish you are after.

try to pull it from its tunnel. Instead lift out the lump of sand that the worm is in and break it open to release it.

Digging yellowtails Because of the yellowtail's wetter habitat it is best to use a small lug spade. These can be bought from good tackle shops. Using a lug spade makes the job a lot easier. Follow the worm's tunnel down from the cast, quickly taking out small spits of sand so that the hole doesn't fill with water.

Mackerel as bait

It's a potent fish attractor and fairly easy to get hold of. When fresh, mackerel is one of the sea angler's most successful baits – oily and enticing to all manner of sea fish.

▼ *Feathering for mackerel – the fast-moving fish are drawn to the hooks and feathers which give off air bubbles as they descend – and are instantly caught. Watch out for sharp hooks swinging on board.*

To stock up with enough mackerel for a good day's sea fishing, the usual technique in summer is to drop a weighted trace carrying six hooks – each whipped with coloured feathers – over the side of a boat. If you manage to locate the shoals then you're soon hauling in strings of fish – a ready supply of bait full of flavour. Feathering from harbours and shore can also be fruitful.

Fresh fish is definitely best but if you can't get it, mackerel frozen soon after catching can make reasonable bait. Shop-bought or frozen mackerel generally lacks a firm texture and has less juicy fish appeal.

Mackerel on board
Once you have your mackerel there are several effective ways of presenting it.

Flappers Boat anglers after conger rely heavily on a 'flapper' bait to get into contact. Push the point of a knife through the mackerel's body just behind the top of the head. Then, using the backbone as a guide, slice the blade along each side until it emerges at the tail. Cut through and remove the backbone as near to the head as you can. This leaves you with a soft bait consisting of two succulent flaps of flesh, naturally attached to the mackerel's head.

Push the point of a size 9/0 or 10/0 hook through the mouth and upwards through the head, so that you get a secure hold in the toughest part of the bait.

Inverted flapper Alternatively, sever the baitfish's head and tail and remove the backbone, leaving two flapping sides connected by the tail section. Hook it first through the tail and a second time further down the body.

Fillet o' fish A side of mackerel cleanly removed is an excellent bait for specimen pollack and coalfish at wreck sites. Hook through the pointed end of the fillet for a

◀ *Small pieces of mackerel cut crosswise from a side are used to catch red and black bream, whiting and pouting. Fresh mackerel flesh stays firm for about six hours and can be cut precisely with a sharp, thin-bladed knife.*

Preparing a side of mackerel

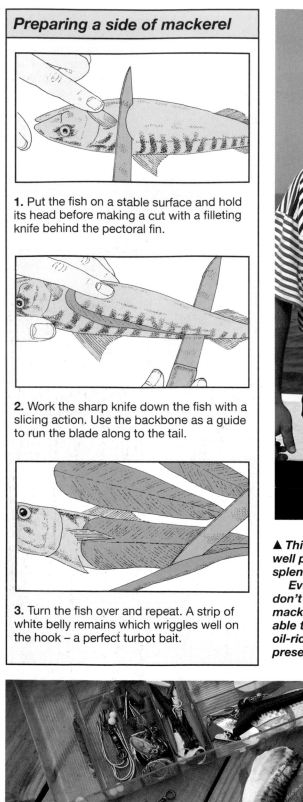

1. Put the fish on a stable surface and hold its head before making a cut with a filleting knife behind the pectoral fin.

2. Work the sharp knife down the fish with a slicing action. Use the backbone as a guide to run the blade along to the tail.

3. Turn the fish over and repeat. A strip of white belly remains which wriggles well on the hook – a perfect turbot bait.

▲ *This pair of anglers are well pleased with their splendid plaice.*

Even bottom fish, which don't feed naturally on mackerel, don't seem to be able to resist the blood and oil-rich flesh of a well presented mackerel bait.

natural swimming action.

Back-to-back baits are particularly successful when you're after turbot, blonde and thornback rays and brill.

Using the tip of a sharp knife, lightly score the inside flesh down the entire length of a side of mackerel. Then fold the fillet shiny side inwards, leaving the fleshy side outwards. A back-to-back bait is very effective when predators are reluctant to feed.

Landlubberly morsels

Shore anglers also make great use of mackerel bait. Flapper style is best for conger as it stays securely on the hook during the rigours of casting.

Long, thin strips can be legered singly or in association with marine worms, squid or crab to make an attractive cocktail. Or fish them on a sliding float rig for bass, pollack, coalfish, garfish, mullet and even other mackerel.

Mullet method Fish for mullet with a flake of mackerel flesh on a small hook, presented in a cloud of pulped mackerel groundbait.

◀ *Head and tail-end mackerel flappers – this light shark rig combines a size 8/0 hook with a long 150lb (68kg) mono trace.*

Whole flappers are also effective baits for conger, skate and tope.

Sandeels

Although some anglers still regard them as a specialist commodity rather than an all-round bait, sandeels have gained popularity in recent years, says top sea matchman Chris Clark.

There are two types of sandeels, the lesser and the greater (launce). The lesser reaches 20cm (8in) in length while the greater can grow to 32cm (13in).

In most boat fishing situations using a live sandeel is often more effective than fishing with its frozen counterpart. When shore fishing, though, you can't cast effectively with a live sandeel.

Few tackle shops have the facilities to keep live sandeels, so blast-frozen ones are a must if you're not in a position to collect your own.

Finding sandeels

Collecting sandeels is quite easy, given the right tidal and weather conditions. Sandbars exposed during spring low tides often have large numbers in the summer.

As the tide ebbs away, the sandeels bury themselves a few inches under the moist sand. Dig them up with a fork or a rake, and put them (no more than 30 or so) in a bucket of sea water with a portable aerator.

▼ *A tried and tested bait for pollack and bass, sandeels also tempt specimen brill such as this one.*
Though live sandeels are more effective, frozen ones are easier to carry when boat fishing.

Sandeels die quickly if they are not kept in well-oxygenated water.

As you fork over the top few inches of sand, look for flashes of silver: you have to be extremely quick when grabbing sandeels because they try to bury themselves as fast as you uncover them.

Storing live sandeels for any length of time is difficult. Ideally you need a large tank filled with water and an aerator – both placed in a fridge to keep the water as cold as possible. If the water temperature starts to rise, bacteria multiply rapidly, killing the fish.

Storing sandeels

Whether you catch sandeels or buy some from a ˙fishmonger, you can freeze them quite successfully. First kill the eels by hit-

Floatfished sandeel

bead and stop knot

pike float

bead

BB shot — 75-90cm

swivel

30-40cm

Use lesser sandeels which are less than 7.5cm (3in) long or cut greater ones into slivers for specimen mackerel.

◄ *Sandeels swim in huge shoals. When threatened by predators such as pollack, coalfish, bass, dabs, brill and plaice, these wriggling, silver-sided creatures burrow into the sandy sea, making a fast, headlong getaway.*

ting them over the head with a small stick (or priest). Rinse them in fresh water and dry them before laying them *individually* on dry newspaper. Place them in the freezer. Once frozen, wrap them in plastic and pack as required.

Using sandeels

Presentation is vital when fishing with dead sandeels. If you're legering on the beach for rays or doggies with lesser sandeels, pass the hook into the mouth and then down the entire length of the eel's body so that the hookpoint emerges about 12mm (½in) from the tail. Wrap the sandeel with shirring elastic to secure it.

Cut greater sandeels into chunks and tie on to the hook with knitting or shirring elastic. Fillet the larger ones.

For float fishing pass the point of a size 2 hook through the eyes and then about 12mm (½in) farther down, just past the gill cover. It's essential to make sure the hookpoint isn't masked. Impale a sandeel not longer than 7.5cm (3in) on a small hook.

▲ ▶ *This is a popular way of hooking a sandeel for boat fishing (above). It allows the tail to sway enticingly in the current. Catch greater sandeels (right) by using a string of feathers, bounced off the bottom.*

Fishing with feathers

Feathers have tickled the fancy of many a fish. Mike Millman reveals how to fish 'holiday feathers' for mackerel.

As long ago as the 17th century, feathers were being used as a means of catching fish in the sea. Today strings of feathers which have either six or twelve hooks – tied to short snoods (hooklengths) – are made by the tens of thousands. They are used principally to catch mackerel. It is likely that the fish are fooled into thinking a string of feathers is a shoal of small prey.

The most commonly used feathers are often called 'holiday feathers' – because of their wide use during short summer fishing trips for mackerel. 'Holiday feathers' consist of a string of six plain or multi-coloured feathers whipped to size 1/0 hooks.

A good trim

There is often too much feather on a commercial hook. A well-used set of mackerel feathers – in which the feather content has been worn down to little more than a wisp – seems to catch a lot more fish. Therefore a good trim with a pair of scissors dramatically improves a string's catching potential.

A string of feathers, with a weight, simply dropped from the side of the boat *will* catch. But your chances of success are much

▲ *A 'full house' of mackerel. Feathering might be considered unsporting – especially with this heavy gear – but it produces a large supply of mackerel to use as bait.*

◄ *Feathers also catch cod – try three feathers on a string, fished deep. Mike recommends catching bottom-feeding cod on size 8/0 feathered hooks, with added squid.*

improved by 'loading' the feathers with oxygenated bubbles before they sink into the depths.

To achieve this you cast the string out so that the weight strikes the water hard, creating the necessary disturbance. In calm conditions you can see the value of this as the feathers bubble while they sink. Mackerel, which have an incredible turn of speed, often stop the string as it plummets down.

Suddenly, everything goes light for a second or two, then you feel the weight as you put the reel into gear and the rod takes the burden. Six good mackerel on at the same

'Holiday feathers'

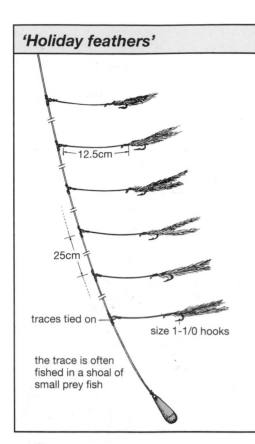

12.5cm

25cm

traces tied on —
size 1-1/0 hooks

the trace is often
fished in a shoal of
small prey fish

▲ *A string of mackerel feathers with size 1/0 hooks. The bold colours readily take the fancy of hungry fish.*

Tip Fishy tails

When fishing larger feathers over rough ground try adding king ragworm to the hooks. This ensures that there is plenty of tail to wave attractively as the feathers are worked upwards.

▼ *Larger, multi-coloured feathers appeal to cod and, when fished around wrecks are excellent for pollack and coalfish.*

time – all of them trying to dash about – puts quite a strain on the tackle. A 'full house' – every hook with a taker – can take some bringing up if the mackerel are large.

Experienced boat anglers only use 'holiday feathers' when they are catching large numbers of mackerel for bait – it is considered 'unsporting' in normal angling terms. A string of feathers can also be used to catch mackerel very effectively from the shore, as long as there is a reasonable depth of water. Steep shelving beaches are ideal for this type of fishing.

Big predators

Big, fast predators like pollack and coalfish can be caught on strings of feathers close to the sea bottom. These species are fooled by a size 6/0 hook heavily laden with different coloured feathers which slick down when wet. These are whipped to the shank of the hook with light monofilament and treated to a coating of instant glue. A 5cm (2in) length of bicycle valve tubing worked down over the whipped shank protects the binding and adds to the attractiveness of the offering. This type of feathered hook is usually fished on a long flowing trace called a flying collar.

Mike once fished a wreck with a three hook rig and 10/0 hooks. At 69m (228ft), three ling hit – a catch of 47kg (105lb)!

'Cornish wreckers'

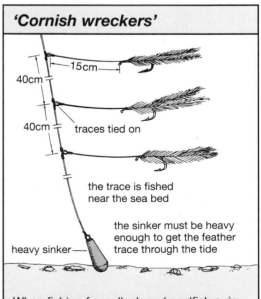

15cm

40cm

40cm

traces tied on

the trace is fished
near the sea bed

the sinker must be heavy
enough to get the feather
trace through the tide

heavy sinker —

When fishing for pollack and coalfish a rig with just three feathers and size 6/0 hooks is effective. This is called a 'Cornish wrecker' because the trace is popular for wreck fishing off Cornwall. The trace is carried down by a heavy weight at high speed. If the hooks are not taken on the way down, the trace is jigged back from the bottom.

Jigging

The jigging of artificial lures to catch predatory fish is a method as old as angling itself. Mike Millman looks at using an old technique with modern lures.

Jigging is a method of catching fish that has been around since man first started using hooks. The word 'jig' simply means jerky motion. In terms of fishing, that refers to any bait or lure that is used in a jerky way – a plain un-baited hook can be a 'jig' if it is made to dance around on the end of the line.

Simple jigs

One of the most basic forms of jig fishing at sea is working a string of feathers. The monofilament trace usually carries three, six or twelve feathered hooks which are lethal for taking mackerel, garfish and small pollack or coalfish.

Although still very effective, the simple team of dyed chicken feathers has now been superseded by the use of man-made materials such as 'Mylar' (braided tinsel) and 'Flectolite' (shiny plastic foil).

The newcomers

The latest variation on this theme has just arrived from the Far East – the oddly named 'shrimp rig'. Odd, because the plastic bodies are in fact shaped like mini-fish, not shrimps. Half the body is luminous, as are the small beads at the head of each lure,

and the tails are made of tinsel.

Another variation of this lure is the 'Hokkai', which also has synthetic feathers in its tail. The effectiveness of this lure has already been established, particularly on large bass, and bigger versions for cod and pollack will doubtless appear soon.

Other newcomers have arrived from America, where lure fishing has always been popular. Most of them are of the lead-head type and have built-in hooks with their points upwards. This makes them much less prone to snagging on weed or on

▲ *These two Jigga lures are being used on short paternosters above a pirk – a set-up similar to 'killer gear'. Jerk them up and down over rough ground and wrecks to provoke cod and pollack into striking them.*

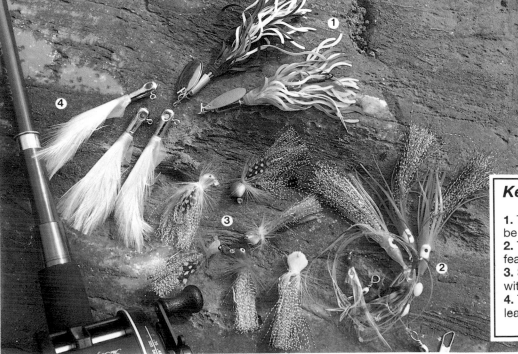

Imported jigs

Recently introduced from the USA are two new lures suitable for jigging.
● **'Ripple Fin'** has two metal barrels mounted on a wire with a spinning blade at one end and a muppet-like rubber frill concealing a treble hook at the other.
● **'Supersquid'** is a muppet type lure with tinsel in the tail. You can add lead to the body.

Key to selection of jigs

1. Two Ripple Fin lures – they can be used as spinners or jigs.
2. Three Supersquid lures – the feathered hooks hang from the tail.
3. Six Porky jigs – leadheaded lures with fluorescent skirts.
4. Three Bonito jigs – more leadheads that fish point-up.

New jigging feathers from the Far East

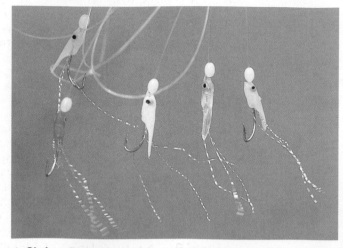

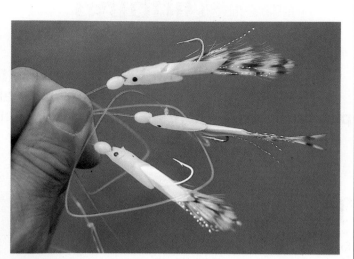

1. Shrimp Rig Strings of five plastic mini-fish with luminous beads and Mylar tinsel tails are mounted on size 4 hooks and 25lb (11.3kg) line. They are absolutely deadly for mackerel and garfish.

2. Hokkai lures Strings of three plastic mini-fish with luminous beads and feather and Mylar tinsel tails are mounted on size 1/0 hooks and 25lb (11.3kg) line. They catch when other types of feathers don't.

rough bottoms and also gives them a very attractive nose-down action.

Leadhead lures

One of the most popular of these self-weighted lures is the Porky jig which features a fluorescent skirt of feathers and Mylar tinsel. The built-in hooks vary in size from 1s to 2/0s according to whether they are 15, 25 or 40 gramme size.

Porky jigs are at their most effective when used on light spinning tackle and retrieved in a jerky sink-and-draw type action, which bass and pollack find irresistible. They can also be used as a team – two or three lures fished on short paternosters above a small pirk.

The Bonito is a similar but less sophisticated lure. Also a leadhead type, this has coloured feathers with a fish shaped white nylon covering and red jewelled eyes.

Another variation on the leadhead concept is the Jigga lure. This is unusual because the line is threaded through the head itself, rather than attached to an eyelet – this means that you can select the size and type of hook used with it. The feathered bodies have a plastic outer layer and the pointed heads are inset with 'Flectolite'.

Tip *Spice up your jigs*

There are times when even the best jigs won't catch. Try livening them up by baiting with thin strips of fish or squid – this added scent trail often does the trick. Be careful not to overdo it, though – you don't want to ruin the action of the lure, which is the jig's main attraction.

▶ *Jigging one of the sophisticated new lures over rough ground or wrecks is a good way to make contact with big pollack, like this fine 18½lb (8.39kg) specimen.*

Muppet fishing

Artificial squid with sci-fi looks, muppets are powerful lures – top boat angler Norman Message explains how to harness their attractive qualities in the water.

There's no accounting for tastes – especially as far as sea fish are concerned. You can understand how a trout might fall for an exquisite Mallard and Claret, Yellow Humpy or aptly named Irresistible. In fact, it's difficult to see how a discerning trout could resist these delicate artificial flies which imitate insect prey with such finesse.

But by comparison it's hard to imagine the fishy appeal of the boldly coloured, flaccid, faintly comical lures known as muppets. Vaguely squidish in appearance, they don't mimic directly any particular baitfish. However, their effectiveness as sea fishing lures is undoubted – guaranteeing the zany muppet a place somewhere in every sea angler's tackle box.

Muppet on a string

Plastic muppets come in several colours and in three sizes – small, medium and large. They are a must as an extra lure and are used in many combinations for shallow and deep-water fishing.

Pollack, coalfish and cod are rather partial to muppets, and bass, mackerel, ling, pout and many other fish go for them if used with sea baits or pirks.

▼ *It looks as though this fish might have a soft spot for pink blancmange – but in fact it has succumbed to a large and brightly coloured muppet.*

Small muppets are used when boat fishing for pollack, coalfish and bass. They are successful fished in a three-hook combination on 50lb (22.7kg) line, with a lead weight or pirk attached at the bottom. The best hook sizes for these rigs are between 2/0 and 4/0. A good colour for the muppets is fluorescent light green when you're after pollack, and dark red, blue or black for bass and coalfish.

Medium and large muppets are ideal for pollack and cod if you drape them over a large treble 8/0 or 10/0 hook fixed to a large pirk. Red and pink lures on a pirk account for many cod and pollack catches from wrecks or rocky ground. In deeper water, where there is not much light, the colour of the muppet is not as important as the action and shape of the lure as you jig it up and down to attract fish.

▲ *The eyes have it – this platoon of beady-eyed muppets is just the sort of colourful selection that seems to tempt fish. Combined with baits and pirks they take a wide variety of species.*

▲ A recipe for successful fishing at anchor: take one muppet, garnish with fresh mackerel strip, and then present the cocktail on a leger rig with French boom.

▼ A big cod taken on a pirk and red muppet. Fishing over wrecks or rocky ground with this combination produces some good catches of pollack and cod.

Insurance policy

When used at anchor, muppets left to flutter in the tide take a number of species. The best method is to team them with mackerel, lug, rag or even squid baits on a French boom which is fixed on about 1m (3ft) above a leger rig. The trace line can vary from 1-1.8m (3-6ft) depending on the strength of the tide – use longer traces when the tide is strong. This technique is doubly effective because the muppets continue to attract fish even if the baits have

been pinched off the hooks. Pollack, bass, bream, pout and whiting all fall to this particular method.

When fishing three muppets on a three-hook dropper rig, try different colours and find out which one is most effective on the day. Once you know, you can put down all three of the same colour and improve your catch rate. It is handy to make up at least two or three rigs of each colour beforehand, ready for use when needed.

Fit the large muppets to your pirks on the day. To do this make a cut in the top of the muppet's head and push through the treble so the eye protrudes and the hook is covered by the muppet skirt. You can then attach the eye to a split ring on a pirk.

Keep your large muppets in good condition by packing them away in separate compartments or plastic bags in your tackle box until you need them.

Artificial sandeels

Artificial sandeels are one of the most successful lures of all time. The seductive, waggling tail has been the downfall of countless fish. Mike Thrussell explains.

Artificial sandeels are made of rubber and come in a fantastic range of different colours and sizes.

Colour and class

Both bass and pollack take artificial eels at night, picking up on the vibrations set up by

▲ Live sandeels are hard to beat when boat-fishing (especially drifting) for bass. But artificials are more readily available and are easier to cast from shore or boat.

the waggling tail. But the colour of the eel is an important but often overlooked part of shore and boat angling. Pollack tend to prefer red and sometimes yellow by day – though their peak feeding time is at dusk when, against all logic, a black eel proves most deadly. Bass prefer a white eel during the day with again a black one at dusk.

Mackerel go for the brighter colours – red, yellow and fluorescent green eels fished from beaches, harbours and off rocky areas. Late evening into night and dawn are again the best times to use eels.

The artificial eel comes ready provided with a hook that is well hidden in the body. This can be replaced with a smaller one when shore-fishing for small pollack, for example. But if you're fishing over a wreck,

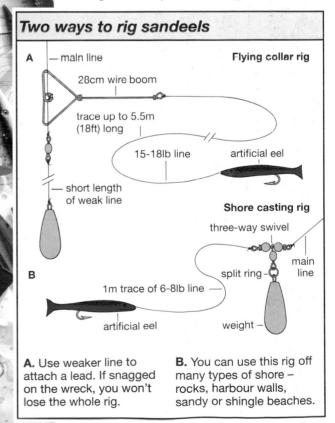

Two ways to rig sandeels

A — main line — **Flying collar rig**

28cm wire boom

trace up to 5.5m (18ft) long

15-18lb line — artificial eel

— short length of weak line

B

1m trace of 6-8lb line

artificial eel

Shore casting rig

three-way swivel

main line

split ring —

weight —

A. Use weaker line to attach a lead. If snagged on the wreck, you won't lose the whole rig.

B. You can use this rig off many types of shore – rocks, harbour walls, sandy or shingle beaches.

◄ Artificial sandeels come in many different colours and sizes. But the effective waggling tail is the most important feature.

Tip _Sizes to suit_

Size one artificial eels are 25cm (10in) long. They represent the offshore launce or greater sandeel which is common over reefs and wrecks. Size two, 20cm (8in) long, is good for bass over inshore rough ground. The small version (7cm/2¾in long) is ideal for mackerel, school bass and small pollack and coalies.

you may want to use a stronger, larger hook. The rubber body is versatile and can accommodate different sizes to meet your needs.

Shore fishing with eels

Artificial eels up to 20cm (8in) or so long can be used for shore casting for bass and pollack from rock marks facing the open sea, very rough, boulder-strewn beaches, harbour walls or breakwaters. Try to fish the eel as close to the sea bed, rocks or weeds as

▲ _This pollack fell for a small, natural-coloured sandeel fished over a rough, boulder-strewn mark._

◀ _Artificial sandeels fished over old war-time wrecks often tempt pollack such as this fine specimen._

possible to maximize your catch. Tackle losses are inevitable, but the fish are there.

If you're after bass, aim to fish near outflowing freshwater streams, over rough ground or alongside rocky promontories where there are small tide races. Alternatively, simply move a few metres along the beach with every cast to cover as much ground as possible.

Boat fishing with eels

Artificial sandeels are also excellent lures for boat fishing. Trolling a freelined eel 80-100m (87-110yd) behind a boat to cover shallow marks usually attracts attention from bass. The ebb tide is usually the best time to use this style of fishing, when bass move back on to the reefs from the beaches.

You can also tempt big pollack and coalfish by using eels over war-time wrecks. A flying-collar rig with a long trace is one of the most popular methods to present the eel. This long trace is needed to get a proper action from the lure and, set up this way, tangles are rare.

Black, red and yellow eels in the longer sizes (15-25cm/6-10in) are best, but coalfish in particular are often caught with small, gaudy fluorescent pink or green eels.

As an alternative you can fish two small artificial eels above a pirk on very short hook snoods. This is called killer gear. It is just jigged up and down close to the bottom until a fish takes one of the lures.

It is an effective way of taking fish, but is considered by many to be unsporting.

Index

Page numbers in *italics* refer to illustrations

Sea

Acknowledgements

Photographs

Allsport title page (left), (John Nicholson) 133; Angling Press Service (Bill Howes) 51(t), 68(t), 131(t), 145; John Bailey 62(c), 86(b), 87; Bob Church 143(b), 144(tl); Bruce Coleman Ltd 20(c); Cully's 64(r); John Darling 23(t), 84(t), 103(r), 173, 174, 180(b), 181, 183(t), 188(b), 194(b), 205, 217, 219(br), 220(cl), 227(t); Eaglemoss (Ian Christy) 110(b), 189, 192(b), (Eric Crichton) 33(t), 34(t), 113, 116(t), 216, (Andy Davison) 12, (Andy Dawson) 16(b), 18(t), 21(l), 60(t), (Peter Gathercole) 79, 81(br), 83(b), 85, 109(t), 111(b), 126(t), 135, 136(b), 138(b), 212(t), (Carl Gedye) 195(c,b), 220(t), (Neil Holmes) 22, 54, 70(tl), 72(b), 89, (Trevor Housby) 171, 211(t), (Neville Kidd) 191, (Dennis Linley) 32(t), 33(c), 38(tr), (Patrick Llewelyn-Davies) 80(t,bl), 110(t,c), 114, 118(t,br), 121(b), 127(b), 132(t), 186(t), 194(t), 208, 214, (Bill Meadows) 80(br), 82(t), 90, (Mike Millman) 18(b), 56(b), 57, (Martin Norris) 14–15, 16(t), 29, 30(t), 67, 69, 93(t), 102(t,c), 103(l), 106, 182, 184, 213, (Nick Randall) 219(t), 234(b), (Clifford Staley) 196(t), (John Suett) 11, 17(b), 19, 20(b), 26, 27, 37(tr), 38(tc), 99, 176(l,tr), 177(b), 178(r), 222(cl), (Steve Tanner) 28, 39(l), 40(bl), 62(t), 63(tl,c), 62–3(b), 64(l), (Stuart Windsor) 49(tr), 50(c,l), 73(t), 81(t,bl), 88(tl), 92(t), 94(t), (Shona Wood) 32(b); Explorer 107; Nick Ferenczy 201(t), 202, 203, 204(c,b); Neville Fickling 40(t), 75, 76(c); Fishpix (Graeme Pullen) 179(b), 196(b), 207(t); Peter Gathercole 95–8, 101, 104(t), 105, 108, 109(b), 111(t), 112(b), 115, 117, 118(c,bl), 119(b), 120, 123, 124(b), 125, 129, 130, 132(b), 137, 139(b), 140, 142(c), 143(t), 144(tr), 146(b), 147, 148, 151, 152, 154(t), 155(b), 157, 158, 159(t), 160(t), 162, 164(b), 168, 170(b); Jim Gibbinson 71, 72(t), 73(b); Jens Ploug Hansen 23(b), 49(b), 51(b), 52, 68(b), 91, 94(b), 185, 188(t); Mike Heliwell 25, 204(t); David Houghman 210(t); Trevor Housby 59(b), 65, 78, 86(t), 100, 172, 175(l), 176(br), 212(b), 225, 227(b),

232(b); Kevin Hyatt 128(b), 159(b), 165(t); Bob James 55(t); Dennis Linley 88(tr,b); Paul Losik 138(t); Graham Marsden 35, 47(b), 66; Mike Millman title page (top right), 17(tl), 36, 37(b), 175(r), 177(t), 179(t), 180(c), 187, 193, 195(t), 198, 207(b), 209(tl,c), 218, 219(bl), 220, 221(c), 224(b), 226(c), 228, 229–230, 231(l), 232(t), 233(b), 235; Natural Science (Neil Bartrop) 119(t), (P. Broadbent) 199, (Tony Davies-Patrick) title page (bottom right), (Ray Forsberg) 39(r), 221, (P. Sheehan) 112(t), (Dave Smyth) 122(b), 136(t), 197, (Alan Spence) 104(b), 170(t), 206(b), (P&S Ward) 43, 44(b), 47(t), 59(t), 8(b); Ian Neale 128(t); Janet Oddy 13, 31; Arthur Oglesby 121(t), 127(t), 153, 154(b), 167, 169; On Reflection 192(t); Oxford Scientific Films (Roger Jackman) 226(t); John Roberts 122(t), 149, 150, 155(t), 161, 165(b), 166; Kevin Smith 24(t,cl), 41–42, 44(tr), 45, 46,48, 50(t), 53, 55(b), 56(t), 178(l), 183(b), 222(t); Swanpix (Graham Swanson) 102(b), 146(t), 163, 164(t; Russell Symons 124(t), 131(b), 223; Dave Tait 160(b); Mike Thrussell 211(b); Mick Toomer 215, 224(t); Jim Tyree 116(b), 126(b), 139(t), 142(b); Alain Urruty 34(b); Ken Whitehead 44(tl), 58(t); John Watson 58(b), 74; Phil Williams 209(tr), 226(b), 231(r), 233(t), 234(t); John Wilson 6, 21(r), 24(cr), 28(tr), 30(b), 33(b), 40(br), 49(tl), 60(b), 61, 70(tr,b), 76(b), 77, 82(b), 83(t), 92(b), 93(b); Alan Yates 186(b), 200, 201(b), 206(t).

Illustrations

Wendy Bramall 162–3; Peter Bull 22, 26–7, 33, 76, 81, 83–6, 187–90, 100, 108, 116, 125, 141–2, 148–50, 156–8, 166, 180, 190–1(b), 197–202, 206–224, 233; Eaglemoss (Michael Cooke) 40, 56–7, 72–4, 107, 114, 167, 187, 190–1, 194, 203, 228, (Mei Lim) 50; David Etchell 144–5; Linden Artists (Craig Warwick) 28, 184; Denys Ovenden 168-9.